GCSE ICT

Information and Communication Technology

Complete Revision and Practice

Contents

Section One — Computers and Hardware

Section Two — Operating Systems and Applications

Section Three — Spreadsheets and Databases

Section Four — Word Processing and Desktop Publishing

Section Five — Presentation and Web Software

Contents

Published by CGP

Editors:
Murray Hamilton and Andy Park.

Contributors:
Colin Harber Stuart, Charley Darbishire, Simon Little and Richard Vickery.

Proofreading:
Glenn Rogers.

With thanks to Jan Greenway for the copyright research.

ISBN: 978 1 84762 179 5

Printed by Elanders Ltd, Newcastle upon Tyne.
Clipart from Corel®

Based on the classic CGP style created by Richard Parsons.

Computers

ICT... Information and Communication Technology. Or as I like to call it... Computers and stuff.

Microprocessors Made the Digital Age Possible

1) Microprocessors (microchips) are in every computer in the world — they're basically the brains of a computer, where all the data is processed.
2) In a computer they're responsible for running computer programs, responding to user input and pretty much everything else that makes a computer what it is.
3) A computer's main processor is the CPU (central processing unit).
4) Microprocessors are installed on circuit boards, along with a load of other chips, wiring and electronic components.

A typical circuit board.

Computers Contain a CPU... Plus Various Other Things

You can't see all the bits listed below in the picture... but they're all in there somewhere.

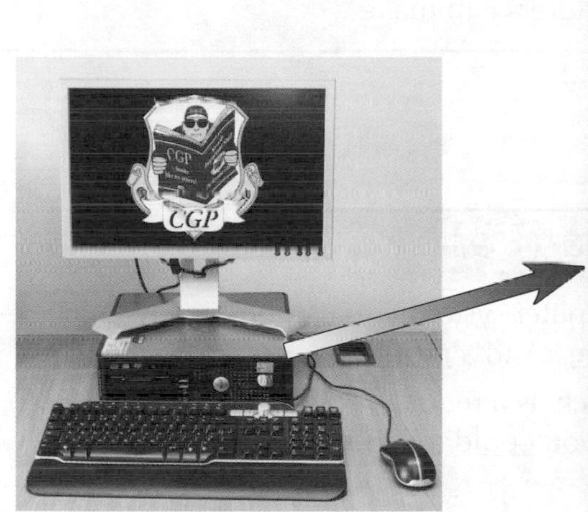

Take a computer apart, and you can see all its bits...

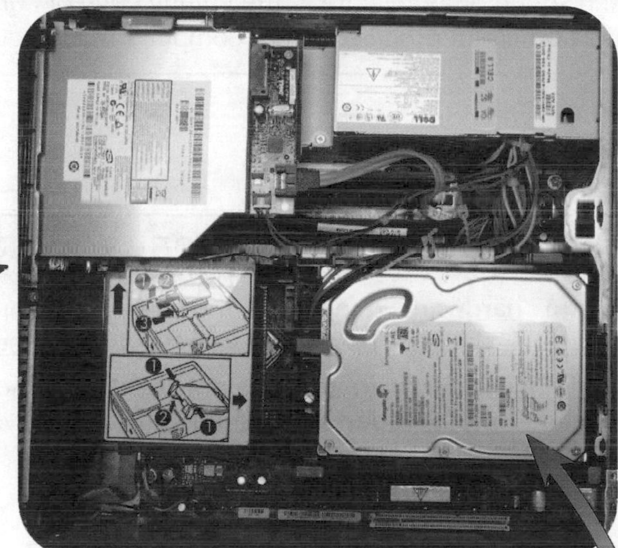

Motherboard
The main circuit board of a computer. It holds the CPU, the memory chips, and various connections.

Sound card
A circuit board that deals with the input and output of sound.

Video card
A circuit board that generates video output.

Internal memory
ROM and RAM (page 16).

Wireless card
A device that picks up wireless signals.

Backing storage
— the hard drive (pages 17-20).

A CPU is a bit like the brain of a computer

A nice and simple page to ease you in with. You don't need to know how to put a computer together (fortunately), but make sure you know the main parts that you find in one, and what each part does.

Computers

Computers are basically collections of various bits of hardware and software.

There are **Computers**... and **Computers**

Computers don't always look the same. Computers can range in size from the mainframes used by businesses (about the size of a small house) to the tiny processors inside your phone.

1) Companies doing a lot of processing (e.g. banks, search engine firms and e-commerce firms on the Internet) need a lot of computing power. They use either mainframes or servers.
2) Mainframes were first developed in the 1960s — they're big and reliable, and often contain multiple copies of each of their parts, so if one fails then they can just switch to another.
3) Servers are fast PCs without most of the bits that normally let you talk to the computer, such as keyboards and screens. Servers can be connected together so they act like a single machine — making it easy to increase or decrease the amount of processing power available by just adding or removing servers. It also means that it usually doesn't matter if any individual machine fails.
4) You wouldn't necessarily know a lot of computers even exist. Embedded computers are inside everyday objects such as washing machines, TVs, central heating systems, cars, phones, watches...
5) And supercomputers are at the cutting edge of computer technology. They contain the fastest, most powerful processors that computer manufacturers can make.

Hardware Means **Equipment** You Can Touch...

1) The term "hardware" refers to all the parts of a computer system you can physically touch. So a keyboard is a piece of hardware. As is a mouse. And a monitor.
2) A hard drive is hardware too. It's not as easy to touch as a mouse — you'd probably need to take your computer apart first. But if you did that, you could touch it, so it's hardware.

...**Software** Means **Programs**

Software means the programs that a computer runs — they're sets of instructions that get all the different bits of hardware to work together. Computers use two kinds of software...

1) An operating system (OS) — this is the software that controls the whole computer system, e.g. Windows®, UNIX®, Mac OS® X. The OS is responsible for running the other type of software...
2) Application software — this means things like word processors, spreadsheets, games, and so on.

Make sure you know the difference between hardware and software

Some people say they don't own a computer. I mostly don't believe them, since microprocessors and computers are inside so many things these days. Make sure you know all this stuff.

Computers

Here are a few different types of computer that you'll need to know about.

Laptops and *Netbooks* are Portable Computers

Computers all used to be hefty things that you could only move around if you owned a forklift. Those days are gone...

Laptops (or Notebooks) are pretty small — not much bigger than this book (but usually slightly thicker). They're very portable — they'll fit in a small bag.

Netbooks are smaller — about the size of a piece of kitchen towel (but, again, usually slightly thicker...). They're very very portable.

Handheld Devices are Smaller Still

Tablets

Traditionally, devices that could be held in just one hand were called "Palmtops".

- The first palmtops were called PDAs (personal digital assistants), and often had a touch screen and a lot of the same software as bigger computers, like word processors, spreadsheets and digital organisers.
- PDAs aren't used much now because they've been replaced by tablets and smartphones.
- Tablets are bigger than traditional PDAs (but smaller than laptops), and have powerful processors and high resolution screens, as well as access to the Internet.
- Because of this, they can download and play music and videos, and run a wide range of software, including games and custom made applications for both work and leisure.
- Some handheld devices can be used to store and read a large number of books — these are known as e-book readers, and are cheaper and lighter than other tablets.

Smartphones

Think "mobile phone meets computer".

- Smartphones have their own operating system and can have various applications loaded onto them — this makes them much more flexible than conventional phones.
- They'll often have touch screens (that can be used as a QWERTY keyboard), loads of memory, Internet and email capabilities, personal organiser, navigation system, camera, media players (for music and video)... and so on.

Input Devices

An input device is any hardware which is used to enter data into the computer system.

QWERTY Keyboards are the Most Common Input Device

1) QWERTY keyboards are the most common type of keyboard. The name comes from the first row of letters on the keyboard.

2) Each key is connected to a switch which closes when the key is pressed. This sends a signal to the CPU based on the key's location.
3) QWERTY keyboards are based on the way typewriters were designed.
4) A problem is that keying in can be slow unless the user has been trained or knows how to type.

Concept Keyboards are Faster but More Limited

1) Concept keyboards are typically found in shops and restaurants. Each switch has a symbol (or word) on it, representing a piece of data (e.g. the price) stored in the computer.
2) For example, if you go to a fast-food restaurant and order a cheeseburger, the assistant will press the picture of that burger. The CPU then tells a display panel to show the correct price and sends a message to the kitchen and stock-control system.

Concept keyboards are great if you want to key in similar information over and over again.

Mice are Used to Move a Pointer on the Screen

Most people find using a mouse easy. A mouse has two main parts:

1) There are usually two or three buttons. When the pointer is over an icon, menu item, or the edge of a picture, the mouse buttons can be clicked or double-clicked to give the computer a command. A button can also be held down to drag something across the screen.

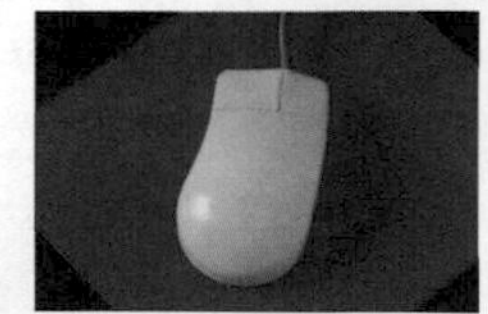

2) Mice tell the computer the direction and speed they are pushed. This is used to move the pointer on the screen. Optical mice have an optical sensor underneath and work out their movement by watching how the surface below them moves. Older mice use a ball. The ball rotates when the mouse is moved and sensors measure the movement of the ball in two directions.

Computers are mainly controlled with keyboards and mice

Nothing too tricky here. But make sure you know the difference between both types of keyboard and their benefits and problems. You've also got to know the main parts of a mouse, but there's only two...

Input Devices

Laptops usually have Touch Pads or Trackerballs

1) Touch-sensitive pads look like small screens. You move your finger across the pad to move the pointer. They use less space than a mouse but usually don't work if you wear gloves, making them unsuitable for many scientific environments.
2) A trackerball works in the same way as a ball mouse, but the ball's moved by hand, so it takes up less space. Most people find using them a bit fiddly, and not that accurate or quick.
3) Pointing sticks are worked by putting a finger on them and pushing in some direction, which moves the pointer. They're really really small, not very accurate, and a bit weird.

Graphics Tablets make Drawing Easier and More Accurate

1) Graphics tablets (sometimes called digitisers) are like a pen and paper. They're made of a touch-sensitive surface (like the piece of paper) and a rigid stylus (like the pen).
2) The user presses on the surface with the stylus, and the touch-sensitive pad registers its position, and displays it on the screen.

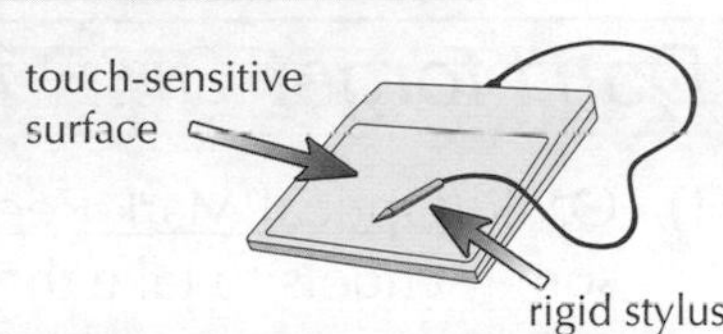

A Joystick can Input Movement

1) These are mainly used to play computer games — but they can also be used to move a computer-controlled device such as a robot or a hospital body scanner.
2) The joystick is fixed to a base but can be moved in any direction. The computer gets information from sensors on the joystick, which tells the computer how to update the screen display or move a robotic device.

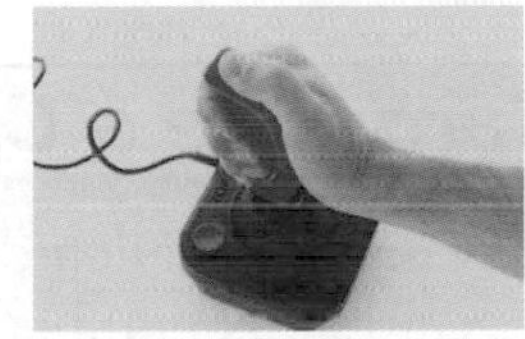

Scanners Convert Images into Digital Data

1) A scanner converts pictures into digital data — different parts of the picture are given different codes depending on their colour and brightness. The computer then builds up a 'map' of the information based on these individual 'bits' of data.
2) A problem is that these bitmap files can be very large and so take up a lot of memory. A benefit is that the scanned image can be manipulated and edited easily and quickly.
3) Most scanners are flatbed devices, which are usually a few centimetres tall and slightly larger than an A4 piece of paper.

Graphics tablets make it easy to draw things using painting software

It's important to remember that even though all of these devices look different and are used in different ways, they are all designed to do the same basic task — to get data into a computer.

Input Devices

OCR Software can Read Text

1) OCR stands for Optical Character Recognition. OCR software takes scanned digital information and looks for familiar patterns that might make up letters or numbers.

2) The software then creates a text file that can be edited using word-processing software.

3) This makes it quick and easy to enter large blocks of text. But the software is not perfect, so the result needs to be proofread.

Don't forget OMR for Registers

1) OMR (Optical Mark Recognition) is used in some schools to take the class register.
2) The teacher fills in different boxes with a pencil if a pupil is present or absent. A scanner then reads the carbon in the boxes.
3) The system is quick and accurate — but only if the OMR sheet is filled in properly.

y Darbishire
ash
Park
Little
Rogers
Thompson

Cards use a Chip or a Magnetic Stripe on the Back

1) Chip and PIN cards have a computer chip which stores account information and the card's PIN number (in encrypted form). To use the card, the customer has to enter their PIN, which is checked against the PIN stored on the chip.
2) Before chips, account information was stored in a short length of magnetic tape sealed onto the back of the card.
3) All new cards have chips, and many also have a magnetic stripe for use with older tills.

Police use OCR software to automatically read car number plates

You might have done a multiple-choice test where you had to mark your answers on an OMR sheet, and you've probably seen a chip and PIN card before — but OCR software might be new to you. Anyway, make sure you learn about all of these input devices before you move on to the next page.

Input Devices

Only two pages of input devices to go — admittedly there are nine more devices to learn still...

1 Digital Cameras

Digital cameras are a bit like scanners. They save an image as a series of dots called pixels. The image can then be uploaded to a computer and edited using photo-editing software. Most digital cameras can also record video clips, but dedicated video cameras are a better bet if you're going to be recording a lot of video footage.

Benefits — photographic film is not needed and the image is available for immediate use. It can also be sent via an e-mail attachment to anywhere in the world.

Problem — high-resolution images use lots of memory.

2 Web Cams

Web cams are basically digital cameras, but are usually used to take pictures and video footage that's going to be sent via the Internet.

3 Bar-code Readers

Bar-code readers are used in supermarkets and libraries.
They are used to read a bar code which contains data about the product being scanned.

Benefits — it makes buying goods faster and reduces the chance of human error.

Problems — the system is expensive and depends on the data in the bar code and the computer system being accurate.

4 Touch Screens

Touch screens are a bit like concept keyboards — but instead of pressing a key, you touch the picture or word on the screen. They're used a lot in information centres and quiz machines in pubs.

Benefits — easy to use and you can have different options each time the screen display changes.

Problems — more expensive than a keyboard, and they get dirty and sticky from being touched.

Input Devices

5 Microphones

Microphones are becoming increasingly used as an input device.
They are used to input data into voice-recognition systems, which convert sound into text or commands for the computer. They are also used to record sound so it can be stored digitally — which means you can do things like send it over the Internet.

Benefit — you can use dictation instead of having to type.

Problem — sound data uses a lot of memory.

6 Sensors

Sensors are hardware that record environmental information and convert it to computer data. Examples include temperature sensors, light sensors and infrared sensors used in burglar alarm systems. Sensors will be covered in the section on data logging (page 82).

7 MIDI Instruments

These instruments can be used to enter music into a computer package, e.g. a keyboard can be played and the notes recorded on the computer, where they can be edited.

Benefit — the sound of the notes can be changed easily, e.g. from a piano sound to a saxophone sound.

Problem — the computer software can be expensive.

8 Remote Controls

Remote controls allow you to control devices like TVs, DVD and music players, and video games from a short distance away. They usually work using infrared radiation.

9 Interactive Whiteboards

Interactive whiteboards look (at first) like normal, low-tech whiteboards that you can only write on with a pen. But in reality, they're fancy hi-tech things that are attached to a computer. The output from a computer (that would normally be shown on a monitor) can be projected onto the whiteboard. And the whiteboard also works like a touch screen, allowing you to use your finger or a pen like a mouse pointer.

You'd have a pretty full desk if you owned all of these devices...

I had no idea that so many input devices existed... Don't get overwhelmed though — all you need to know is a device's name, what it's used for and any advantages and disadvantages it has.

Warm-Up and Worked Exam Questions

Well that was a bit of a huge chunk of revision. Hopefully you've still got the will to carry on — there's quite a bit more to go... For now, have a go at the following few pages of questions. If you get one wrong, go back and learn the stuff again before having another go at the question. It's the best way to do it.

Warm-Up Questions

1) What is a server?
2) Describe how a keyboard works.
3) What are sensors?

Worked Exam Questions

1 Bridgette is paying for some clothes in a shop. She was given a 10% discount. Suggest three data input devices that might have been used during the transaction and explain what they might have been used for.

A bar-code reader ✔[1 mark] might have been used to scan the clothes' data, e.g. price, into the cashier's computer. ✔[1 mark]

A chip and PIN card reader ✔[1 mark] might have been used to collect Bridgette's bank account details. ✔[1 mark]

A touch screen ✔[1 mark] might have been used by the cashier to apply the discount to Bridgette's purchases. ✔[1 mark]

You have to use your brain a bit for this one — don't pick input devices like interactive whiteboards because you won't be able to justify your answer.

(6 marks)

2 (a) (i) Describe OCR software.

OCR stands for Optical Character Recognition. ✔[1 mark] OCR software takes scanned digital information and looks for patterns that might make up ✔[1 mark] letters or numbers.

(2 marks)

(ii) Describe OMR.

OMR stands for Optical Mark Recognition. ✔[1 mark] A special sheet is marked and an OMR scanner reads the sheet for any marks and records them. ✔[1 mark]

(2 marks)

(b) Give one disadvantage of OCR software

The output needs proofreading by a human to check it's OK. ✔[1 mark]

(1 mark)

(c) Give one use of OMR.

to collect class register information ✔[1 mark]

(1 mark)

Exam Questions

1 Five types of portable computer are labelled with the letters **A**, **B**, **C**, **D** and **E**. Write one letter in each row of the table that best matches the description.

A e-Book reader **B** Smartphone **C** Laptop **D** Netbook **E** PDA

	Description	Letter
(i)	Mobile phone with a touch screen that can run many applications.	B
(ii)	Portable computer with components found in a desktop computer, e.g. a full-sized keyboard and screen.	D
(iii)	Handheld device used exclusively to store and display a large number of books.	A

(3 marks)

2 Tom is building a PC. He has already bought a CPU and a hard drive.

(a) Suggest three other components that Tom will need to buy for his PC.

Tom will need a monitor, mother board, sound card and wireless card

(3 marks)

(b) (i) What is a CPU?

Central processing unit

(1 mark)

(ii) Describe what a CPU does.

(2 marks)

3 (a) Describe the difference between hardware and software.

Hardware are the things you can touch. Software are the programs that run the computer

(2 marks)

(b) Give two examples of hardware and two examples of software.

Hardware	Software
keyboard	microsoft word
monitor	microsoft excell
speaker	microsoft publisher

(4 marks)

Exam Questions

4 Chippy's Pizza Shack is a fast food restaurant in Blackpool. Staff use a concept keyboard to enter customer orders onto the computer system.

(a) What is a concept keyboard?

A concept keyboard is

(2 marks)

(b) State one benefit to the restaurant of using a concept keyboard.

(1 mark)

5 Tick **two** boxes to show which of the following are **not** input devices.

	Tick **two** boxes
Touchpad	
LCD monitor	✓
Microphone	
Webcam	
Laser printer	✓

(2 marks)

6 An artist is drawing a picture in a graphics software package on her laptop using a trackerball. She is finding it quite difficult to draw something exactly how she wants.

(a) (i) Describe how a trackerball is used.

A trackerball a is a ball that is moved by hand to move the cursor on on the screen

(2 marks)

(ii) Suggest an alternative input device that could be better for the artist to use.

a stylus

(1 mark)

(b) The artist uses a digital camera to take photographs which she edits in a graphics software package.

(i) Give one advantage of using digital cameras over traditional film cameras.

A digital camera image can be uploaded to a computer

(1 mark)

(ii) Give one other input device that can be used to input images.

A scanner

(1 mark)

Output Devices — Printers

An output device is any hardware used to communicate the result of data processing. Printers are used to produce a permanent hard copy of the information on paper.

Laser Printers are Great but Expensive

Laser printers work in a very similar way to photocopiers. They have four main parts:

1) Electrostatic rotating drum — has an electrical charge.
2) Laser — 'etches' onto the drum a negative image of a page by removing electrical charge.
3) Toner cartridge — contains ink. As the drum passes over the toner cartridge, ink is attracted to charged areas of the drum, and then transferred onto the paper.
4) Fuser unit — heats the paper to fuse the ink onto it.

Advantages

Very high resolution — typically 600 dots per inch (dpi) or more, so they can print high-quality documents.

Very fast — over 10 pages per minute (ppm).

Laser printers are very quiet.

Disadvantages

Expensive — though they're getting cheaper.

Lots of complex equipment inside — so expensive to repair.

Inkjet Printers are a Good Compromise

1) These are the cheapest kind of printer, but they can produce good quality output.
2) The main component is the printhead. This has lots of tiny nozzles or spouts through which small jets of ink are sprayed onto the paper.
3) There are three different ways of controlling the flow of ink:

i) The nozzles can be controlled by crystals inside the printhead, which change shape when an electrical current is passed through them.

ii) The ink can be heated so that it expands and pushes through the nozzles.

iii) Continuous flow printers squirt ink continuously from the nozzles, then unused ink is electrically charged and diverted back by charged plates.

Advantages

Good resolution — usually 300 to 600 dpi, so can print good quality documents.

Cheap to buy — the cheapest are under £30.

Small — so ideal for home desk use.

Disadvantages

Slow(ish) — colour printing often less than 4 ppm.

Expensive to run — the cartridges cost more (per page) than laser printer cartridges.

Nowadays inkjet printers can cost less than a pair of trainers

Different printers are suited to different situations. Inkjets are great for good quality, affordable printing — but not a lot of it. Lasers print loads of pages of professional quality documents quickly.

Output Devices — Printers

Just a few more things to learn about printing and then it's on to some more types of output devices...

Buffering and *Spooling* Help make Printing Easier

Computers process data faster than printers can print it. There are two ways to prevent hold-ups:

1) A printer buffer is memory that stores the pages that have not yet been printed. It is found inside the printer. This means the user can do other things while waiting for the printed document.

2) Spooling is when the document to be printed is saved onto the hard disk before being held in a print queue. This frees up the CPU to continue processing data. Again, this means the user can get on with other tasks without waiting for the printer.

Graph Plotters are Specialised Printers

1) Page (laser) printers are good for most things but they're often not accurate enough for precision drawings such as architects' plans — and they can't print on big enough bits of paper.

2) The most common type of graph plotter is a flatbed plotter. The paper lies on a flat surface and a plotter arm moves over it from left to right. On the plotter arm is a pen holder which moves up and down the piece of paper. In this way the pen can draw accurate lines in any direction.

3) As colour page (laser) printers get cheaper and better there will be less demand for small graph plotters.

Learn the difference between buffering and spooling

There was a time when you had to keep a document open while you printed it — otherwise if you closed it, the printer would just stop. With the invention of buffers and spooling, this problem is a thing of the past. Graph plotters can print huge documents, e.g. wall posters, with ease.

Other Kinds of Output Device

You might already be familiar with the output devices on this page — there's nothing overly complicated, so with a bit of old-fashioned hard work you'll be done with this page in no time.

Monitors give a Visual Display

Monitors are the most commonly used output device.

1) They're used when visual information is needed but a permanent record isn't.
2) Most monitors these days are flat-screen LCD models, but older computers used heavy, bulky cathode-ray tube (CRT) ones.
3) There are two important ways that monitors differ from each other — size and resolution.

CRT monitors are generally much bigger and heavier than LCD monitors.

i) Size — measured in inches across the diagonal. A typical general PC monitor has a size of at least 19 inches. Most laptops have a screen about 15 inches across.
ii) Resolution — measured by the number of pixels or dots that make up the image viewed on the screen. Most new monitors can show at least 1280×1024 pixels.

Graphics designers and desktop publishers who want to see a whole design or page in great detail should use a large, high-resolution monitor.

Speakers Output Sound

1) Computer speakers (especially the ones built into laptops) may not be the best quality possible.

2) New speakers can easily be attached to improve sound quality or volume.

Digital Projectors Show Output on a Big Screen

1) Digital projectors are used to project output that would normally appear on a monitor onto a big cinema-style screen (or a wall) instead.

2) They're useful if you have to present information to large numbers of people.

3) They're fairly light and portable, but can be quite delicate and easy to break.

CRT monitors are preferred to LCD monitors in some industries...

... like in printing, because they generally show colours more accurately. But that doesn't change the fact that they are heavy and hard to move around — unlike their trim LCD cousins.

Other Kinds of Output Device

It's the final page of output devices. But not boring, run-of-the-mill output devices like printers and monitors. No, this page is about robots and stuff...

Computers can Control **External Devices**

1) All output devices are activated by signals which come originally from the CPU. These signals can be used to control devices outside the computer.
2) For example, computer signals can switch things like lights and buzzers on and off. You just need a control interface to connect these output devices to the computer.
3) On their own, lights and buzzers aren't massively exciting. But if you string a few of them together and add an appropriate input device (e.g. a motion sensor), you can end up with a burglar alarm system, for example.

Actuators Can be Made to **Move**

A control interface can also be used to operate actuators — output devices that are able to move and perform simple mechanical tasks. There are three main types of actuator:

1) Motors are powered by an electricity supply.
   a) Stepper-motors are ones where the motor moves in a series of tiny but accurate steps. Flat-bed scanners are usually powered by stepper-motors.
   b) Servo-motors are ones where the motor moves continuously at high speed. These are used in computer-operated drills, for example.

2) Hydraulic actuators are powered by liquid pressure controlled by the computer. This makes them slow but very powerful, so they're useful for heavy lifting equipment.

3) Pneumatic actuators are like hydraulic ones but are powered by air pressure instead. They're less powerful than hydraulic systems but more responsive, and are often used to power robots on fast-moving automated production lines.

Robotic Arms are a Type of Output Device

1) Once you can use a computer to control physical movement, the world is your oyster. This is because it's only a small step from that to things like robotic arms, and more...
2) Take a computer, some actuators, and connect them up using a few gears, levers and the like, and you have a device that can grip an object. Or, if your engineering skills are more advanced, you can build a device that can build a car — the principle is essentially the same.

Robotic arms are just a big combination of actuators

You probably won't see robotic arms on a daily basis, but that's not to say that they won't come up in your exam — learn this page from top to bottom, including the three types of actuators.

Storage Devices — ROM and RAM

ROM and RAM are two types of computer memory. They're similar but different.

RAM is Temporary Memory

1) RAM is short for Random-Access Memory. It's memory that can be read from or written to.

2) There are two types of RAM — volatile and non-volatile.

3) Volatile RAM keeps its contents only while power is supplied to it. If you cut off the power then anything that's stored in it is lost.

4) Non-volatile RAM needs power to change its contents, but things that are stored in it stay there even if the power is switched off.

5) Lots of people confuse RAM and the hard drive, but they're different. Hard drives are a permanent data store, while RAM is a temporary store of data that the computer can access more quickly.

But if a computer doesn't have as much RAM as the computer would like to use (e.g. while running lots of programs) then it'll use the hard drive as a kind of 'overflow' memory — but data stored there will be much slower to access. That's why adding more RAM to a computer can influence its processing power, speed, and how many programs it can run at the same time.

ROM is Permanent Memory

1) ROM is short for Read-Only Memory — it's permanent memory and won't be lost in a power cut, so it's a type of non-volatile memory. The amount of ROM in most computers is small compared with the amount of RAM.

2) ROM contains the instructions that enable the operating system to be loaded into RAM from the backing store (i.e. hard drives etc.) when the computer is switched on.

3) However, sometimes the computer operating system is stored on ROM. This is especially true for mobile devices, like phones and PDAs (see page 3).

Adding more RAM to your computer can improve its performance

You're often told about a computer's memory size in adverts — this is how much RAM the computer has. It's quite easy to confuse this with hard drive size, as they're both measured in bytes. But they're very different. ROM is also different from RAM, and you need to know what the differences are.

Data Storage — Backing Storage

A backing store (also known as a secondary store) is any data-storage area that the CPU uses outside of its ROM and RAM. And the good news is, there are lots and lots of types to learn.

Data is stored in **Bytes**

1) Computers consist of a number of electric circuits, and each circuit must either be on or off.
2) This is why computers use a binary code (i.e. they use only 2 digits) to represent data. Usually, a circuit that's switched on represents 1, and a circuit that's switched off represents 0.

Morse code works in a similar way — it's either a dot or a dash.

Bit	Each individual 1 or 0 is called a bit — short for binary digit.
Byte	8 bits is called a byte.
Kilobyte	1 kilobyte (1 KB, or simply 1 K) is about a thousand bytes. To be exact, 1 KB = 2^{10} = 1024 bytes.
Megabyte	1 megabyte (1 MB) is about a million bytes (it's actually 2^{20} = 1 048 576 bytes).
Gigabyte	1 gigabyte (1 GB) is about a thousand million bytes (it's actually 2^{30} bytes).
Terabyte	1 terabyte (1 TB) is about a million million bytes (it's actually 2^{40} bytes).

Hard Disks are the Main **Data Store**

1) Hard disks are usually found inside computers. They're stacks of magnetised circular metal plates. Each plate is divided into concentric tracks and sectors — and data is stored in the sectors (usually on both sides of the individual plates).

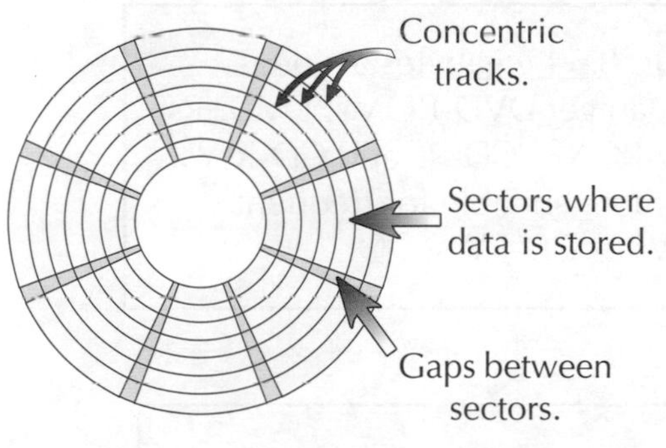

2) Read/write heads float just above the surface of the disk. They're so close that a speck of dust would ruin the hard drive — so the disk drive is kept in a sealed unit.

3) Hard drives are usually housed inside a computer. However, you can also get external hard drives for additional storage — these are also useful if a hard drive needs to be swapped between different computers.

4) The main benefit of hard drives is that they have a large capacity — hundreds or thousands of gigabytes (1 gigabyte = 1024 megabytes) are now common. But if there's a problem with the hard drive, all of the data stored on it may be lost.

A petabyte is 1024 terabytes — about a quadrillion bytes...

You need to learn the table of memory units — don't be put off by the big numbers, it's pretty straightforward when you break it down. And don't forget about hard disks — they're very important.

Data Storage — Backing Storage

CDs, DVDs and Blu-Ray™ discs are found nearly everywhere — and they're all types of optical disc.

Optical Discs are the Main External Backing Store

Optical discs include Compact Discs (CDs) and Digital Versatile Discs (DVDs). They store digital data as pits (i.e. little indentations) on the surface of a reflective disc. The data is read by moving a laser beam across the surface of the disc and reading the change in position of the reflected beam.

There are three different types of CD:

1) CD-ROMs hold around 650 megabytes, but you can't write to them (see page 16 for more on ROM).

2) CD-Rs (the R stands for 'recordable') are sold as blank CDs, and can have data written onto them... but only once. After that they work in the same way as CD-ROMs. Both CD-ROMs and CD-Rs are known as WORM discs — "Write Once and Read Many times".

3) CD-RWs are also available. RW stands for Re-Writable. They're like a CD-R but can have old data deleted and new data written onto the disc.

DVDs are like CDs but hold much more data — up to 8.54 gigabytes a side. As a result they can store whole films digitally. You can get DVD-ROMs, DVD±Rs and DVD±RWs. These work in the same way as CD-ROMs, CD-Rs and CD-RWs. DVD-RAMs are like DVD±RWs but are made to be more suitable for frequent updating and changing of data than either DVD±RWs or CD-RWs.

Blu-Ray™ discs are like DVDs but again hold much more data — nearly 6 times as much as a standard DVD. They're used for storing films in high definition.

Each type of optical disc is read with a different type of laser

Lots of people think that digital distribution (i.e. over the Internet) of things like films and music will mean that these optical discs won't be needed any more. But that won't happen any time soon, and definitely not before your exam — so make sure you know about each of the different types of disc.

Data Storage — Backing Storage

Excellent — there are more types of backing storage for you to enjoy. Once again, make sure you know how each one works and what its uses are.

Solid-State Drives are a More Robust Alternative

1) Solid-state drives perform the same function as a hard drive, but they have no moving parts, so they're not affected by movement or shocks. This makes them ideal for use in mobile devices.
2) They also have quick access times (i.e. they can read data very quickly).
3) However, they're more expensive (per unit of storage) than a hard drive.

Flash Memory is a Type of Solid-State Drive...

1) Flash memory is a type of non-volatile memory which can be used to store gigabytes of data.

2) Flash memory is a lot slower than the computer's main RAM, but is often faster than a hard disk.

3) It's very stable and doesn't break easily. It does 'wear out' eventually, though.

...and is used in Memory Sticks and Memory Cards

1) Flash memory's often sold in pen-sized devices that you can easily connect to your computer using a USB socket (so they're often referred to as pen drives, memory sticks or USB drives).
2) They allow you to easily transfer data between computers.
3) Some operating systems, such as Windows® 7, even let you use memory sticks as a temporary storage area between RAM and the hard disk. That can lead to a faster computer.
4) The main disadvantages are that they are easily lost or stolen.
5) Flash memory is also used to make small memory cards. They come in lots of different shapes and sizes, but most are close to rectangular and about the size of a coin.
6) Memory cards are used by digital cameras and some mobile phones and MP3 players. Many computers come with slots for memory cards, which means that you can use them for reading and writing files just like a memory stick.

USB stands for Universal Serial Bus — it's a standard connection that most computers support.

Solid-state drives are quite expensive, but they're quick and reliable

Before solid-state USB drives came along, you had to carry data on CD, Zip disk or even a floppy disk — but times have changed and you need to know all about solid-state drives and flash memory.

Data Storage — Backing Storage

Two more data storage mediums to go — one quite old (magnetic tape) and one quite new (online storage). Both need to be learnt before you can say that you've finished the first section...

Magnetic Tape *can Back Up Large Amounts of Data*

1) Magnetic tape is often used when large amounts of data need to be backed up.

> Backing up means making copies of files that can be stored somewhere safe.
>
> The idea is that they can be used if the original gets lost or damaged for some reason. Back-ups need to be kept secure — ideally in locked fireproof rooms in a different location.

2) With magnetic tape, data is written to and read from tape in the same way as in a video recorder.
3) Very large amounts of data can be stored relatively cheaply.
4) However, access time is slow, because the read/write head can't go directly to a particular piece of data — you have to wind through the whole tape. This is called serial or sequential access.

> In contrast, disk drives and flash memory give direct access to data — much handier.

On-line *Storage is Good for* ***Backing Up*** *and* ***Easy Access***

1) On-line storage means storing data on the file servers of an ISP, an Internet Service Provider (see page 94 for more info), instead of on your own computer's hard disk.
2) You can use on-line storage to:

> back up your files

> share your files with other people (e.g. holiday photos)

> access your files from any computer with Internet access

On-line storage companies usually charge by the gigabyte

If you need to back up loads and loads of data, magnetic tapes are what you want — then you can store the tapes safely. But if you need to get easy access to your files, online storage is the way to go.

Warm-Up and Worked Exam Questions

Another big chunk down — it's time to see how you got on with output devices and data storage...

Warm-Up Questions

1) What does ROM stand for?
2) How many bytes are in one kilobyte?
3) Explain why magnetic tape is often used as a back-up storage medium.

Worked Exam Questions

1 Nilesh gives presentations around the country to groups of people who have signed up to his company's services. He uses an LCD monitor to show the presentation slides.

(a) Suggest another visual output device that Nilesh could use for his presentations.

digital projector ✔ [1 mark]

(1 mark)

(b) Describe one advantage and one disadvantage of the device you suggested in part (a) over Nilesh's current output device.

Advantage *Digital projectors display images at a large size,* ✔ [1 mark] *so it will be easier for people to see Nilesh's presentation.* ✔ [1 mark]

Disadvantage *Digital projectors are quite easy to break,* ✔ [1 mark] *so if Nilesh is regularly travelling with the projector he might damage it.* ✔ [1 mark]

(4 marks)

2 Many desktop computers contain:

- an internal hard disk
- a DVD writer

(a) (i) Which of these would you recommend to back up data? Explain your answer.

The DVD writer because DVDs can be stored away from the original data. ✔ [1 mark]

(1 mark)

(ii) Which of these would you recommend to store commonly used applications software and data? Explain your answer.

The internal hard disk because it can store more software in one place ✔ [1 mark] *and the data on it is easier and quicker to access than on DVDs.* ✔ [1 mark]

(2 marks)

(b) Some newer computers contain solid-state drives. Give one advantage and one disadvantage of solid-state drives over hard disks.

Advantage *They can read data much more quickly.* ✔ [1 mark]

Disadvantage *They are much more expensive per unit of storage.* ✔ [1 mark]

(2 marks)

Exam Questions

1 Gemma is trying to decide whether she should buy an inkjet printer or a laser printer.

(a) Give two advantages and two disadvantages of inkjet printers.

Inkjet printers have good resolution and they are cheap to buy. But they are slow and expensive to run

(4 marks)

(b) Give two advantages and two disadvantages of laser printers.

Laser printers have very high resolution and they are fast. But they are expensive and they have complicated equipment

(4 marks)

(c) A salesman in the printer shop was telling Gemma about buffering and spooling.

(i) Describe the difference between buffering and spooling.

(2 marks)

(ii) Describe the advantage of buffering and spooling to a computer user.

(1 mark)

(d) Gemma's boyfriend is an architect who uses a graph plotter at his workplace. Suggest one reason why he might need to use a graph plotter rather than an inkjet printer.

Because a graph plotter draws accurate line

(1 mark)

2 (a) What is an actuator?

A actuator is a motor that converts energy into motion

(1 mark)

(b) Describe two types of actuator and what each type might be used for.

(4 marks)

Exam Questions

3 Michael's mobile phone has a slot for a flash memory card.
Give one advantage and one disadvantage of flash memory cards.

....

....

(2 marks)

4 Four types of optical disc are labelled with the letters **A**, **B**, **C** and **D**.
Write one letter in each row of the table that best matches the description.

A CD-R **B** CD-RW **C** DVD-ROM **D** DVD±RW

	Description	Letter
(i)	Stores more than 4 GB of data and can be rewritten many times	
(ii)	Stores around 650 MB of data and can be rewritten many times	
(iii)	Sold as a blank disc that stores around 650 MB of data and can be written to once	

(3 marks)

5 A school's computer contains two gigabytes of RAM.

(a) (i) How many megabytes are in one gigabyte?

....

(1 mark)

(ii) Does one gigabyte contain more or fewer bytes than one terabyte?

....

(1 mark)

(b) (i) What is RAM?

....

(1 mark)

(ii) Explain how adding more RAM to a computer can improve its performance.

....

....

....

....

(4 marks)

(c) Describe what ROM is used for.

....

....

(2 marks)

Revision Summary for Section One

Section One is pretty important, I reckon. It gives you all the information you need on the bits that make up a computer system. And now you've learnt all the stuff, it's time to test yourself with some fiendishly tricky questions — so you can see how much of this stuff you've really understood. This might all sound a bit scary, but then again, it's better to find out what you don't know now, rather than in the middle of your GCSE exam. That way you can do something about it. So your basic aim is to get every question right — even if it takes you a couple of attempts.

1) What's a CPU? Where would you find one inside a computer?
2) What is a mainframe? What's an embedded computer? What about a supercomputer?
3) What's the difference between hardware and software?
4) Describe: a) a laptop, b) a netbook, c) a PDA
5) Explain the difference between a smartphone and a "normal" mobile phone.
6) What are the first six letters on a normal keyboard?
7) How are concept keyboards different?
8) Describe how a mouse works.
9) Explain one difference between a touch-sensitive pad and a mouse.
10) What type of file is created when an image is put through a scanner?
11) What do the letters OCR and OMR stand for? What do they mean?
12) List five other input devices — and explain how they work.
13) Doris has been asked to perform the following tasks. For each one list the input device that she should use:
    a) type text to create a letter,
    b) record a sound message to appear on a website,
    c) take a photo of herself and e-mail it to a friend.
14) How does a laser printer work? Give two advantages and one disadvantage of laser printers compared to inkjet printers.
15) Why are inkjets the most popular printers for home use?
16) What is the difference between buffering and spooling? Why is each one useful?
17) What are two important ways that monitors differ from each other?
18) Explain what a digital projector does.
19) What are the three main types of actuator called? How do they differ from each other?
20) What is the difference between ROM and RAM?
21) Explain the terms: a) bit, b) byte, c) megabyte, d) terabyte
22) What is a hard disk? How do they work?
23) What does WORM mean? Give the names of two types of WORM discs.
24) What's so flash about flash memory? And what is flash memory used for?
25) Which method is quicker when accessing data — serial or direct access? Why?
26) Give three uses for on-line data storage.

Operating Systems

The Operating System (OS) is the software that enables applications and the rest of the computer system to work. The most popular types of OS are Windows®, Mac OS® and Linux.

There are *Different Types* of Operating System

All OSs have the same function — they talk to the various bits of a computer (see page 1) so applications and hardware can run properly. But there are different ways that an OS can work:

Interactive OSs, as the name suggests, allow users to interact with programs — they can alter the result of the program while it's running. This is different to some older and specialised OSs, where programs run without allowing the user to affect the final outcome.

The Windows® OS is interactive and multi-tasking.

Multi-tasking OSs can run many programs at the same time. That means that they have to share out resources such as the available memory and CPU time. If more than one program wants to communicate with a peripheral (e.g. if two programs want to access the Internet at once), then the OS has to make sure that's shared too.

Multi-user OSs allow many people to log into a computer and use it at the same time. A multi-user OS has to do similar sharing of resources to a multi-tasking OS. It also has to keep track of multiple workspaces, so that each user has the same experience as they would using an individual computer.

Real time OSs run programs that need to react in a specific amount of time to events occurring in the outside world, e.g. the stock markets or the weather. The OS manages the computer's resources so that programs aren't interrupted, allowing them to meet the deadline for their responses.

You might have heard about 'cloud computing' — online OSs are part of this.

Online OSs are stored on a computer server (see page 2) that doesn't belong to the user. Users' files, e.g. documents, pictures and music, are also stored on the server. Users log in to the OS from any Internet-enabled computer — they can then use the OS as if it was on their own computer.

An operating system basically manages a whole computer

Operating systems are really important — you wouldn't really be able to do anything on a computer without one. Make sure you know what the different types of operating system above are used for.

Operating Systems — Organisation of Data

I'm sure you've wondered how a system stores information, and how it keeps track of where it all is...

Data is Stored in Files and Directories

1) A file is a block of data that's stored under one name, called its filename — e.g. a picture file, or a letter written on a word processor.
2) Some OSs store extra information with the file to identify its type and which program should be used to open it. In Windows®, this information is usually just an extension (an extra bit at the end of a filename). E.g. Microsoft® Word documents have the extension .doc or .docx.
3) A directory is a file, but also a kind of index containing information about other files. A directory tells the OS where on a disk the files are, how big each file is, when it was created, and so on.
4) With some operating systems, the files in a directory are represented by pictures, as shown below. In this type of OS, the directories are called folders.

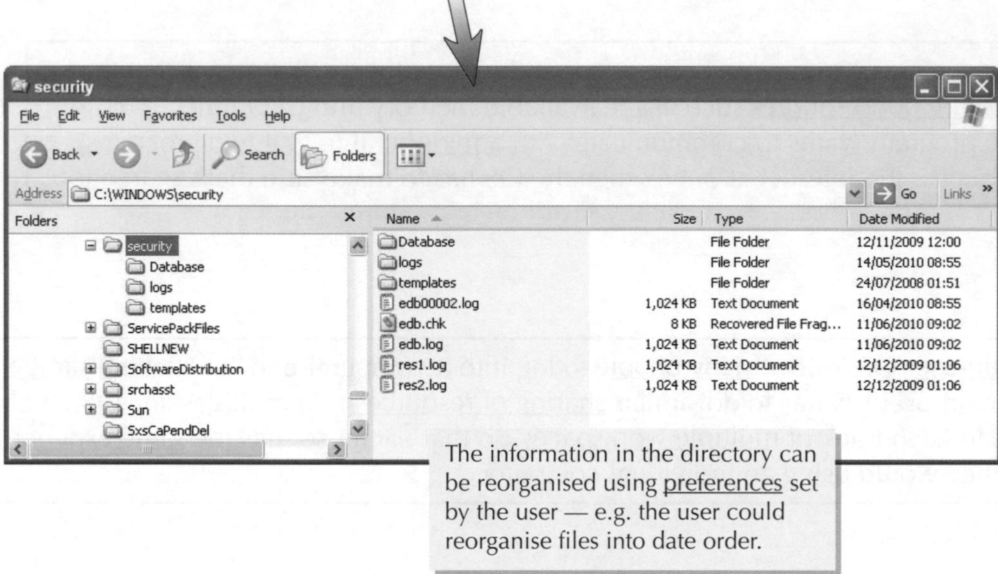

The information in the directory can be reorganised using preferences set by the user — e.g. the user could reorganise files into date order.

5) Subfolders are folders within folders — useful when dealing with loads of files.
6) Every file has a specific filepath, which describes its location. Most filepaths start off with the root directory (the folder which contains everything else), then a number of subfolders, then the filename and its extension. Here's an example:

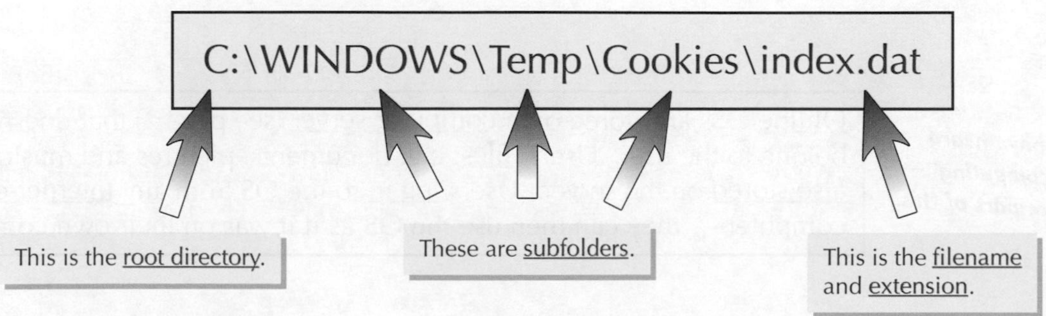

Folders and subfolders keep data organised and easy to find

You're probably used to navigating around folders and files on a computer — this is just some of the theory behind it. It's not really complicated, but make sure you know this page inside out.

Operating Systems — Files

Nearly all the work you can do on a computer involves files — you need to know how they're managed.

Files can be **Created**, **Saved** and **Managed**

1) Most applications (see page 29) have a file menu, with commands that tell the OS to carry out different file-related operations.
2) For example, creating a new file is as simple as using the 'New' command.
3) The 'save' command stores the new file — you'll be asked for a filename and a location where the file is to be stored. After the file has been saved, it can be closed and opened.
4) Opening a file and saving it again replaces the original file with a newer version. The 'save as' command lets you save a copy of the file, while keeping the original.

File management operations controlled by the OS include:

- Renaming — changing the filename of a file.
- Deleting — removing a stored file.
- Copying — making a duplicate of the file.
- Moving — transferring the file to a new location (so it has a new filepath).

Drivers let Operating Systems **Talk to Hardware**

1) Drivers are files that tell OSs how to communicate with computer hardware.
2) Most devices, e.g. printers, come with a disc with suitable drivers on it (or some instructions giving you details of a webpage where you can download the drivers).
3) You need to install the driver on the computer that the device is hooked up to, so the OS knows how to speak to the new device and make it work.

File management is carried out by a computer's operating system

Drivers have a special purpose, but they're just another type of file. All of the usual file management operations can still be done on them, but fiddling with them might cause hardware to stop working.

Operating Systems — User Interfaces

A user interface is the posh term for the way the user communicates with the OS, or other software.

Some User Interfaces use Command-Lines...

1) A command-line interface presents the user with a blank screen. The user types in commands which the OS then carries out.
2) It can take a long time to learn all the commands you're likely to need, but the system can be very powerful.

...but Most use a Graphical User Interface (or GUI)

1) These are the most popular types of user interface — all major modern operating systems use them. A GUI combines a menu-driven interface with icons to represent the main commands.
2) GUIs are more intuitive and accessible than command-line interfaces. For example, menus display lists of commands or options that are selected by clicking them with a mouse, and moving a file is as easy as dragging and dropping it in its new location.
3) GUIs are also known as WIMPs because they make use of Windows, Icons, Menus and Pointers:

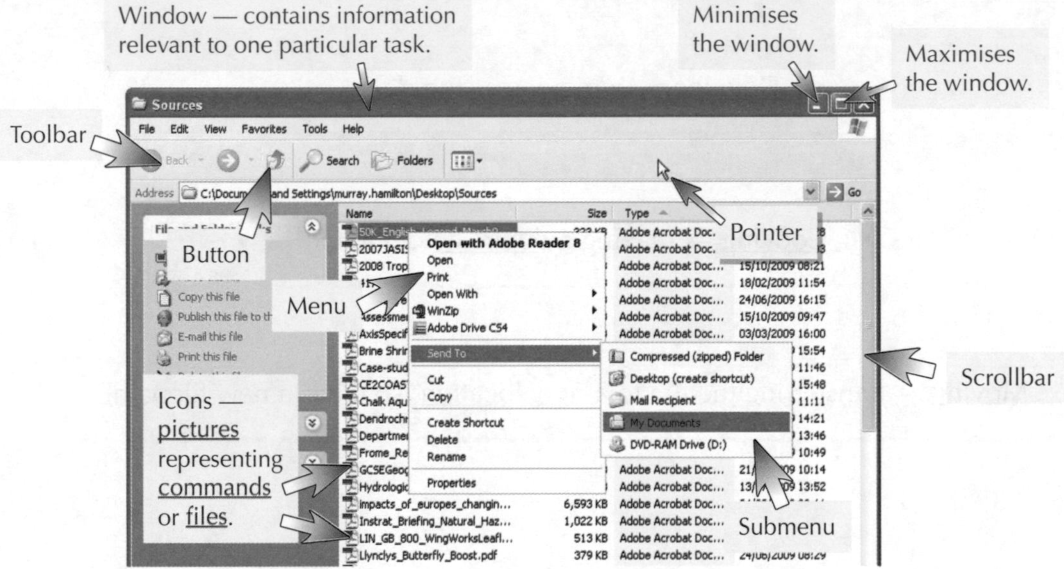

4) Users can customise GUIs to their own personal taste, making them easier to use — for example, by adjusting the volume of sounds or the desktop contrast (so things look clearer).
5) To use a GUI you don't need to learn shedloads of commands. But menu-driven interfaces can be cumbersome to use — and it's not always obvious what the logic behind the menu structure is.

Some User Interfaces Don't Need a Mouse and Keyboard

1) Many user interfaces are controlled using input devices like mice and keyboards, but modern technology has started to move away from them.
2) Touch screens, e.g. in some mobile phones and tablet PCs, allow users to press the device's screen to select options or drag items around.
3) A person's voice can also control software — many mobile phones have voice-activated dialling.
4) Direct neural interfacing is all about controlling a computer with your brain. Very futuristic.

User interfaces have evolved over time

GUIs are everywhere in modern computing, but don't forget about the humble command-line interface.

Applications Software

This stuff is just an intro to applications software — the specifics are all in later sections.

Applications Software has a **Specific Purpose**

Computers can do a lot of things, but for each task there's often a specific piece of software:

Applications software	**Used for...**
Spreadsheet software	Calculating and analysing data.
Database software	Storing large amounts of data.
Word processing software	Making documents, e.g. letters.
Desktop publishing software	Making documents with a flexible layout, e.g. magazines.
Presentation software	Making slides of information to show to people.
Web design software	Making websites.
Audio & video software	Making music and videos.
Graphics software	Making images.
Animation software	Making moving images (2D or 3D).
Programming software	Making other software.

Common Features that **Increase Usability**

Most applications software has the same basic features to make it easier to use:

Feature	**What it does**
Undo/Redo	Reverses or repeats an action.
Cut, copy and paste	Moves or copies things, e.g. text, from one place to another.
Wizards	Walks the user through a complicated action.
Help files	Instructs users on how to use the software.
Drag and drop	Makes it dead easy to move things around.
Find and replace	Searches for specific things and changes them.
Zoom	Enlarges a specific area of a document.
Printing	Creates a hard copy of a document.

Applications software helps you to get certain tasks done

Not many applications do more than one thing — they're usually very specialised bits of kit. But most of them share common features, to make your life (and revision) easier.

Applications Software

Common Features** that **Improve Presentation

Most applications produce output that's designed to be looked at. So most applications allow you to format things so they're pretty and clear.

1) Fonts can be changed, e.g. from Arial to Times New Roman.
2) Text size can be changed, e.g. emphasising headings and subheadings by making them larger.
3) Text can be highlighted. There are four ways to make text stand out:

(i) **bold type** (ii) *italics*

(iii) underlined (iv) colour

4) Line spacing determines how far apart lines of text are. Double-line spacing is much easier to read than single-line spacing — but it uses up much more paper.
5) Alignment and justification affect how each line of text is arranged. This paragraph has been fully justified, so that each line is the same length. Some different types are shown below.

This text is left-aligned.
This text is right-aligned.
This text is centre-aligned.

This text is aligned to the top of the box.
This text is aligned to the centre of the box.
This text is aligned to the bottom of the box.

6) Headers (top of a page) and footers (bottom of a page) show useful information, e.g. titles, dates and page numbers.
7) A page's orientation can be either portrait (tall and narrow) or landscape (short and wide).
8) Margins are blank areas at the edges of pages — they can help 'frame' a page's contents.
9) Inserting images in a document can help make a page more attractive and clearer. Text can then be wrapped around an image (see page 58).

Good formatting makes documents easy to read

You've probably used most of these features to format your work. You need to know their proper names though, and the reason why you would use a particular feature — but that's not too tough.

Everyday Tips and Problems

Try not to say 'yeah, yeah, whatever...' too much when reading this page — it's quite useful, and it could well come up in your exam.

The Basics — Turning a Computer On and Off

1) When you switch on a computer it usually beeps and then loads the operating system — it'll stop loading if you need to log on to access your account.

2) Logging on to a computer requires a user name and password. It's important to remember these as you won't be able to use the computer if you can't log on.

If you can't remember your user name or password, speak to the person who looks after the computer accounts.

3) After you've finished using the computer you need to shut it down. Don't head straight for the socket and turn the power off — computers don't like this.

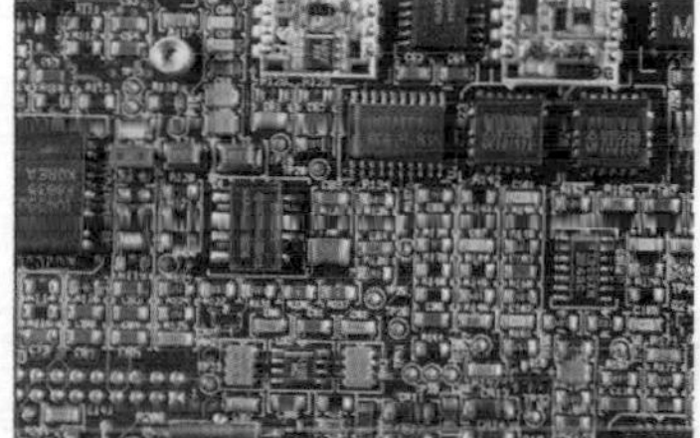

If you don't shut down your computer properly you can damage some of the components.

4) The best way to shut down a computer is by using a menu. Most operating systems give you a few options for this, such as...

- shut down (turn the computer off),
- log off (leave the computer on but let others log on),
- stand by (the computer 'goes to sleep', reducing energy consumption).

Now you can turn a computer on and off, it's all downhill from here...

OK, that seemed like I was stating the obvious, but there's every chance you'll get a question on this stuff — and you don't want to lose out on some marks because you thought you knew it all...

Everyday Tips and Problems

Basic **Hardware** and **Software Problems** can be **Solved**

1) Computers sometimes go wrong. The problem could be serious, and an absolute nightmare to sort out. But very often, the problem can be made to go away quite simply.

2) For example, when software freezes (stops responding to a user's input), or a piece of hardware stops working, there are a few things you should try before you panic too much:

- Restart your system — this will sort a lot of problems out. If you can access the shut down menu, use it. Otherwise hold the computer's power button until it turns off.

- Reinstall software — if a program is frequently not working, you could try reinstalling it. A file might have been corrupted, so installing a fresh version may fix the problem.

- Install patches — if there's a problem with the source code (see page 78) of a program, a programmer might create a patch that fixes the problem. These are usually available from the manufacturer's website.

- Check your hardware — check that you've connected the hardware correctly and that it's turned on. Also make sure that you're not expecting your hardware to do the impossible — e.g. if you're writing data to a CD, make sure the CD has a big enough storage capacity.

- Update drivers — drivers let hardware talk to the operating system. Without the right drivers it might seem like your hardware is broken, even if it's not. Up-to-date drivers are usually available from the manufacturer's website.

3) A lot of other problems (e.g. paper jams in a printer) can be solved easily once you've read the instructions or have been shown what to do.

4) But if you can't sort a problem out on your own, you should always get help from a trained person, e.g. a teacher or ICT professional.

The key to solving computer problems is keeping a cool head

The vast majority of the problems you might encounter when using a computer are pretty easy to solve — if you learn this page from top to bottom you'll probably never need to call a helpline again.

Warm-Up and Worked Exam Questions

This section wasn't very long, but there's still a whole lot of learning to be done. The questions below should put you in the right frame of mind to tackle the exam questions over on the next page.

Warm-Up Questions

1) What is meant when an operating system is said to be 'multi-tasking'?
2) Describe two features of an online operating system.
3) What is a driver?
4) What does WIMP stand for?
5) Give an example of a task that spreadsheets can help with.

Worked Exam Questions

1 A bank uses a real-time operating system with a command-line user interface to monitor global stock markets.

(a) (i) Explain what is meant by the term 'real-time operating system'.

It's an operating system that manages the computer's resources so programs aren't interrupted, ✔ [1 mark] *allowing them to meet the deadline for their responses.* ✔ [1 mark]

(2 marks)

(ii) Give one advantage and one disadvantage of using command-line user interfaces.

Advantage: *they're quick to operate once the user knows the commands* ✔ [1 mark]

Disadvantage: *it takes time to learn all the commands* ✔ [1 mark]

(2 marks)

Command-line user interfaces are the ones you see in lots of films from the 80s. MS-DOS is an operating system that had a command-line interface.

(b) Most other computers in the bank have a multi-user operating system. Describe what is meant by the term 'multi-user operating system'.

It's an operating system that allows many people to log into a computer and use it at the same time. ✔ [1 mark]

(1 mark)

(c) Name two file operations that are carried out by an operating system.

Copying files ✔ [1 mark]

Deleting files ✔ [1 mark]

(2 marks)

Pretty much anything you do to a file is controlled by the operating system so there are a few different answers you could write here, e.g. deleting files, renaming files, or moving files.

Exam Questions

1 Milham School is planning to install a new computer network. The network will be run by an operating system with a graphical user interface (GUI).

(a) What is a 'graphical user interface'?

....

....

(2 marks)

(b) Give one advantage and one disadvantage of using a graphical user interface to run an operating system.

Advantage: ....

Disadvantage: ....

(2 marks)

2 Many different applications have certain features in common so that people can learn how to use them quickly.

Tick **two** boxes to show which of the following features are found in most word processors and desktop publishing software.

	Tick **two** boxes
AutoSum	
Find and replace	
View slideshow	
Export as MP3	
Change page orientation	

(2 marks)

3 Sandy had a problem when he tried to print a document from his word processor. His friend said the problem might have been caused by Sandy never turning the computer off properly.

(a) Describe the correct way to turn off a computer.

....

(1 mark)

(b) Suggest two ways that Sandy could try and fix the printing problem.

1. ....

2. ....

(2 marks)

Revision Summary for Section Two

I know, you're upset that you've nearly finished another section and you're that little bit closer to finishing your revision. Don't worry though, I've got something that'll cheer you right up — a selection of questions to make sure you've understood everything on the last few pages.

1) What is the main function of an operating system?
2) What is an interactive operating system?
3) What is a multi-tasking operating system?
4) If a computer program has to run in fifteen seconds, no more and no less, what type of operating system should be used to run it?
5) What's so special about an online operating system?
6) What is a file?
7) On a PC using a Windows® operating system, where can you find out a file's type?
8) What is a subfolder?
9) What does a filepath describe?
10) Describe the difference between the 'save' command and the 'save as' command.
11) Describe three file operations that are carried out by an operating system.
12) Why do drivers have to be installed when you connect a new device to a computer?
13) How does a user control an operating system through a command-line interface?
14) Give one disadvantage of a command-line interface.
15) What does GUI stand for?
16) Describe two ways in which a GUI is more intuitive than a command-line interface.
17) Name four things that you would expect to see in a GUI.
18) Why do people customise their GUIs? Give one example of such a customisation.
19) Give one disadvantage of a GUI.
20) Describe two examples of how a user interface can be controlled without a mouse or keyboard.
21) What is desktop publishing software used to make?
22) What is programming software used to make?
23) Why are wizards helpful for users of applications software?
24) What feature allows users to enlarge a specific area in an application?
25) Name three ways that text can be highlighted.
26) What's the difference between a header and a footer?
27) Explain the following terms: margins, justification, page orientation.
28) What's the correct way to turn off a computer?
29) Describe three fixes that you can try if you need to sort out a hardware or software problem.

Spreadsheets — The Basics

Most people find spreadsheets a bit scary — very few people really understand them. But they're basically pretty simple. Make sure you learn this page well before moving on to the trickier stuff.

Spreadsheets are **Clever Calculators**

1) A spreadsheet is simply a program that can display and process data in a structured way. Most people think spreadsheets can only process numbers — but they can handle text as well.

2) Spreadsheets can:
   a) record data,
   b) sort data,
   c) search for particular items of data,
   d) perform calculations based on data,
   e) produce graphs and charts.

Data can be sorted in ascending (A to Z, 1 to 10) or descending (Z to A, 10 to 1) order. You can sort data by column and row.

3) Examples of uses include keeping records of patients in a doctor's surgery, calculating the exam results of a group of pupils, and producing graphs based on the results of a questionnaire.

Data is Entered into **Cells**

1) A spreadsheet is made up of tables. Rows and columns divide each table up into individual cells.

2) Each cell in a table can be identified using the column letter and row number as coordinates.

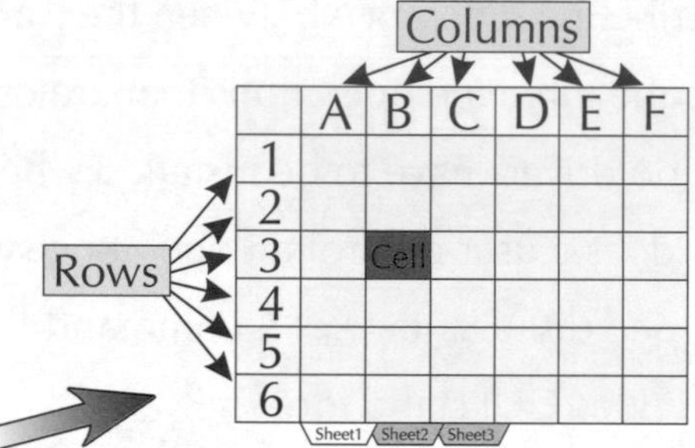

The red cell is in Column B and Row 3 — so its cell reference is B3.

Each Cell can Contain **One of Three** Things

Numerical data

e.g. integers (whole numbers), fractions, numbers with decimal places, dates, times, money, percentages.

Most spreadsheets recognise dates and money and convert them into a suitable number format, e.g. if you enter 23-6, it changes to 23 June.

Text (or Alphanumeric) data

e.g. people's names, titles of songs.

1) Column headings usually contain text.
2) One process that can be carried out on text is sorting it into alphabetical order.
3) The ICT term for a piece of text is a text string.

Formulas

1) These allow results of calculations to be displayed inside a cell.
2) E.g. you could get the computer to add up all the numbers in a column and display the answer in a cell at the bottom of the column.
3) The great thing about spreadsheets is that if any numbers are changed, the results are automatically updated.

Alphanumeric is just a fancy way of saying letters and numbers.

Spreadsheets can be used for more than just lists...

Spreadsheet software is very powerful, which makes it seem complicated. While it's true that some spreadsheets are complex, the basic idea is pretty simple — so get all this info in your brain.

Spreadsheets — Entering Data

Now you know the basics, it's time for the fun part — putting the data in. There's only really one rule to remember when entering data, but it's a pretty important one — so don't forget it...

The Data in Cells can Only be of One Type

The Golden Rule is to put only one piece of data in a cell — this means that you shouldn't mix any of the types of data.

1) If you enter the weight of a kilo of fish as '1000g' then you have numerical data (1000) and text data (g).
2) Spreadsheets treat cells with any text in them as though they contain only text data.
3) This means the spreadsheet will read '1000g' as text — which means you can't do any calculations with it.

The exceptions are things like currencies where the spreadsheet knows that £5 has a value of 5.

Data can be Entered Directly or with Controls

Learn all this stuff about entering data and formatting a spreadsheet:

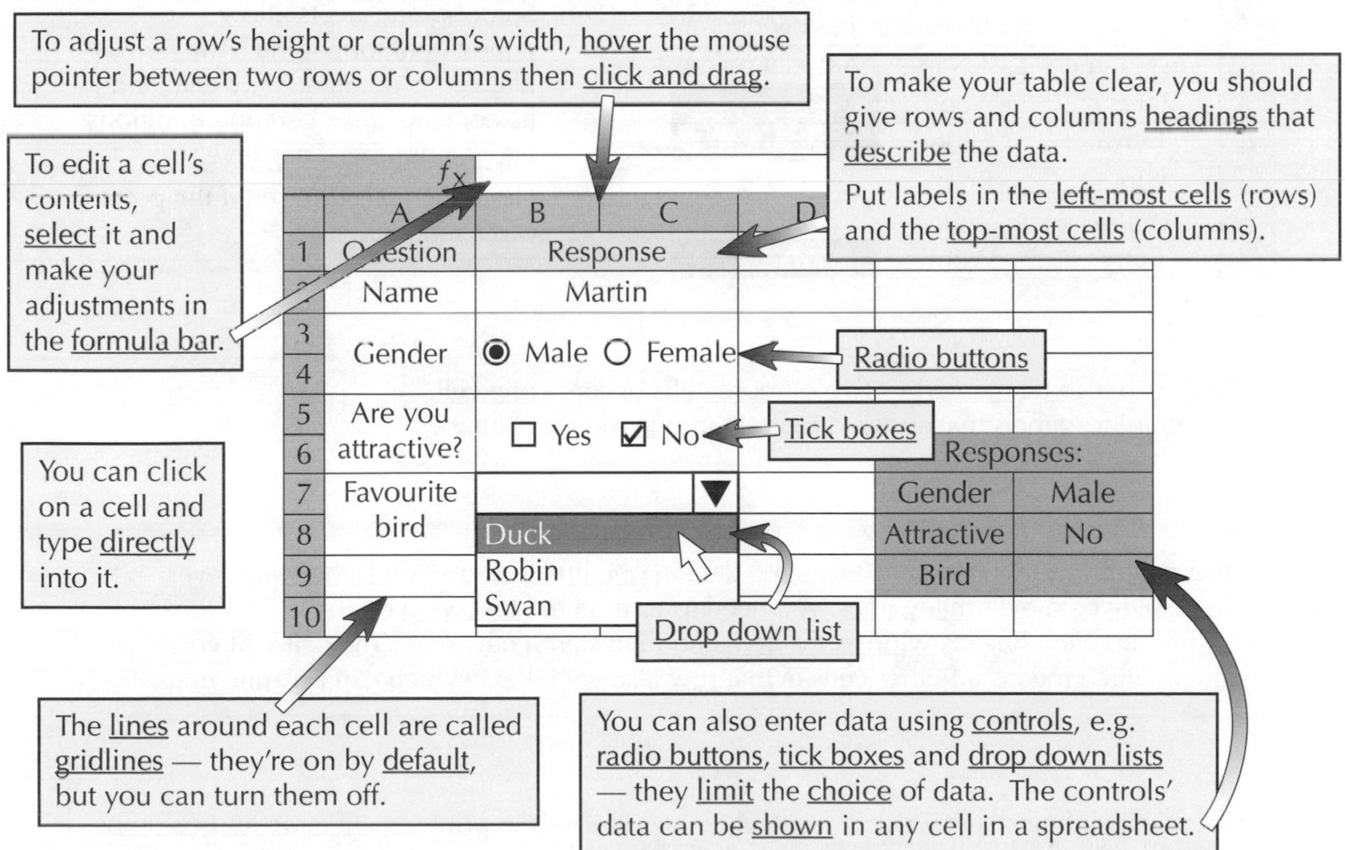

Take a recess — and learn about cells...

The best way to get to grips with spreadsheets (or any new kind of software) is to have a play with them. That goes for the rest of this section — try out the stuff you've learnt on a computer.

Spreadsheets — Formatting Data

After you've put your data in, it's a good idea to format it. A well-formatted spreadsheet is easy to read and helps people to understand the data — so don't go over the top with these options...

Data can be Formatted to Improve its Appearance

1) Data in spreadsheets can be formatted in similar ways to a word processor. Use italics, bold type, different fonts, colours, sizes etc. to make data stand out.

2) The alignment of data can be changed — it's the usual suspects of left, right and centre aligned (horizontal alignment) and top, middle and bottom aligned (vertical alignment).

3) The cells containing the data can be jazzed up a little bit too. For example, different fill colours (or shading) can be applied to them, and borders of varying thicknesses can be drawn around them — these formatting options can help show data more clearly.

	A	B	C
1	ICT Club — membership fees owing		
2	First Name	Last Name	Amount owing
3	Teresa	Wood	£8.00
4	Tanya	Hide	£5.52
5	Arthur	Brain	£0.00
6	Willie	Winn	£0.00
7	Betty	Wont	£33.67

4) Some spreadsheets allow conditional formatting. The format of a cell is automatically changed if its contents meet certain conditions, like if a number's negative. Here, the cells turn red if the person owes money.

5) Cells can also be merged — two or more cells become one cell. It's useful for labels that apply to more than one row or column.

6) You might have noticed cells that store data in one line that goes on forever and ever. To display data over many lines, you need to turn on the text wrap option — the data will fill up each line (as wide as the cell) and then start a new one. The cell will get taller, which means all other cells in that row also get taller. Which can be annoying...

7) If you're printing a spreadsheet, a useful feature to use is to print certain rows and columns on every page. This means you can show labels, making the print-out easier to read.

Data in a spreadsheet can be formatted like text in a word processor

If you don't know this stuff already, get yourself on a computer, load up a spreadsheet and try doing all the things described on this page. It's all good clean fun, and it'll help things to stick in your memory.

Spreadsheets — Simple Formulas

Without formulas, spreadsheets are just fancy tables.

A *Formula* is a Simple Computer *Program*

1) A formula is an instruction to the computer to process data held in specific cells.

	A	B	C	D	E	F
	Exam Marks for 1st Year Mocks					
2	First Name	Last Name	Maths	ICT	English	Total
3	Teresa	Wood	63	45	89	=C3+D3+E3
4	Tanya	Hide	32	54	78	
5	Arthur	Brain	33	53	95	
6	Willie	Winn	24	54	75	
7	Betty	Wont	64	53	88	

Step 1 — Click the cell where you want the answer.

Step 2 — Type an equals sign (=). This tells the computer to expect a formula.

Step 3 — Type in the formula. Here, it would be C3+D3+E3.

2) Simple formulas contain normal maths symbols like +, –, * (for multiply) and / (for divide).

3) For more complicated calculations, spreadsheets usually have a range of built-in functions (e.g. AVERAGE and SINE). You can either type functions in, or choose them from a list.

4) Once you've entered a formula, you can copy it to other cells. So the formula in F3 could be copied to cells F4 to F7 — and the computer would automatically insert the correct formulas for the totals of these rows. This makes spreadsheets an easy way to do lots of similar calculations on a large set of data.

	C	D	E	F
1				
2	Maths	ICT	English	Total
3	63	45	89	=C3+D3+E3
4	32	54	78	=C4+D4+E4
5	33	53	95	=C5+D5+E5
6	24	54	75	=C6+D6+E6
7	64	53	88	=C7+D7+E7

5) Spreadsheets recalculate formulas automatically — e.g. if you change the data in a cell range used by a formula, the formula's result will be updated without you having to think about it.

Formulas can have *Absolute* or *Relative Cell References*

1) In the example above, the formula in F3 (=C3+D3+E3) tells the computer to add together the data in the three cells to the left. If you copy this formula to cell F4, it still adds together the contents of the three cells to the left, so F4 becomes '=C4+D4+E4'. That's why they're called relative cell references — the data used is in the same place relative to the answer cell.

2) Sometimes part of a formula always needs to refer to one particular cell. In this case, you need to use an absolute cell reference — one that won't be changed. The usual way to make a cell reference absolute is to put a dollar sign in front of each part of the cell's coordinates. So B12 is a relative cell reference — but B12 is an absolute cell reference.

3) The spreadsheet to the right uses an absolute cell reference (to represent the % commission a letting agency charges on its properties).

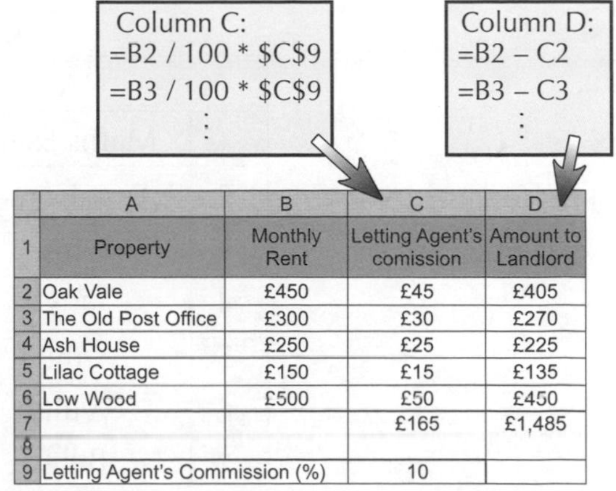

	A	B	C	D
1	Property	Monthly Rent	Letting Agent's comission	Amount to Landlord
2	Oak Vale	£450	£45	£405
3	The Old Post Office	£300	£30	£270
4	Ash House	£250	£25	£225
5	Lilac Cottage	£150	£15	£135
6	Low Wood	£500	£50	£450
7			£165	£1,485
8				
9	Letting Agent's Commission (%)		10	

Formulas can be as simple as adding up a set of numbers

Make sure you understand all the info on formulas. You should be able to write them down as you'd type them. And you need to know the difference between absolute and relative cell references.

Spreadsheets — Functions

You'll need to know about the following functions that are found in most spreadsheet software.

Functions *tell a Spreadsheet* ***How*** *to* ***Process Data***

The examples in this column refer to the spreadsheet at the bottom of the page.

Function	What it does...	Example	Result
SUM	Adds up numbers.	=SUM(C3:C7)	216
AVERAGE	Averages numbers — the mean average.	=AVERAGE(C3:C7)	43.2
ROUND	Rounds numbers to a specified number of decimal places.	=ROUND(43.2,0)	43
ROUNDUP	Same as ROUND, but only rounds up.	=ROUNDUP(43.2,0)	44
MAX	Finds the largest value in a cell range.	=MAX(C3:C7)	64
MIN	Finds the smallest value in a cell range.	=MIN(C3:C7)	24
RANK	Finds the position of a number in a range of numbers after it has been sorted in ascending (1) or descending order (0).	=RANK(C4,C3:C7,1)	2
		=RANK(C4,C3:C7,0)	4
COUNT	Counts the number of cells that contain only numbers (numerical data).	=COUNT(B2:C7)	5
IF	Checks if data matches a condition — result depends on the match being true or false.	=IF(C7>40,"Yes","No")	No

	A	B	C	D
1	Maths Exam Results			
2	First Name	Last Name	Mark	Pass?
3	Teresa	Wood	63	Yes
4	Tanya	Hide	32	No
5	Arthur	Brain	33	No
6	Willie	Winn	24	No
7	Betty	Wont	64	Yes

Colons are used to show cell ranges. E.g. "A1:D7" would include all the cells in the table to the left.

Make sure you know the name of each function and what it does

It's a lot to learn, but the sooner you get started, the sooner you'll be finished. And it's not too hard.

Spreadsheets — Functions

You met the IF function back on the last page. It can be a bit tricky to get your head round, so there's more detail on the function below. You also need to know about the LOOKUP function...

The IF Function uses Logic to Analyse Data

The IF function confuses people — don't be one of them...

1) The IF function gives different results, depending on whether data in other cells matches a condition — e.g. if the number in a cell containing a temperature is negative, the output of the IF function could be "Chilly", while if it's positive, the output could be "Warm".
2) In the spreadsheet below, the percentage scores from a maths exam are in column C. Students with 40% or less haven't passed. The IF function in column D tells the spreadsheet to display the word "No" if the number in column C is 40 or less, and "Yes" if it's above 40.

	A	B	C	D
1	Maths Exam Results			
2	First Name	Last Name	Mark	Pass?
3	Teresa	Wood	63	Yes
4	Tanya	Hide	32	No
5	Arthur	Brain	33	No
6	Willie	Winn	24	No
7	Betty	Wont	64	Yes

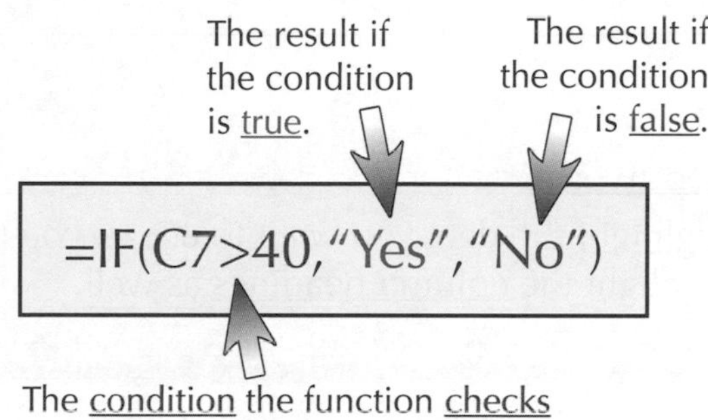

The LOOKUP Function Displays Specified Data

1) The LOOKUP function displays data from a table in another part of the spreadsheet.
2) Here, a shop selling vampire supplies has listed its products at the bottom of the spreadsheet. A user enters a product code into cell B1 — the LOOKUP function automatically displays the product name in B2 and the price in B3.
3) The formulas in cells B2 and B3 are pretty scary — but basically they search the data in cells A6-A12, and display the data in the same row as the relevant product code.

Enter a product code here...

	A	B	C
1	Product Code	26346	
2	Product Name	Garlic repellent	
3	Price	£0.50	
4			
5	Product Code	Product Name	Price
6	12532	Black capes	£25.99
7	65489	Sharp teeth	£5.50
8	26346	Garlic repellent	£0.50
9	57243	Sunglasses	£15.99
10	53289	Assorted bats	£25.99
11	12489	White face paint	£5.99
12	23412	Light meter	£34.50

...and product details appear here.

Where the function looks for the value (the product code column).

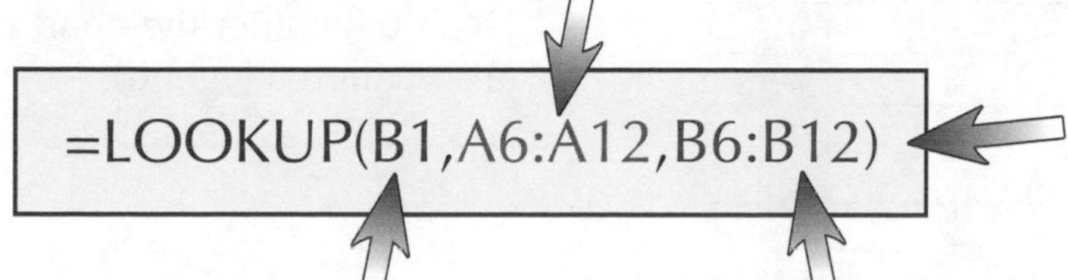

This is the formula in cell B2 — it's the same in cell B3, but the column where the function gets its result from is C6:C12 (the price column).

The value the function looks for (the product code).

Where the function gets its result from (the product name column).

The IF and LOOKUP functions help you to analyse and pick out data

When you break it all down, the IF and LOOKUP functions aren't that bad. You'll need to know how to write each of these functions, as well as all the other ones on the previous page, so get learning...

Spreadsheets — Charts and Graphs

Graphs and charts are quite similar really — they're just ways of communicating data visually.

Creating a Chart is Dead Easy

All modern spreadsheets can produce graphs and charts — but each one uses a slightly different method. The basic idea is always the same though.

Step One:

Get all the data you want to put into a graph into a single block. It's best if the data is arranged in columns.

	A	B
1	Category	Monthly Spend
2	Food	£7.50
3	Magazines	£1.00
4	CDs	£2.00
5	Going out	£4.00
6	Revision Guides	£6.00

Step Two:

Highlight the data you want to use — you might need to highlight the column headings as well.

	A	B
1	Category	Monthly Spend
2	Food	£7.50
3	Magazines	£1.00
4	CDs	£2.00
5	Going out	£4.00
6	Revision Guides	£6.00

Step Three:

Select the type of chart you want — be sensible and make sure it's suitable.

The next page tells you how to pick the best type of chart for your data.

Step Four:

Choose a meaningful title for the chart — one that summarises the contents of the chart, and label any axes.

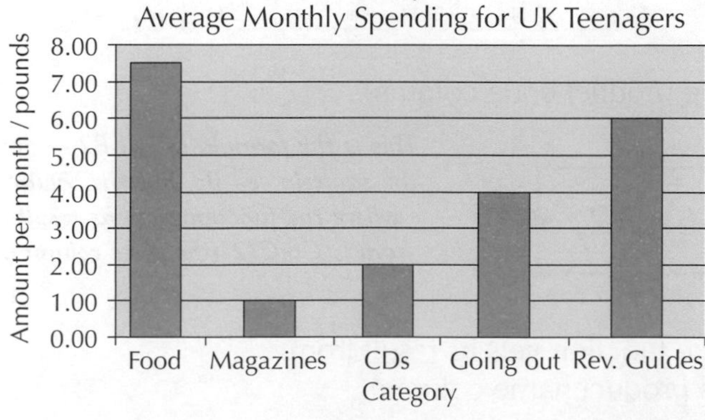

Step Five:

Decide whether the chart needs a key (also called a legend).

Spreadsheet software usually has a chart wizard to help you out

Learn the page then write out the five steps as a flow chart. There isn't really anything complicated about this stuff at all — so get it all lodged in your brain and score some easy marks in your exam...

Spreadsheets — Charts and Graphs

Spreadsheets can create so many different types of graph — but you need to choose the right kind. Sometimes it's just a matter of taste, but sometimes there are definite rights and wrongs.

You need to know which **Charts** are **Appropriate**

1) Bar Graphs display a category on the x-axis and a value on the y-axis. Use a bar graph when each category is discrete (i.e. separate from the others) — e.g. the number of people who take certain shoe sizes.

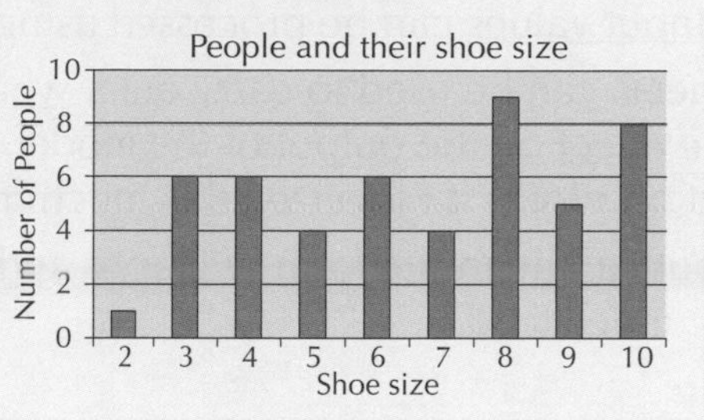

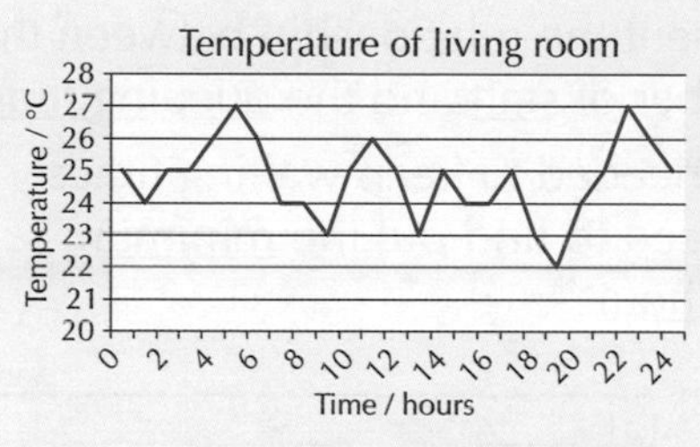

2) Line Graphs are similar, but are used when the data on the x-axis isn't in categories — like 'time' when you show the temperature of a room over a 24-hour period.

3) Scatter Graphs show the relationship between two sets of data — plot one set along the x-axis and the other on the y-axis, and add a trend line to show the relationship more clearly.

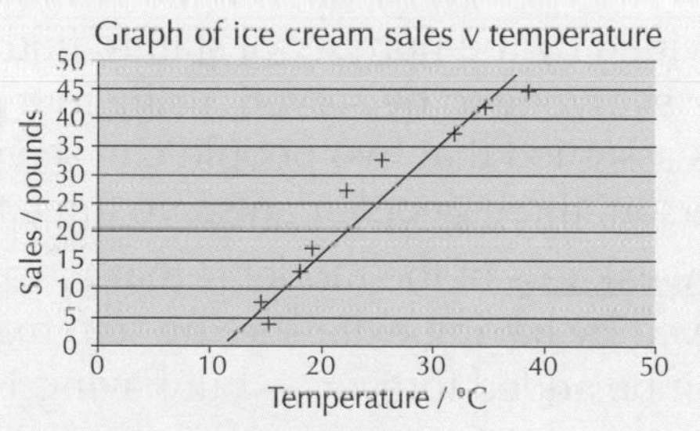

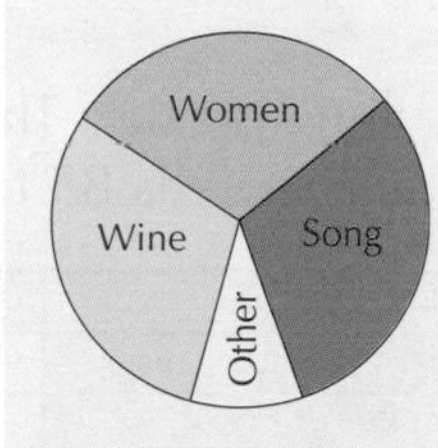

4) Pie Charts show the contributions of categories to a total — e.g. a chart showing what I spend my money on.

It's tempting to try to be too clever, and use fancy graphs that aren't really any clearer than something basic. Again the golden rule is keep it simple — make sure the graph gets its point across, and if possible test your graph by showing it to an intended user.

Appropriate charts make it easy to understand your data

Make a table with these headings: type of chart, description and when to use it — then fill it in. Some spreadsheet software has crazy stuff, like bubble and radar charts — but it's best if you don't use them.

Spreadsheets — Modelling

You could get asked about any kind of model or simulation in the exam. But, boring as they are, spreadsheets come up more often than the others. You have been warned.

Three Reasons *why Spreadsheets make Good Models*

1) Spreadsheets can use formulas to try to describe the rules that a real-world phenomenon seems to follow. Input values can be processed using these formulas to produce output values.
2) Spreadsheets can be used to carry out a what-if analysis. This is when the user changes input values to see the effect on the output of the model. So companies can ask a question like, "What would be the effect on profits if I invested this much money on new machinery?"
3) The output can be in the form of graphs and charts to make the predictions of the model easier to understand.

Example 1 — ***Queues*** *in a School Canteen*

1) A school canteen manager could build a model to represent the relationship between the number of pupils wanting to eat in the canteen, the number of staff and the queuing time.
2) The model could be used to find out the number of staff needed to keep waiting times to a minimum. Taking this one step further, it could be used to find out the minimum number of staff needed to serve all meals in less than an hour.
3) The formula in cell B5 is =B1*(B3/60)/B2.
The total time needed for one person to serve all the pupils is equal to the number of pupils (in cell B1) multiplied by the time taken to serve each pupil (in cell B3, divided by 60 to make it minutes). This is then divided by the number of staff to find how long it takes for everyone to be served, using four people.
It's assumed that two people can serve meals twice as quickly as one person, three people can serve three times as quickly, and so on.

	A	B
1	Number of pupils	600
2	Number of staff	4
3	Average time to serve a meal (seconds)	20
4		
5	Total serving time (minutes)	50

=B1*(B3/60)/B2

4) A weakness of the model is that the assumption about serving times is questionable — the time saved by having extra serving staff may not be this simple. The model also assumes that serving staff can be added forever — but having 100 serving staff would create obvious problems.

Example 2 — ***Profitable*** *Pizzas*

1) A pizza business could build a model to show its profit from selling pizzas. The owner enters data into cells B1 to B4, then the model calculates the data in cells B5 to B7.
2) The firm could then change any of these variables to see the impact of these changes on its profit — e.g. the effect a reduction in sales to 400 and an increase in production costs of 50p per pizza would have on profits.
3) This could be extended to give a direct link between the price of pizzas and the number sold.

	A	B	
1	Production cost per pizza	£2.00	
2	Other business costs	£1,000	
3	Selling price per pizza	£6.00	
4	Number of pizzas sold	500	
5	Total costs	£2,000	=B2+(B1*B4)
6	Total profit	£1,000	=(B3*B4)-B5
7	Profit per pizza	£2.00	=B6/B4

Watch out for weaknesses in your models

Spreadsheets are quite useful — once you've got your head round how they work. And that's the tricky bit. If you're still struggling with them, go back over the first few pages of this section.

Warm-Up and Worked Exam Questions

So that's spreadsheets. Time to take a breather and check you know it all. The usual drill — some quick easy questions, a nice worked example, then some exam questions for you to try.

Warm-Up Questions

1) Name three things that can be stored in a cell of a spreadsheet.
2) What is a spreadsheet formula?
3) What type of graph would you use to show how the temperature of a swimming pool varies during a day?
4) What's the difference between a relative and an absolute cell reference?

Worked Exam Questions

1 A school tuck shop keeps a record of its sales on a spreadsheet. Part of this spreadsheet is shown below. The amount of money customers spend on each product is calculated using a formula.

	A	B	C	D
1	**Tuck Shop Sales**			
2	Product	Number of units sold	Cost per unit	Amount spent by customers
3	Apples	16	£0.10	£1.60
4	Chocolate bars	35	£0.40	
5	Cream eggs	23	£0.40	
6	Crisps	23	£0.35	
7	Peanut bars	32	£0.40	
8	TOTAL			

(a) What formula has been entered in cell D3?

*=B3*C3* ✔ [1 mark]

(1 mark)

*Remember * for multiply and / for divide...*

(b) The following formula could be entered into cell D8: =D3+D4+D5+D6+D7. Suggest a better formula to enter in this cell.

=SUM(D3:D7) ✔ [1 mark]

(1 mark)

(c) Suggest three ways in which the appearance of this spreadsheet could be improved.

1. *Highlight the column headings, e.g. by using bold text.* ✔ [1 mark]

2. *Centrally align the data.* ✔ [1 mark]

3. *Merge cells A1:D1.* ✔ [1 mark]

(3 marks)

Exam Questions

1 The spreadsheet opposite is used to keep a record of ticket sales for a play.

	A	B	C
1		**Ticket Sales**	
2	Ticket Cost	£2.50	
3			
4	**Day**	**Number of tickets sold**	**Total**
5	Monday	101	£252.50
6	Tuesday	120	
7	Wednesday	105	
8	Thursday	98	
9	Friday	120	
10	Total		
11	Average		

(a) The formula =B5*B2 is entered in cell C5 to calculate the total sales (in pounds) for Monday night. However when this formula was copied and pasted into cell C6 it gave a value of £0.00.

(i) Explain why this happens.

....

....

....

....

....

(3 marks)

(ii) Write a formula for cell C5 that also gives the correct value when copied into C6.

....

(1 mark)

(b) The organisers want to see a chart showing how the number of tickets sold varies from night to night. What type of chart would be most suitable? Explain your answer.

....

(2 marks)

2 Miss Keeley is a maths teacher. Part of her spreadsheet showing the examination marks for her class is shown. A function is used in column C to work out whether the pupil has passed or failed the exam. The minimum pass mark is given in cell B2.

	A	B	C
1		**Marks in Exam**	
2	Pass mark	50	
3	**Name**	**Mark**	**Grade**
4	Chloe	56	fail
5	Davina	76	
6	John	45	
7	Patel	49	
8	Sam	95	

(a) The formula in cell C4 is =IF(B4>=50,“fail”,“pass”). It gives the wrong output. Correct the formula so it shows that Chloe has passed.

....

(1 mark)

(b) Miss Keeley may need to change the pass mark in cell B2. She wants column C to update automatically when she changes cell B2. Write down a formula that could be entered in cell C4 and then copied to cells C5 to C8 to achieve this.

....

(2 marks)

Exam Questions

3 Five spreadsheet functions are labelled with the letters **A**, **B**, **C**, **D** and **E**.
Write one letter in each row of the table that best matches the description.

A AVERAGE **B** MAX **C** ROUNDUP **D** COUNT **E** MIN

	Description	**Letter**
(i)	Rounds numbers up to a given number of decimal places.	
(ii)	Finds the largest value in a cell range	
(iii)	Finds the number of cells in a range that only contain numerical data.	

(3 marks)

4 A band is raising money by selling T-shirts with the band's logo on. The predicted sales and profits are stored in a spreadsheet. Part of this is shown in **Figure 1**.

	A	B	C
1	Predicted T-shirt sales		
2	Month	Number of shirts sold	Total profit
3	April	250	£250.00
4	May	360	£360.00
5	June	350	£350.00
6	July	500	£500.00
7	August	210	£210.00
8			£1,670.00
9	Cost of making one T-shirt	£3.50	
10	Selling price of one T-shirt	£4.50	
11	Profit per T-shirt		

Figure 1

(a) (i) The profit made on each shirt is stored in cell B11. It is calculated by subtracting the cost of making the T-shirt from its selling price. Using **Figure 1**, write the formula to calculate the profit made on each T-shirt.

....

(1 mark)

(ii) Using your answer to **(a) (i)**, write down a formula that could be in cell C3.

....

(2 marks)

(b) Describe how the band could use the spreadsheet as a model to explore how the cost of making a T-shirt affects the total profit.

....

(1 mark)

Databases — The Basics

Databases are stacks of fun. I think you'll enjoy the next few pages...

A Database is a Store of Data

1) Databases are used to store lots of data in an organised way.
2) Databases hold data in one or more tables.
3) Each table is organised into fields (columns) and records (rows).
4) Column headings are called field names.

In this table, each column is a different field... *Field name* **Primary key**

... and each row is a record.

Item of data

First Name	Last Name	Department	Payroll Number	Date of Birth	Salary
Doug	Witherspoon	Catering	100345	26/09/64	£19,000
Neil	Beforem	Customer Service	100346	12/08/76	£15,000
Anita	Dear	Marketing	100347	23/05/83	£18,000
Phil	Ordabuk	Sales	100348	30/03/77	£17,000
Bill	O'Verdue	Finance	100349	22/05/79	£15,000
Stan	D'Alday	Porter	100350	06/11/80	£8,000

5) Each table has a primary key. It's a field which can uniquely identify any record in the table. There can only be one primary key per database table. In the table above, the primary key is the payroll number field — no two people have the same payroll number.
6) The big benefit of databases is that you can search them quickly to find specific data, or use them to generate reports — e.g. which books in a publisher's database have sold the most.

Databases can be Flat-File or Relational

Flat-file Databases

1) All the data's organised into one table, which can be viewed by opening one data file.
2) Flat-file databases can be created using all database programs and most spreadsheets.

Relational Databases

1) Relational databases store the data in separate tables.
2) All the data's linked together by key fields.
3) Linking tables together means that important information, such as customer addresses, only needs to be stored once in the database — this reduces data redundancy.
4) It also makes it quick and easy to update information if some of it is wrong — it'll only need changing in one table.

Databases are designed to store loads of data

Now you know the basics of databases. If you don't, return to the top of the page and start again. Repeat this process until you know it all — but there's not that much to learn, so it won't take too long.

Databases — Entering Data

Simple databases are pretty easy to make, but you need to think about it a little before you jump in...

Well-Structured Fields are Really Important

1) The first step in creating a database is to decide on what fields you need. And once you've decided that, each field needs a name, a data type and a format.
2) The data type is dead important, as different processes can be performed on different types of data. The most common data types are in the box — most programs allow others, e.g. pictures, audio and video.

Text e.g. Banana
Number e.g. 20 (integer) or 24.41 (real)
Date e.g. 26-09-82 or 26/09/82
Time e.g. 10:04
Currency e.g. £50.00 or $34.69
Boolean e.g. true or false

Boolean means there are only two possible values — e.g. yes or no, on or off, 1 or 0, etc.

A new Database starts with a Table

1) Databases usually have a design view. This is where you set up your table.
2) The design view lets you create fields, name them, give them a data type and set the primary key — you can't input any data in this view.
3) You can also set up data validation rules in the design view. They help to reduce mistakes when data is being entered:

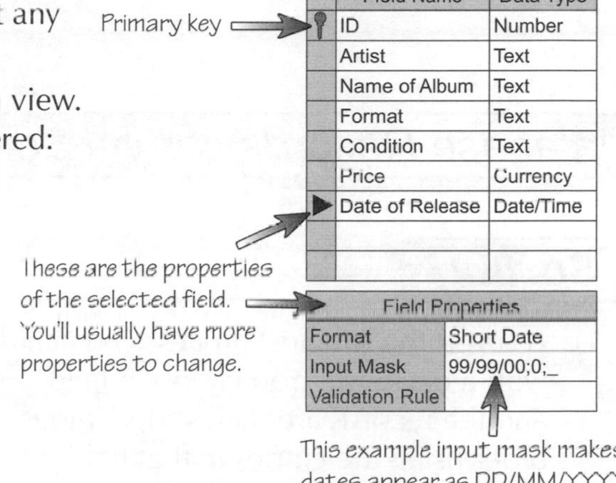

List	This only allows data from a list of options to be entered.
Range check	If the data falls outside of a certain range, e.g. between the years 1900 and 2010, then it can't be entered.
Input mask	This forces data to be entered in a certain format, e.g. DD/MM/YYYY for dates.

4) Once the table has all of its fields, head over to the datasheet view — it looks like a spreadsheet:

ID	Artist	Name of Album	Format	Condition	Price	Date of Release
1	Jerry and the Garglers	Throat Tunes 2	LP	VG	£3	08/08/2008
2	Linda Belinda	Equine Escapists	LP	EX	£4	19/12/2003
3	Going-Going-Gones	Under the Hammer	CD	EX	£5	06/11/2007
4	Tyrone Warbler	Mellow Bliss	CD	G	£2	19/12/2002
5	Jane's Obsession	What's the Use?	LP	M	£6	24/01/2001
6	Janglebirds	Jingle and Desperate	CD	G	£4	01/02/2003
7	Fertiliser	Non-Organic Rock	CD	VG	£2	11/05/2004

5) In this view you can input data, amend data that already exists, and delete data, e.g. redundant data (data that appears in more than one table in a relational database). Just click the data or cell you want to work with.

Don't forget — relational databases have more than one table

Databases would be pretty useless without any data in them. Fortunately, entering data is the easy part — the bit you have to make sure you understand is how you set up a table with the right data types.

Databases — Entering and Accessing Data

Having to enter data in the datasheet view can be a bit tricky, especially if there are loads of records. Forms make the whole process a lot simpler, and you can make them look really nice too.

Forms are a User-Friendly Way to Edit and Enter Data

1) Forms can be used to enter and edit data in a table. The idea is that they're clearly designed and user-friendly to make this as easy as possible.
2) Forms have to be linked to a table — this tells the form which table's data it should be editing or adding to.
3) Forms also have a design view to adjust their layout.
4) Forms can contain text boxes (for typing into), or tick boxes and lists for users to choose options from. You can even display input masks in your text boxes.
5) Forms allow users to move through the existing records in a database table and edit them. They also let users create new records in a table.

Database Records can be Sorted and Filtered

Sorting

1) A sort is the simplest process you can do with a database. You choose a field, and the records are then sorted into order using the entries in that field.
2) Sorts can be done on text fields and numerical fields. With text fields, entries are sorted into alphabetical order.
3) Sorts can either be in ascending order (the lowest value first), or descending order (the highest value first).

First name	Last name	Team	Value
Boris	Batley	Blood and Thunder	£60
Basher	Best	Workington Warriors	£40
Freddy	Beech	Joshy's Giants	£15
Knuckles	Borissov	Higgie's Hairy Men	£5
Smasher	Bentley	Burton's Brigade	£3.50

These Fantasy Tiddlywinks League players are sorted in order of transfer value — most valuable first.

Filtering

1) When you're viewing a table, you can apply a filter to see only records that match certain conditions (e.g. players with a value of £60). You can use more than one filter at once.
2) One filtering method is to show records that do or don't match the currently selected data item. You can also filter records by selecting a number of criteria to look for.
3) To view all the records in a table again, just turn the filter off.

Forms have to be linked to a table in order for them to work properly

Databases are a bit like a swan. The tables do all the hard work but they're not great looking (like a swan's legs). Forms are the pretty bits that are on show (the bit of a swan above the water).

Databases — Accessing Data

As well as knowing how to enter data in a database you need to know how to interrogate one.

Database Records can be *Searched*

1) One way to search a database is to use a query.
A query is basically a list of the things you want the database to look for.
2) Query results are displayed as a separate datasheet — the table that was queried (searched) remains unchanged and separate from the results. This is different to how a filter works.
3) Simple queries tell the database to look for records that meet just one condition.

Simple Queries

This could be to list all the records of players whose transfer value equals £40 — the query is:

Value = £40.

Operator	Finds values ...
=	equal to
<	less than
>	greater than
<>	not equal to
<=	less than or equal to
>=	greater than or equal to

4) It's also possible to do wildcard searches. These are where you only know part of the value to search for — maybe you can remember that a tiddlywinks player's last name begins with 'Be', but can't remember the full name. You need to use the word 'LIKE' together with the * wildcard.

Wildcard Searches...

Use * to stand for anything. E.g. in

Last name LIKE "Be*",

the asterisk can stand for anything (or nothing). The results will include Best, Bentley and Beech, but not Batley or Boris.
And if you searched for

Team LIKE "*gi*",

the results will include Joshy's Giants and Higgie's Hairy Men.

*The * wildcard matches any number of characters. You could also use the ? wildcard — it matches a single character.*

5) You can also do complex searches — these are when you use AND, OR and NOT to find records that meet more than one condition.

Complex Searches...

These search for data meeting more than one condition. You might need to find all the tiddlywinks players called either Boris or Beryl. So your search criteria would be:

First name = "Boris" OR First name = "Beryl"

Or maybe you need to find players called Boris who also have a transfer value over £50.
In this case the search is:

First name = "Boris" AND Value > £50

Or maybe you're looking for people not called Boris whose transfer value is not over £20.
You could use:

NOT (First name = "Boris") AND Value <= £20

When you use a search engine you're basically querying the Internet

You can use the results of a database query to create mail-merged letters (see page 62).
Make sure you know all the different ways to access data, including filters and types of queries.

Databases — Reports

A report is the result of a database query that is intended to be seen by someone else. They can either be screen-based or printed depending on what the user needs.

*Reports can be in **Record** or **Column Format***

1) Record-format reports display each record of data completely separately. They're useful if you want to view each record on its own.

   This record format report has been designed to be used as a reminder slip to send to customers whose payments are overdue.

   You can format reports by using different font sizes, colours, headers and footers, and so on. If the database format options are limited, you could export the data into a word processor or desktop publishing package where you have more options.

Mortgage Payment Reminder Notice

Name and Postal Address	Account No.
Yoda Murky Swamp District Dagobah System MS5 6RP	07293

Date of Issue:	Amount due
23 June 01	26p

We have still not received payment of the amount shown above.
Please pay this bill immediately.
If you are having difficulty paying, call us on 1236329012.
Your hut may be at risk if you do not keep up with payments.

2) Column-format reports display the data in a big table, with all the information shown underneath the field headings. This is more useful if you're interested in comparing values in particular fields across different records.

Account No.	First Name	Date of Issue	Amount Due
07293	Yoda	23 June 01	26p
26438	Darth	4 May 01	13p
14472	Luke	23 April 01	68p
91772	Han	5 June 01	84p

Most database software lets you specify which fields will be displayed in the report.

*Reports can be **Really Snazzy***

1) You can use calculations in your report. For example, a publisher might use a database to store details about the weekly sales of books, with each week's sales in a separate field. The database could then add together the weekly sales for each book and display this on a report as total sales.

Month	Chocolate teapot sales	Motorbike ashtray sales	Waterproof teabag sales
January	15 000	12 000	16 000
February	20 000	17 000	21 000
March	8 000	5 000	9 000
April	10 000	7 000	11 000
May	6 000	3 000	7 000
June	10 000	7 000	11 000
July	30 000	27 000	31 000
August	28 000	25 000	29 000
September	30 000	27 000	31 000
October	13 000	10 000	14 000
November	14 000	11 000	15 000
December	6 000	3 000	7 000

MONEYBAGS INC.
Annual Report

Product	Sales
Chocolate teapot	190 000
Motorbike ashtray	154 000
Waterproof teabag	202 000

Boring

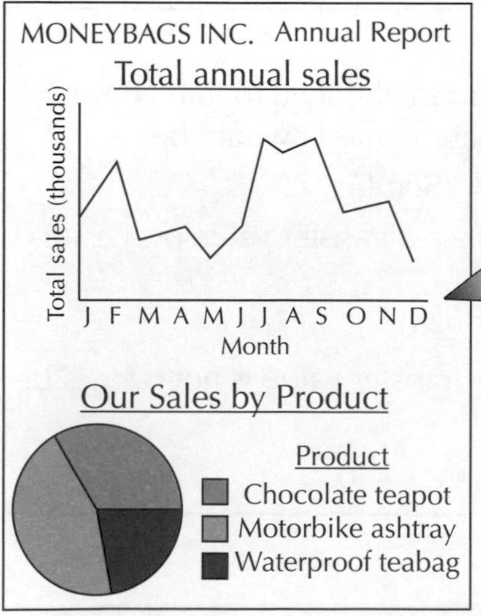

Amazing

2) You can also use charts and graphs in reports. Just select the fields you want to display, select the chart type, give it a title and Bob's your uncle.

Just one final note on reports. If you've got a database with lots of tables, you can use any of the data from any table in a single report. At the same time, you can use the data in a single table to produce lots of different reports. Report creation tools in database software are really flexible.

Warm-Up and Worked Exam Questions

It's hard to get really excited about databases, but you're likely to get questions on them in your exam — so you might as well just get on and learn all this. Starting with the warm-up questions...

Warm-Up Questions

1) What is a database?
2) Describe the difference between the design and datasheet views of a database table.
3) What are the two main ways of setting out a database report?

Worked Exam Questions

1 A garage keeps details of cars for sale on a database. An extract is shown below.

Year	Type	Engine size (cc)	Colour	Mileage
2001	4X4	2200	Black	12000
2002	Estate	1600	Grey	14000
1999	4X4	2000	Red	34000
2000	Saloon	2000	Green	35000
1999	Estate	1600	Blue	40000
2000	Saloon	1800	Green	54000
2001	Supermini	1200	Red	55000
1999	Estate	1700	Green	66000
1998	Hatchback	1400	Red	123000

(a) How many fields and how many records are shown?

Fields: *five* ✔ [1 mark]

Records: *nine* ✔ [1 mark]

(2 marks)

(b) On which field is the table sorted? Say whether it is ascending or descending order.

'Mileage' field. ✔ [1 mark]

It's sorted in ascending order. ✔ [1 mark]

(2 marks)

Remember — ascending is lowest value first (A to Z) and descending is highest value first (Z to A).

(c) How many cars would the following searches find from the extract above?

(i) Colour = "Red" OR "Blue" .... *4* ✔ [1 mark] cars

(ii) Colour = "Green" AND mileage < 60000 .... *2* ✔ [1 mark] cars

(iii) NOT (Type = "4X4") AND Year >= 2000 .... *4* ✔ [1 mark] cars

(3 marks)

Exam Questions

1 Timothy is creating a database. He is choosing one of the fields to be a primary key.

(a) What is a 'primary key'.

A primary key is a field that can uniquely identify any record in the table

(2 marks)

(b) (i) Timothy decides he should create a relational database.

Explain what is meant by the term 'relational database'.

Data stored in different tables

(1 mark)

(ii) How can a relational database be used to reduce data redundancy?

relational databases only need to be stored once

(2 marks)

(c) There is a 'Date' field in the database. Give **two** data validation methods and explain how they would prevent errors when data is being entered into the 'Date' field.

Method 1 The forces data has to be entered in a certain format

Method 2 The data has to be in a certain range

(4 marks)

2 Five features are labelled with the letters **A**, **B**, **C**, **D** and **E**.
Write one letter in each row of the table that best matches the description.

A Form
B Field
C Report
D Record
E Query

	Description	Letter
(i)	A way of presenting selected data in a database	C
(ii)	A row in a database	D
(iii)	A set of conditions used during a database search	E

(3 marks)

Revision Summary for Section Three

You should be getting used to these pages by now. All you've got to do is answer every one of these little gems — then check and see if you were right. If you get any wrong — just do them again.

1) What is the smallest part of a spreadsheet called?
2) Which row is cell G14 in?
3) What is a text string?
4) How many different items of data should be entered into a single cell?
5) Name two ways that you can enter data into a cell.
6) What feature of spreadsheet software can be used to edit a cell's contents?
7) Explain fully what conditional formatting is.
8) Describe three other ways to format the data in a spreadsheet.
9) What does "absolute cell reference" mean?
10) What function will Farmer Kevin put into cell B5?

	A	B
1	**Cow**	**Selling price**
2	Daisy	£48.26
3	Buttercup	£58.69
4	Boris	£2.50
5	Total income	

11) What does the function =IF(C2>15000,"No pay rise","Pay rise") mean?
12) What does the LOOKUP function do?
13) Explain the difference between a bar graph and a line graph.
14) Explain the difference between a scatter graph and a pie chart.
15) Dodgy Dave wants to use a spreadsheet to help him model the profits from his second-hand balloon business. Give one way he could do this.
16) What is what-if analysis? How could it be used to help model the effects of an increase in patients on waiting times at a doctor's surgery?
17) What might be the primary key in a database listing information about different books?
18) Explain the difference between a flat-file database and a relational database.
19) Name three data types that can be given to a database field.
20) Describe two types of data validation rules.
21) What are database forms used for? Describe two characteristics of a form.
22) Who will appear at the top of a list sorted in descending order of last name: Alice Zybrynski or Zack Alphonsus?
23) How are queries and filters different?
24) What's the difference between > and <>?
25) What is a wildcard search? How could one be used to search for all people whose last name begins McD?
26) What are AND, OR and NOT used for?
27) Describe one way that you can make a database report snazzier.

Word Processing and DTP — Uses

I've shortened Desktop Publishing to DTP — if you worked this out, your prize is a page of revision...

Word Processors and DTP Software are **Different**

Here are some loose definitions of a word processor and DTP software:

A word processor allows users to write, edit and format text documents.	DTP software allows users to create publications that contain text and images.

As technology has advanced, word processors have become able to deal with images, in similar ways to DTP software. However, there's still one major difference between most word processors and DTP software...

DTP Software is usually **Frame-Based**

1) Frame-based software means that information is put on pages in blocks (called frames).
2) Frames can be moved or resized. This means that it is very easy to edit a DTP document by moving pictures or blocks of text around. Frames can also be moved from page to page.
3) DTP works rather like creating a noticeboard — you have a set of different pieces of information which you can move around until you're happy with the overall layout.

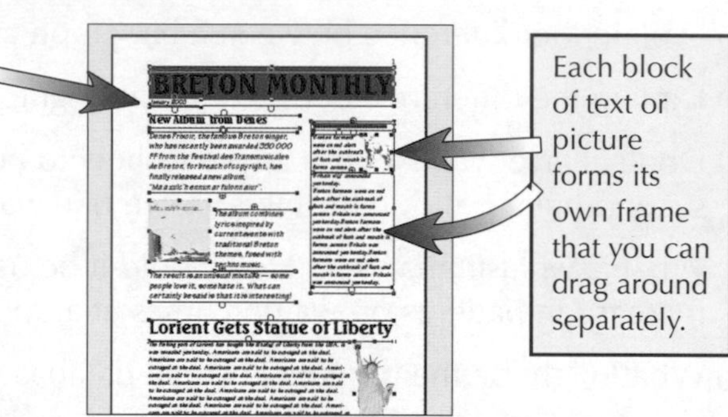

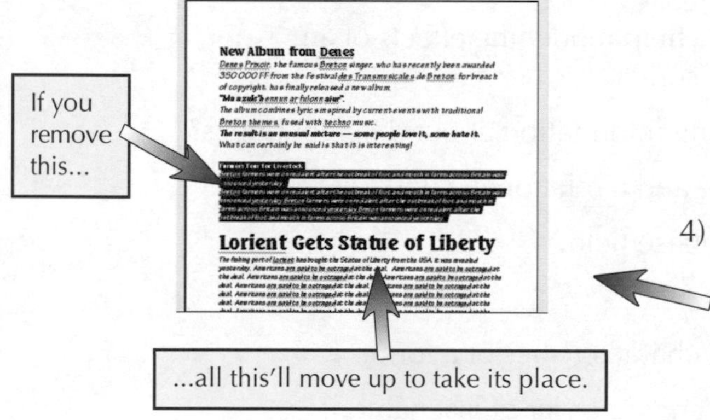

4) Most word processors are not frame-based, so the position of one thing depends on the position of everything else. That means moving one thing might make a whole load of other stuff move as well. This doesn't happen with DTP.

Some **Uses** of Word Processors and DTP Software...

You'd use a word processor for documents that are mainly text:

letters	essays	memos	reports

You'd use DTP software to make documents that contain images and text, and that need a flexible layout:

posters	catalogues	leaflets	magazines
flyers	newspapers	brochures	business cards

These are the uses that the software was designed for — you can make a poster using a word processor, but it's easier to make it with DTP software.

Get yourself in the right frame of mind...

Loads of people think they're experts at using this software — but exam questions are often answered badly. That's because they don't know the basic facts — so get learning. No excuses.

Text Formatting

As well as the common features mentioned on page 30, you can format text in the following ways...

Lists Help to Structure Text

1) Lists are useful for text that can be split up into steps or parts — it makes it easier to read. There are two main types of list:

1) Numbered lists...	• Bulleted lists...
2) ...where each point...	• ...where each point...
3) ...has a number.	• ...has a bullet symbol.

2) You can also format lists, e.g. use different bullet symbols, letters instead of numbers, full stops not brackets, etc.
3) Most word processors and DTP software can handle sub-numbering — it lets you add more levels to a main point. Here's an example:

> 1) This is the first point that I want to mention.
>   i) This point is related to point 1).
>   ii) As is this point.
> 2) This is the next main point that I want to make.

4) The different levels usually have different characters — here, the sub-numbering is done in Roman numerals. (The same kind of thing can also be done on a bulleted list.)

Page and Line Breaks Split Up Text

Page and line breaks are just where a new page or line starts. They're usually put in automatically, when a line or page is full. You can also add them manually to help break up big blocks of text.

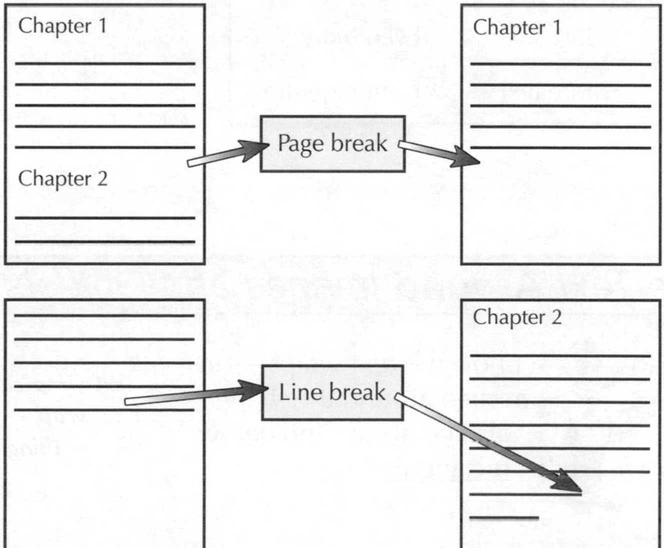

Structured text with clear breaks is easy to read

There's usually a button that you press to turn lists on, then the software will automatically format the list for you — numbered lists will be in numerical order and bullet characters will be put in for you.

Text Formatting

As well as the stuff on the last page, you need to know about indents, tabs and text wrap.

Indents and *Tabs* set *Positions* for Text

If you've used a word processor or DTP software, you might have noticed a ruler near the top of the screen. Sometimes the ruler has got weird shapes on it — these are indents and tabs.

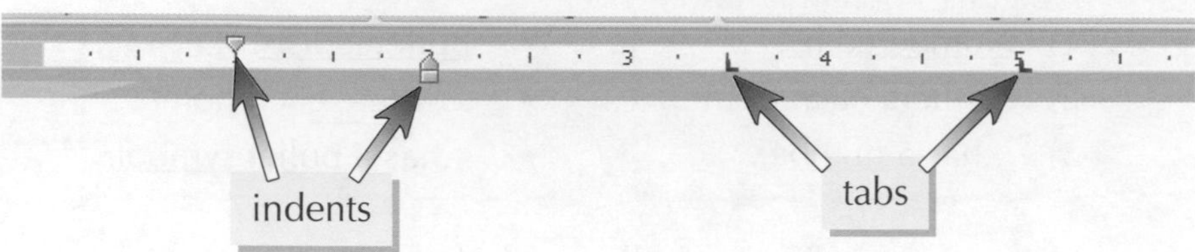

Indents

Indents determine how close to the edge of the page the text can go (or in DTP software, how close to the edges of the text's frame).

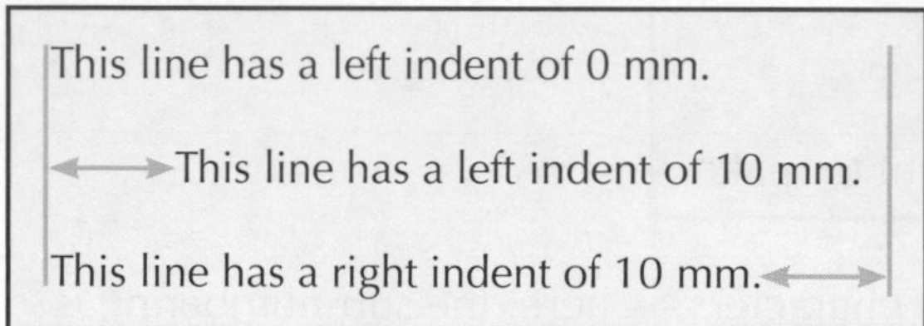

Tabs

Tabs are stops along the ruler that text can be moved to by pressing the Tab key (usually above Caps Lock). They're used to line up bits of text vertically.

	Tab at 25 mm v	Tab at 50 mm v
Some text	More text	Even more text
Some text	More text	Even more text

Text Wrap Feeds Text *Around* Images and Objects

Most software allows you to set how the text wraps — in this example, the text is nestled around the shape of the duck, but it could also be above and below him or wrapped around his rectangular frame.

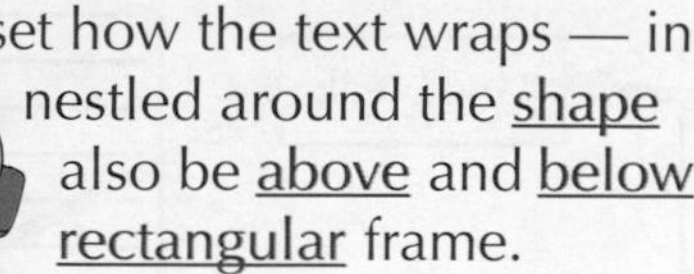

Text wrap can also be called auto wrap — they're the same things though.

Make sure you know the difference between indents and tabs

Text wrap is really useful when you want to spread some text around an image with an odd outline. It saves you having to mess about with the return key, trying to get your lines to end in the right place.

Improving Presentation

Now you know how to format text, here are a few tricks to make documents look a bit snazzier.

Tables, Borders and Columns can Help Readability

1) Tables are a good way to present lists of numerical or text information, e.g. lists of names and addresses.

2) Most word processors and DTP software will let you create tables from scratch. And when you paste in data from a spreadsheet it's often formatted into a table (although only the values will be carried across — things like formulas will be lost).

3) Just like with spreadsheets (see page 38), you can merge the cells in a table. If you change your mind, you can split them up into single cells again.

4) Amazingly, you can format the different parts of a table — border thickness and colour, cell fill colour, vertical alignment, etc. can all be adjusted to suit the document.

5) Putting borders around tables, pictures, whole pages or blocks of text helps break up the information on the page — which sometimes makes it easier to read. Or you might just want to make things look nice and pretty...

Wordprocessing Weekly News

Typists around the country were staggered to learn yesterday that text can be arranged automatically in columns.

"I'm staggered," said 38-year-old Ian Denting. "If these newfangled word processors keep going at this rate then I'm going to become marginalised."

Nelson Column, of London, said it had "absolutely nothing to do with me."

6) Columns can be created so that the text flows down the page and jumps automatically to the next column. This is great for newsletters and newspapers.

Tables can be formatted in similar ways to spreadsheets

The key to all these features is using them wisely — tables may improve readability, but don't go crazy and put everything in one. The same goes for columns — not every document will need them.

Improving Presentation

You might not have used the following features before, so give this page a thorough read...

Layering *and* ***Grouping*** *Help When Creating Documents*

1) Most word processors and DTP software let you stack things on top of each other.

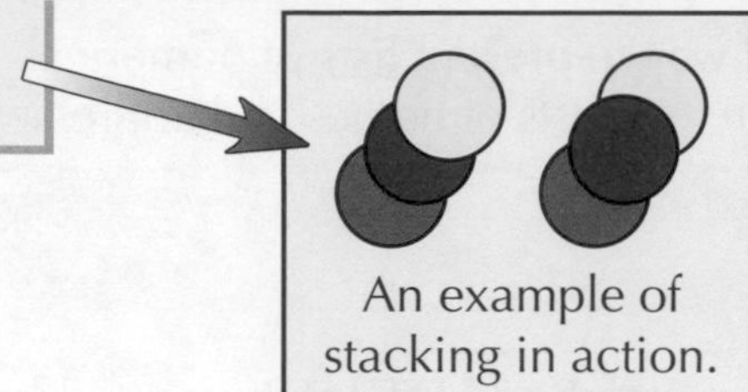

An example of stacking in action.

2) Adjusting the stacking order changes how these things overlap.

3) Layering takes the idea of stacking one step further. Layers are like separate transparent sheets which you can create different parts of a page on. The layers are stacked on top of each other.

4) You can adjust the stacking order of layers, and you can also turn them on and off — this makes it easy to hide parts of a document.

5) Grouping means a number of separate items are treated as one thing.

6) The good thing about grouping is that it's not permanent. You can ungroup objects and they'll be treated as separate things again.

Grouping is useful for keeping items together if you move things around a lot.

Watermarks *draw* ***Attention*** *to the Page*

A watermark is an image or text that appears behind the main text in a document. For example:

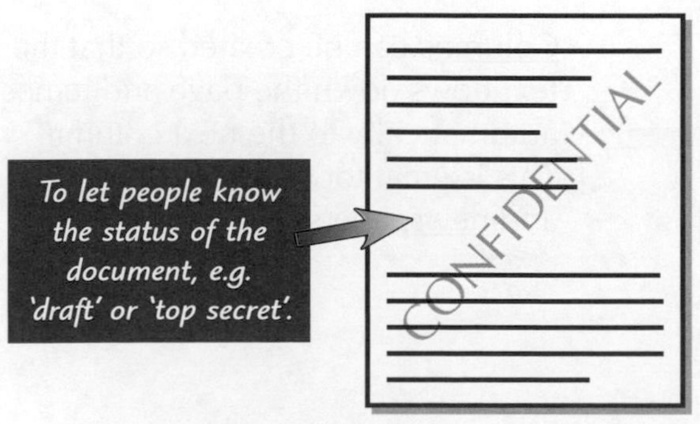

To make documents look nicer, e.g. to make a love letter even more sickly sweet than it already was.

Try not to overdo it with the watermarks...

Word processors and DTP software have loads of options to make your documents look nice, but luckily you only need to know about the ones above and on the previous page — get them learnt.

Advanced Features

Some more features for you to learn about. Although it says 'advanced', it's not really that difficult.

Headings and Subheadings Break Text into Logical Chunks

1) A heading describes the main topic — this page's heading is 'Advanced Features'. Subheadings are separate topics that are part of the main topic — the green boxes on this page.
2) You can assign styles to headings and subheadings. A style is a set of formatting options that can be applied to text. Styles are useful for two main reasons:

- They help give documents a consistent appearance, which makes documents look more professional.
- They let you change the look of a whole document really easily — you just update the styles instead of every single piece of text in the document.

Style sheets contain information about all the different styles used in a document.

3) Word processors and DTP software can also use styles to generate a table of contents — you tell it what styles to include, and it sorts everything out automatically.

Sections Split Documents into Parts

1) You can split a document up into sections.
2) This creates different parts that can have their own page numbering — e.g. one could have Roman numerals (i, ii, iii...), while another could have letters (a, b, c...).
3) Different sections could also have their own headers and footers.

A fancy word for the numbering of pages is pagination — word processors and DTP software let you fiddle with pagination to your heart's content.

Mind Your Language with Spelling and Grammar Checkers

Grammar and spelling checkers should improve your written communication — but there are potential problems.

SPELLING CHECKERS:

1) They come in different languages. Many words are spelt differently in different parts of the English-speaking world — e.g. labor (American English) and labour (UK English). So if you live in the UK, check that you're using UK English.
2) They only recognise misspelt words — not their context. This is a problem with words like 'were' and 'where'. If you use the wrong one, the spell-checker won't find a problem.
3) Sometimes the dictionaries contain mistakes. A version of one well-known word processor's spell-checker contained a misspelling of 'liaise'.

GRAMMAR CHECKERS:

Grammar checkers can be unreliable and give confusing advice. This is because good grammar depends on context — and most software isn't yet powerful enough to take this into account.

Check the Word Count

1) Sometimes you need to know how many words you've written, e.g. in a piece of coursework.
2) Automatic word counting is an option in most word processors and DTP software.

Mail Merge

Mail merge lets you merge data from a data source (e.g. spreadsheet or database) into a word processor or a DTP document. This is incredibly useful if you need to send out stacks and stacks of standard documents with just a few details (like the name and address) changed each time.

First, You'll Need Some **Data** to Merge...

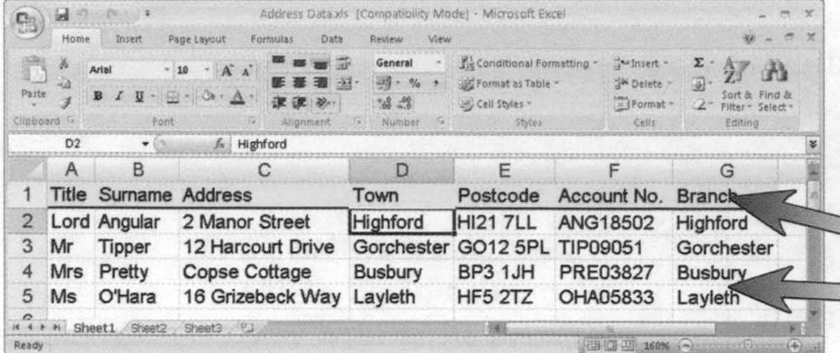

	A	B	C	D	E	F	G
1	Title	Surname	Address	Town	Postcode	Account No.	Branch
2	Lord	Angular	2 Manor Street	Highford	HI21 7LL	ANG18502	Highford
3	Mr	Tipper	12 Harcourt Drive	Gorchester	GO12 5PL	TIP09051	Gorchester
4	Mrs	Pretty	Copse Cottage	Busbury	BP3 1JH	PRE03827	Busbury
5	Ms	O'Hara	16 Grizebeck Way	Layleth	HF5 2TZ	OHA05833	Layleth

Organise Your Data

You'll need the source of the data that you want to merge into your document. Here, the data's in a spreadsheet.

The first row shows the names of the data fields. Other rows each contain one complete record (see page 48 for a definition).

...Then You Need a **Document**, Complete with **Merge Fields**...

Write the Document and Add the Fields

Here's a standard letter that needs to go to all the customers whose details are in the above spreadsheet.

But there are some details missing that will be different for each customer — the name, address and account number, for example. Instead of filling these details in, fields have been inserted — these are the things inside <<double angled brackets>>.

Inserting the field names can be a bit fiddly, and usually involves a few different menus. But the basic idea is always the same — you're creating links from your letter to a field in your data source.

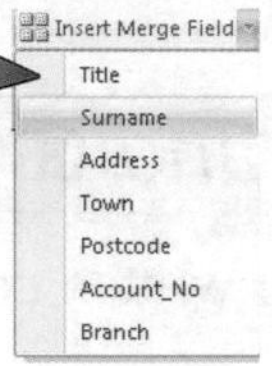

Mail merges can also be used for invoices, payslips, membership cards and name badges.

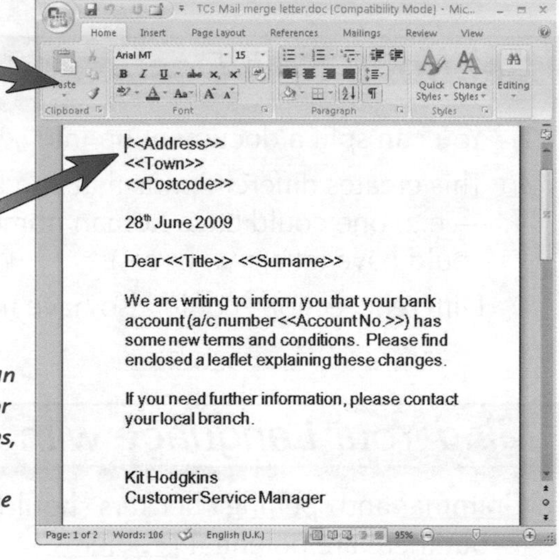

<<Address>>
<<Town>>
<<Postcode>>

28th June 2009

Dear <<Title>> <<Surname>>

We are writing to inform you that your bank account (a/c number <<Account No.>>) has some new terms and conditions. Please find enclosed a leaflet explaining these changes.

If you need further information, please contact your local branch.

Kit Hodgkins
Customer Service Manager

...Then **Merge** Data and Document

You've done the hard bit — this bit's pretty easy.

Merge the Data

It's pretty straightforward to merge the data and print your documents. The field names are replaced by data from one record in the data source.

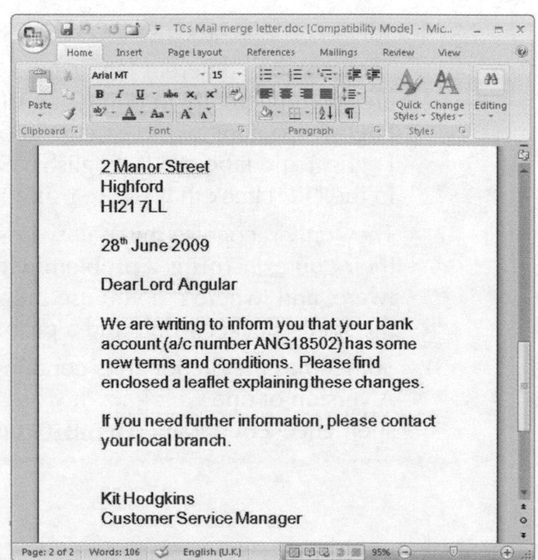

2 Manor Street
Highford
HI21 7LL

28th June 2009

Dear Lord Angular

We are writing to inform you that your bank account (a/c number ANG18502) has some new terms and conditions. Please find enclosed a leaflet explaining these changes.

If you need further information, please contact your local branch.

Kit Hodgkins
Customer Service Manager

Mail merge is an example of importing data — inserting data that was created using a different software application. But you can only import data if it was saved using a file format that the word processor or DTP software can recognise.

Remember, you need to insert merge fields — you can't type them

Mail merge looks more fiddly than it is — the key is practice, so try it out until you've got it nailed.

Warm-Up and Worked Exam Questions

Hopefully this short-ish section didn't just pass you by in a blur — you've got a few questions to answer before you can move on to the next section. If you get any wrong, go back and learn the stuff again.

Warm-Up Questions

1) What does DTP stand for?
2) What is a page break?
3) Name the feature that tells you how many words you've typed in a document.
4) Briefly describe how you create a mail merge.

Worked Exam Questions

1 Frank is making a catalogue.

(a) What software would be suitable for making the catalogue? Explain your answer.

Desktop publishing software ✔ [1 mark] *would be suitable. This is because it's frame-based software,* ✔ [1 mark] *which means images and text can be moved around easily to create the best-looking layout.* ✔ [1 mark]

(3 marks)

You could make the catalogue with a word processor (since they can produce colourful documents that include text and images), but they can be a bit more fiddly if you want to use a 'fancy' layout.

(b) Suggest a suitable way of presenting the following information in the catalogue:

(i) Step-by-step instructions.

a numbered list ✔ [1 mark]

(1 mark)

(ii) A page of contact names, numbers and addresses.

a table ✔ [1 mark]

(1 mark)

This is another question where you have to decide what is 'suitable' — there might be more than one correct answer.

(c) Frank is going to use styles when making the catalogue.

Give **two** advantages of using styles.

1. *Styles help to give documents a consistent appearance,* ✔ [1 mark] *which makes them look professional.* ✔ [1 mark]

2. *Styles let you change the look of a document really easily* ✔ [1 mark] *— you just update the styles rather than the individual bits of text in the document.* ✔ [1 mark]

(4 marks)

Exam Questions

1 Word processors and desktop publishing software are designed to produce different types of documents.

Tick **two** boxes to show which of the following documents are most suitably produced using desktop publishing software.

	Tick **two** boxes
Letters	
Essays	
Posters	
Magazines	
Memos	

(2 marks)

2 Five features are labelled with the letters **A**, **B**, **C**, **D** and **E**.
Write one letter in each row of the table that best matches the description.

A Text wrap **B** Grouping **C** Indent **D** Watermark **E** Tab

	Description	**Letter**
(i)	Makes the selected objects in a document be treated as one object.	
(ii)	A point that determines how close to the edge of the page text can go.	
(iii)	Feeds text around images and objects in a document.	
(iv)	An image or text that appears behind the main text in a document.	

(4 marks)

3 Angela has created a document in a word processor. She ran a spelling check before printing it out, but when she read the document she found a few spelling and grammar errors.

Suggest **two** reasons why the errors were not caught by the spelling checker.

1. ....

....

2. ....

....

(4 marks)

Revision Summary for Section Four

Another section down, another set of questions to test just how much knowledge you have gained. The usual terms and conditions apply — have a go at these questions and if you get any wrong, head back to the page in question and learn it all again until your brain is swollen with information.

1) Describe the main difference between word processors and DTP software.
2) Give three uses of word processors.
3) Give three uses of DTP software.
4) Name the two main types of lists.
5) What is sub-numbering?
6) What do indents determine?
7) What are tabs used for?
8) Give two ways you could break up a big block of text.
9) Name the text formatting feature that lets you nestle text around an image.
10) What might you use to display a long list of names and telephone numbers in a document?
11) Give two ways that borders can improve presentation.
12) What is a layer? What are layers used for?
13) Explain what grouping is.
14) Give two reasons why watermarks are used on some documents.
15) What is a heading? How is a subheading different?
16) In DTP or word processing, what is a style?
17) Describe one reason why styles are useful.
18) Give one reason why a document might be split up into sections.
19) Describe two reasons why spelling checkers aren't completely reliable.
20) What two things do you need before you can carry out a mail merge?
21) What happens when you merge the data in a spreadsheet with merge fields in a letter?
22) Explain what is meant by importing data.

Presentation Software

Presentation software is used to give talks and display ideas. You need to know its main features.

Presentations are Created as a **Series of Slides**

1) Presentation software creates a series of slides in a single document. Each slide contains a number of frames (a bit like DTP software, see page 56).
2) Each slide usually contains text or images — but you can put movies and sound on slides too.
3) The software makes it easy to insert and delete slides, and to change their order.
4) The really clever thing about presentation software is that you can animate things — e.g. make them move around and flash and spin... and so on.
5) This helps to capture an audience's attention and can help presenters make their points.

Animations and **Transitions** bring Slides to Life

1) Animations make the frames on a slide arrive on screen in different ways. For example...

① A line of text can appear one word at a time, or the whole line can fly into place from either side.

② A picture can grow, shrink, rotate or move along a set path.

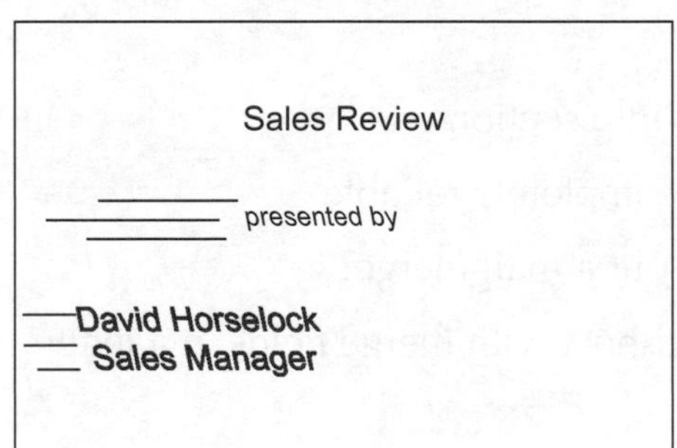

- We need to hit sales targets.
- Sales currently down by 13%.
- Action plan being drawn up.

Greater Sales = Greater Profit = Greater People

③ The bars of a bar chart can appear one at a time.

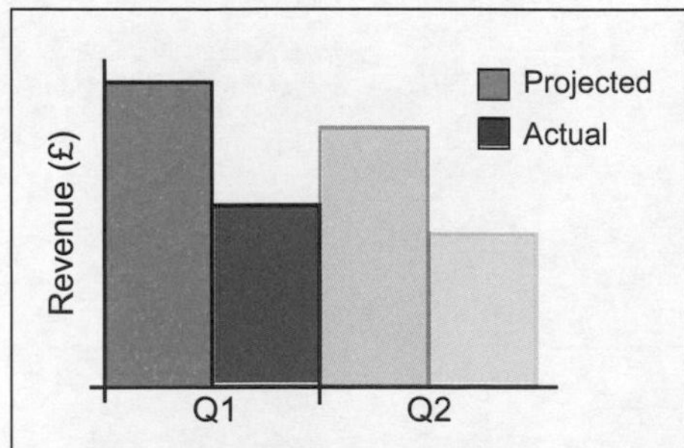

2) Transitions are effects that change how each new slide appears. For example, new slides can fade in, or the slides can open and close like shutters or curtains.

Presentation Software

Timings Automate Animations and Transitions

1) Animations and transitions are usually triggered by clicking a mouse button or by pressing a keyboard key.

2) But most presentation software lets you set timings for these events too. You could set up the timings so all you have to do is start the presentation and it'll run through all of the slides and animations automatically.

3) You can also add a timing to individual frames or slides, e.g. if you want to show a slide for exactly ten seconds.

For Fancy Slides, add **Hyperlinks**, **Buttons** and **Multimedia**

1) Hyperlinks are a way of moving around a presentation (instead of just moving through all the slides in the planned order). They're useful if you want to jump to a particular slide, e.g. to refer to some figures on the last slide or to view the first slide again.

2) Hyperlinks are attached to objects, e.g. some text or a picture — you just click the hyperlink to be taken to the destination slide.

3) Some hyperlinks look like animated buttons that seem like they're being pushed in when you click them.

4) Most presentation software lets you add multimedia clips to presentations, e.g. video clips and sound effects.

5) You can change:

- when the clips start (e.g. when the first slide appears or when the presenter clicks a button),
- how loud the volume is,
- whether the clip starts again once it reaches the end, or just stops.

Do a presentation — don't make an exhibition of yourself...

None of this stuff is complicated, but don't assume that you know it already. When you're ready to learn some more, move on to the next page — you'll have to do your own transition, I'm afraid...

Presentation Software

There are just a few more features in presentation software that you need to know about....

*Presentations can be **Viewed On-Screen** and on **Paper***

1) You can view your presentations on a monitor — but for large audiences, you might need to project the presentation onto a large screen.

2) You can also print paper handouts of the slides for members of the audience, or for the presenter.

- Each page of the handouts might show more than one slide.
- Handouts can be annotated (show extra notes as well as what's on the slide — e.g. the presenter can add reminders of what to say).

3) Handouts make it easier to follow a presentation, and people can scribble their own notes on the printout too.

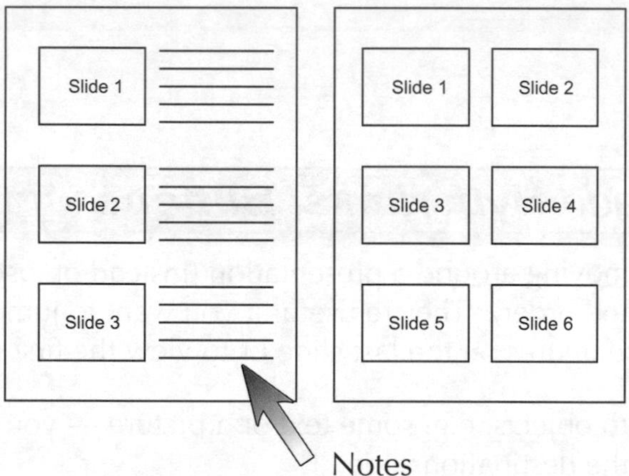

***Consistent Colour Schemes** and **Simple Layouts** are Good*

1) The most effective and professional-looking slides use a good, consistent colour scheme, and they have a simple layout.

2) Most presentation software has a selection of ready-made colour schemes to use on your slides. You select a colour scheme, and the software will automatically apply the right colours to slide backgrounds and text.

A good colour scheme is a set of colours that look good together.

3) You can usually select a template layout for your slides, e.g. one with just a title and a text frame, one with two columns, a blank one, etc.

See page 69 for more about templates.

The key is using all of these features in moderation...

It's quite easy to make a presentation look awful — billions of different animations, transitions and colours just put people off and then the presentation ends up being useless. So be warned...

Web-Design Software

Making a website used to be the preserve of the supergeek — now everyone's at it...

Web Design Software is a Bit Like a Word Processor...

1) For the most part, using web design software is similar to using a word processor (see page 56). You can add text, pictures and so on in much the same way.
2) The end result is a website, made up of individual web pages.
3) The software will also convert your website to HTML, the standard code that web browsers (see page 96) understand.
4) Here are two features that you'll find in most web design software:

HTML stands for HyperText Markup Language — you might not need to know this, but I knew you were wondering what it meant.

Master pages: these are pages containing objects that need to appear on all pages. They save a lot of effort and they're good for consistency, e.g. so things are in the same place on each page.

Templates: these are pages that are partially completed — you just amend the headings and change the text etc. for each particular page.

5) The above features give a consistent look to your pages, which makes them look professional.

...with Added Web Features

You can use these things on websites to make them more fancy — otherwise they'll just be like a text document that's been put on the Web, which is boring...

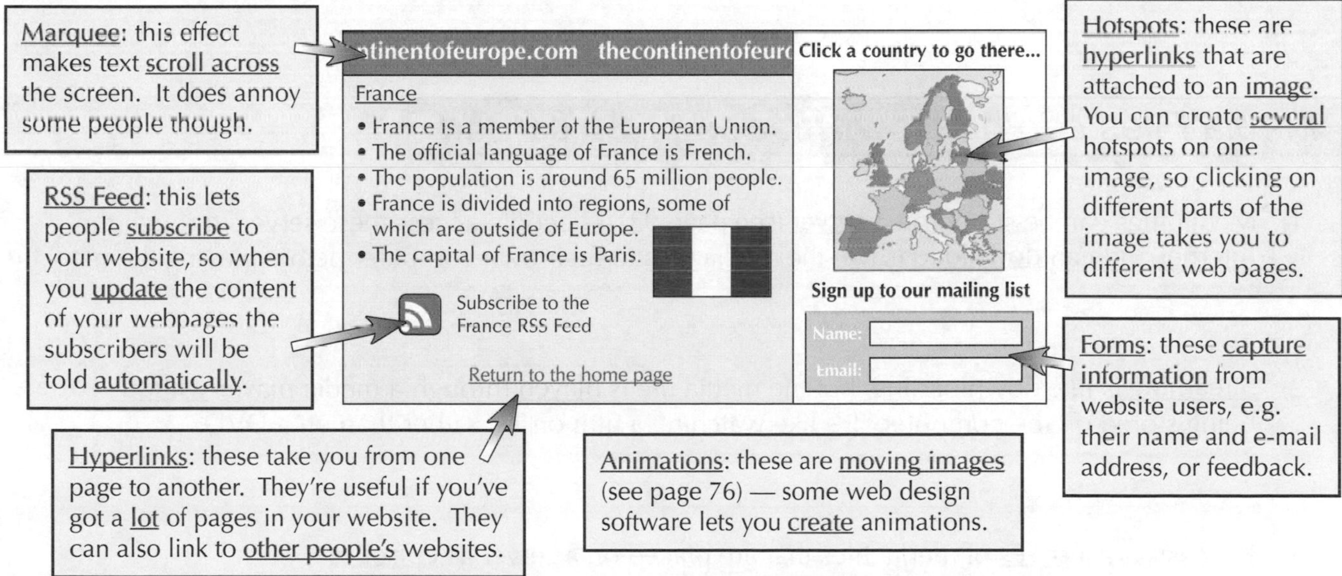

Navigation Bars and Counters are Useful Features

1) You could include a navigation bar on your website. It's a menu of hyperlinks that is on each page of a website, to make it easier for users to find what they want. Usually the pages that people want to visit frequently are on the navigation bar, e.g. the home page or search page.
2) Counters are useful to see how many visitors you've had to your website. Some counters will ignore repeat visitors, so you know how many individuals have visited your website.

You can make a web page with a text editor — if you know HTML...

You've probably been on a website before, but you might not have made one. Even if you have, make sure you learn the stuff on this page from top to bottom — it might come up in your exam.

Audio and Video Software

If you want to learn about audio and video software, you've come to the right place. Step right in...

Media Players — You know what they are...

1) You need a media player to watch a video (e.g. a DVD or a video file) or listen to some audio (e.g. a CD or MP3 file).

2) Media players can be a separate piece of hardware (like a DVD player under your telly), or a piece of software installed on your computer. They all have the same basic features.

- Play/Start
- Stop
- Pause
- Fast forward
- Reverse
- Volume adjustment
- Mute (i.e. no sound at all)

3) Some have extra features, like the ability to display subtitles.

4) Most software media players also let you create playlists, which are custom lists of media files that the media player will play in order.

*Media Files can be **Downloaded** or **Streamed***

1) Media files can be stored on a server (see page 92) — people access these servers through the Internet and can download (save) the media files to their own computer before playing them.

2) Streaming is like downloading, but the media file is played through a media player without being stored on the computer. It's like watching a film on TV, rather than on a DVD.

3) Podcasts are a series of media files that are placed on a server as episodes. People can download podcasts at any time and play them in any suitable media player, not just the well known one that the name suggests...

4) Podcasts can be used for loads of things — news reports, comedy shows, educational material... In a nutshell, they're a modern and convenient way of broadcasting.

Don't confuse downloading and streaming — they're different things

This is one of those pages where you've probably experienced everything that's on it in everyday life — but you need to make sure you know the right words to describe all of this audio and video stuff.

Audio and Video Software

Creating and *Editing* Media Files is a bit more *Interesting*

You'll need a selection of hardware and software to create and edit media files on a computer, e.g:

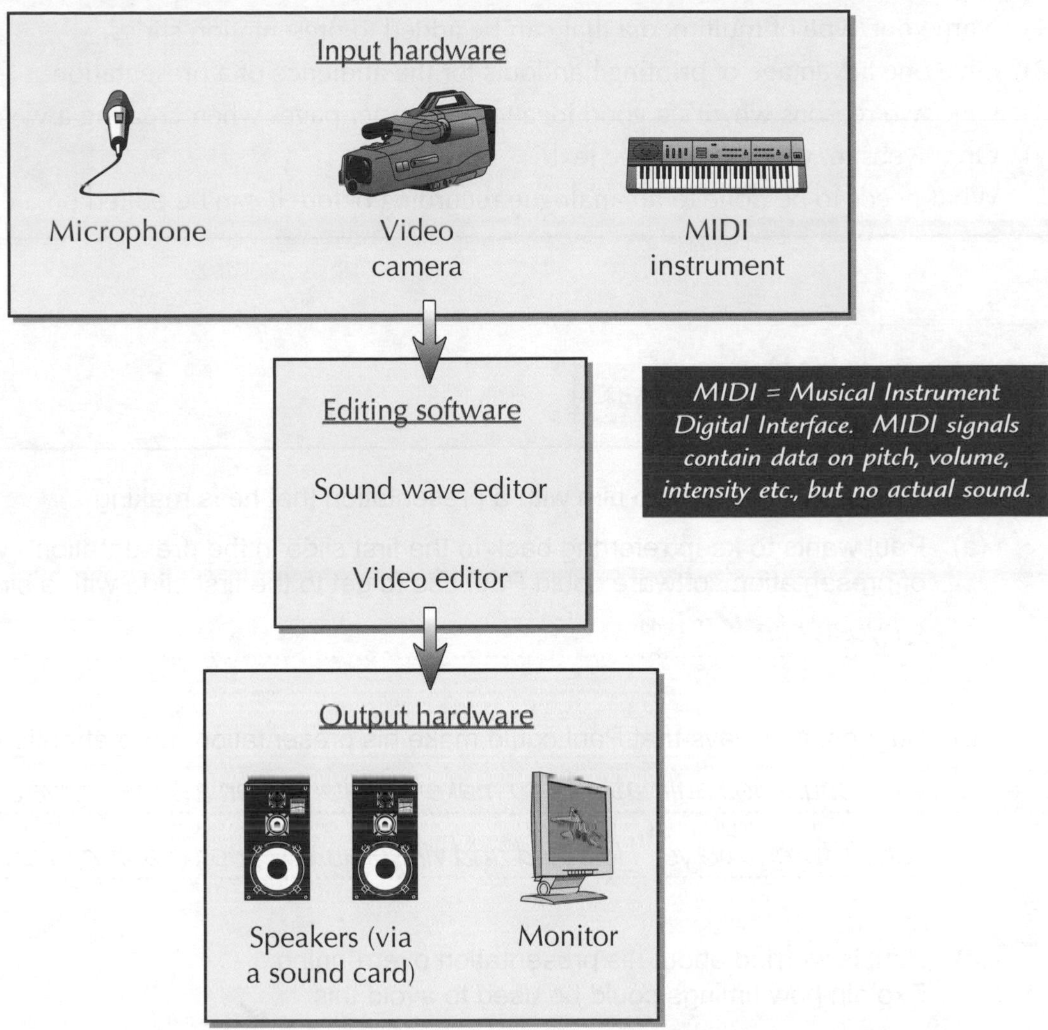

MIDI = Musical Instrument Digital Interface. MIDI signals contain data on pitch, volume, intensity etc., but no actual sound.

1) Media can be recorded in analogue or digital formats — but before you can edit an analogue recording on a computer, you'll need to convert it to a digital format. See page 83 for more on this.

2) It's also possible to compose music using software. Some software lets you add notes to an on-screen stave pretty much like you would with a pen and paper — it can then play the piece back to you.

A musical stave

3) Sound-wave editors let you adjust sounds in all kinds of fancy ways (e.g. you can add different effects, change the tempo, and all sorts).

With the right hardware and software, it's easy to make media files

After you've made something, you could upload it to a media-sharing website for all the world to see...

Warm-Up and Worked Exam Questions

Three types of software down, three types of software to go — but not before you see how much of the last few pages you can remember. As always, if you get any wrong you should learn the page again.

Warm-Up Questions

1) Name one type of multimedia that can be added to presentation slides.
2) Give one advantage of printing handouts for the audience of a presentation.
3) Give two reasons why it's a good idea to use master pages when creating a website.
4) On a website, what is marquee text?
5) What needs to be done to an analogue recording before it can be edited on a computer?

Worked Exam Questions

1 Paul has asked you to help him with a presentation that he is making.

(a) Paul wants to keep referring back to the first slide in the presentation. What feature of presentation software could Paul use to get to the first slide with a single click?

hyperlinks ✔ [1 mark]

(1 mark)

(b) Suggest two ways that Paul could make his presentation more attention-grabbing.

He could use animations to make the frames on a slide arrive on screen in different ways. ✔ [1 mark] *He could add video/audio clips to some of the slides.* ✔ [1 mark]

(2 marks)

(c) Paul is worried about his presentation overrunning.
Explain how timings could be used to avoid this

Timings automate animations and transitions. ✔ [1 mark] *Paul could use timings to automate the whole presentation so that it ends after a particular period of time.* ✔ [1 mark]

(2 marks)

(d) The presentation is being given to Paul's business partners. Describe two features of presentation software that could be used to give a consistent and professional look.

1. *Colour schemes* ✔ [1 mark] *can be applied to slides. The presentation software will automatically apply the right colours to slide backgrounds and text.* ✔ [1 mark]

2. *Layout templates* ✔ [1 mark] *can also be applied to slides. These automatically set up the position of things like text boxes and columns on the slides.* ✔ [1 mark]

(4 marks)

Exam Questions

1 Five features of websites are labelled with the letters **A**, **B**, **C**, **D** and **E**.
Write one letter in each row of the table that best matches the description.

A Counter **B** Hyperlink **C** Form **D** RSS Feed **E** Navigation bar

	Description	**Letter**
(i)	a menu of hyperlinks to make it easier to move around a website	
(ii)	a way of capturing information from visitors to a website	
(iii)	a way of automatically telling subscribers that a web page has been updated	
(iv)	keeps a record of how many people have visited a website	

(4 marks)

2 Tick **two** boxes to show which of the following features would be available on a DVD player.

	Tick **two** boxes
Print	
Mute	
Export	
Fast forward	
Redo	

(2 marks)

3 (a) What is a podcast?

....

....

(2 marks)

(b) How is a podcast different to streamed media?

....

....

(2 marks)

(c) Suggest one advantage to the audience of a podcast over a live broadcast.

....

(1 mark)

Graphics Software

These pages are for all you budding Rembrandts — you'll soon know all about graphics software...

Images are Stored as either **Bitmap** or **Vector** Data

Bitmap Images — made with **'Painting' Software.**

1) The graphic is saved as a series of coloured dots (pixels) in a file called a bitmap. These files are large — each dot in a red circle would be saved individually.

2) To edit the image, you basically alter each dot, but there are lots of tools to make this easier.

Resolution means the number of pixels making up the image. The more pixels used, the sharper the image — but the bigger the file. If you change the size of the image, the software has to add or remove pixels to fit the new size — this reduces the image quality, making things blurry.

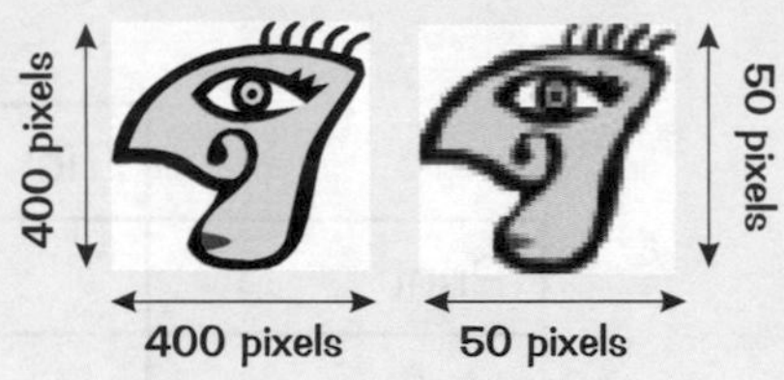

Vector Images — made with **'Drawing' Software.**

1) The image is saved as coordinates and equations (e.g. a red circle might be represented by its radius, the coordinates of its centre and a number for its colour).

2) Vector images are much easier to edit than bitmap images — you can resize them without reducing image quality and you can manipulate the individual objects (e.g. squares, circles) that make up the image, e.g. change their colour, give them an outline, etc.

Modern graphics software can work with vector and bitmap images

Bitmap and vector sound like complicated computer words, but don't be put off. Keep reading over the page until you know the differences between bitmap and vector images — then move on.

Graphics Software

You can *Create Images* or Use *Existing Ones*

1) The drawing functions of graphics software let you draw pretty much anything you can imagine. This can be quite time-consuming, so you might want to...
2) ...use existing images — but images that exist on paper, e.g. photos and drawings, need to be converted to a digital image before you can use them — this is what a scanner does. You can also upload images from a digital camera to your computer, which the software can work with straight away.

Another option is clip art graphics — digital images that have been made by someone else for you to use.

Tools for Creating and Editing Images

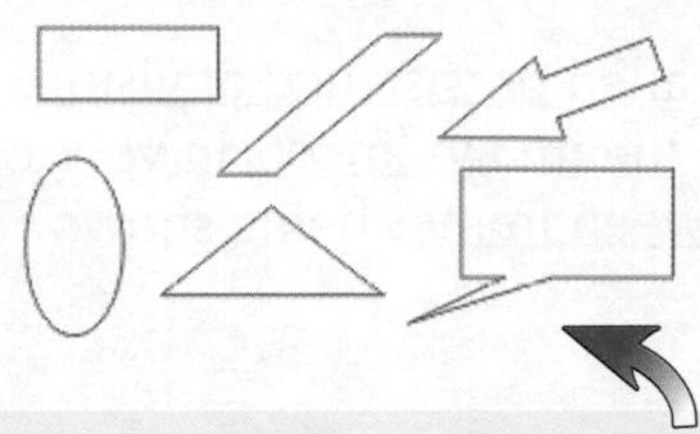

Graphics software has tools to draw simple shapes like squares, rectangles, circles, triangles, and so on. You can then edit these basic shapes to make arrows, speech bubbles and other more complex designs.

Because most vector graphics (except basic shapes) consist of separate objects, it's easy to change the colour of certain parts of the graphic, like this jacket and trousers, by recolouring individual objects.

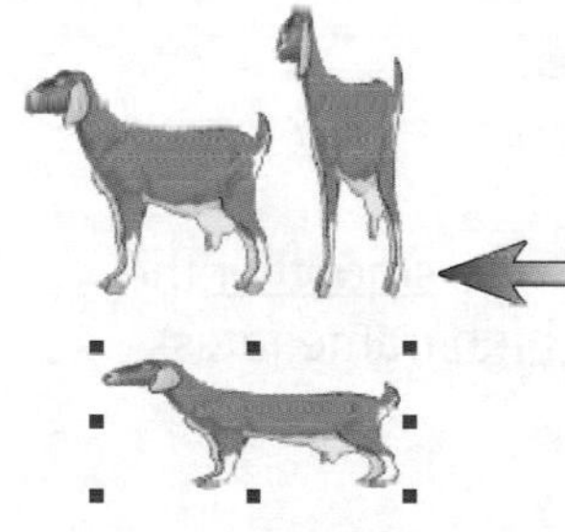

You can change the size of any object by dragging one of the handles (around the outside of the image) outwards or inwards. But if you don't keep the proportions the same, you can end up with very stretched or squashed images.

It's also possible to construct an image using different objects — the seal originally balanced a ball but that part of the graphic can be removed and replaced with pretty much anything.

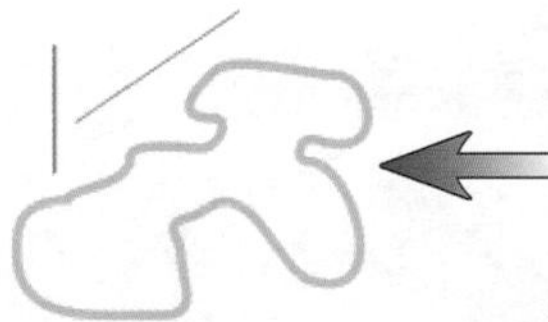

Straight lines and freehand lines can be drawn with different properties — e.g. thickness and colour can be changed.

Brush

Air brush

Eraser

In painting software, you can freehand draw with a brush or air brush. You can also erase pixels.

Fill and shading tools let you change the colours and backgrounds of objects. You can have patterned fills as well as single colours and gradients (transitions from one colour to another).

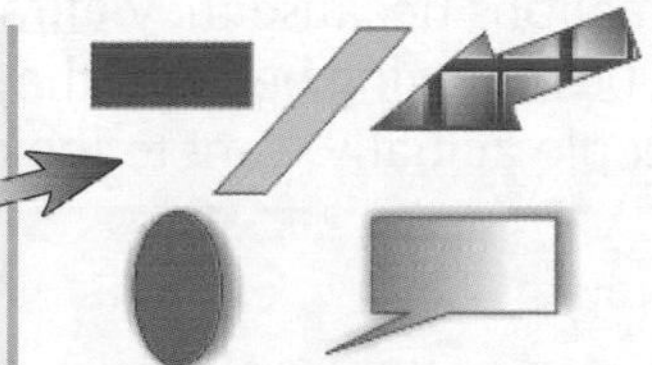

There are other fancy things that graphics software can do...

... for example, make objects transparent, distort them and clone (duplicate) them. It's all clever stuff.

Animation Software

Not all exam boards expect you to know about animations. But just in case yours does...

Animations are Made Up of Frames

1) Animations are a collection of frames — a frame is basically an individual image.
2) When an animation is played, each frame is shown, and then hidden, in turn.

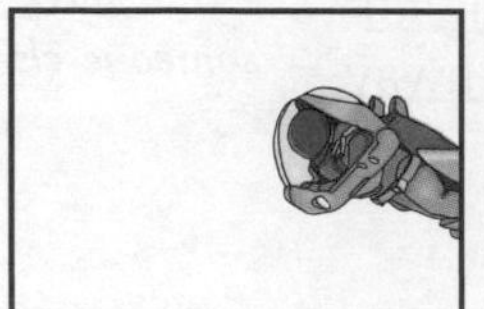
Frame 1

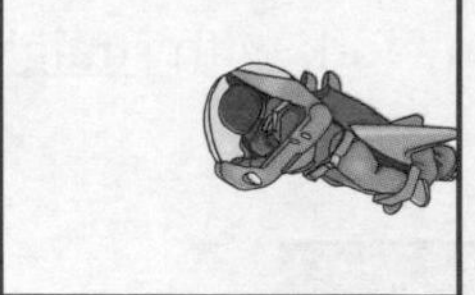
Frame 2

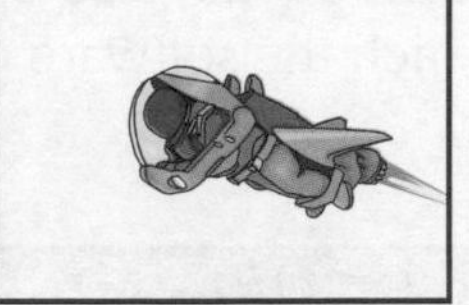
Frame 3

Frame 4

3) The animation looks like it's moving because of something called persistence of vision. When an image appears in your vision and then disappears, the image lingers in your eye for a few milliseconds. The lingering image fills the gap between frames being shown, so you think you're watching a continuously moving image.

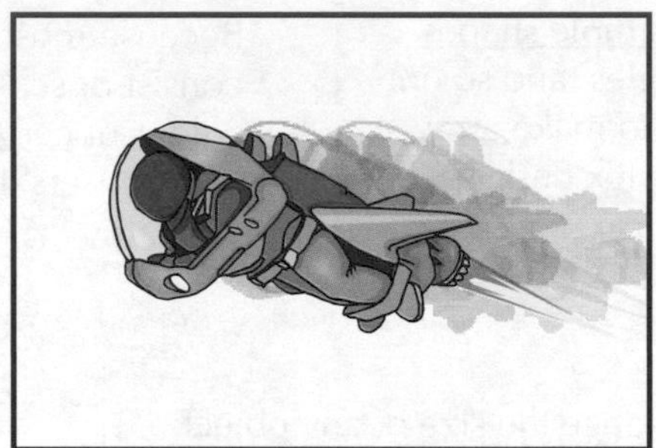

4) The frame rate is the number of frames per second. The higher the frame rate, the smoother the animation (up to a point — your eyes can't tell the difference between really high frame rates).

Animations have a Number of Uses

1) Animations are useful for teaching because they can show processes in motion, rather than just describe them with words and static images.

2) Many adverts on websites are animations because they attract people's attention — but they can be annoying because they can get in the way of the things people actually want to look at.

3) 3D animation has allowed film-makers to create realistic special effects for films. However, it's expensive and time-consuming to make them look convincing.

Animation Software

Animation *Techniques* have *Changed Over Time*

1) Early animations were done in flip books — they're essentially notebooks, and each page is a frame of the animation. To 'play' the animation you rapidly flip through the book.

2) Stop-motion animation was next. It's where a physical object is photographed, then moved, then photographed, then moved... each photo is a frame of the animation. The photos are shown in quick succession to make an animation.

3) Key frame animation uses animation software. Animators set up the key frames, which show the start and end of a piece of action, and the software then works out the frames in-between — this is called 'tweening'.

Claymation™ is a form of stop-motion animation, using models made out of modelling clay or similar. Wallace and Gromit™ films are made in this way.

4) 3D animation is the most recent development. Animators use animation software to pose 3D models (created in a computer) in each frame. 3D animation software lets you change viewing angles easily — with 2D animation you'd have to redraw everything to change angles.

A few *Features* of *Animation Software*

Looping — the animation starts again when the final frame is reached.

Onion skinning — a faint outline of the previous frame is shown so it's easier to draw the next frame.

Rotoscoping — showing the frames of live action video so they can be traced. This can create more natural looking animations, but it's a slow process.

Make sure you know some pros and cons of using animations

The best way to start an animation is by making a storyboard — a set of still images that mark out key points in the animation. It'll help you to focus your ideas and make the whole process easier.

Programming Software

Just what you wanted to know about — software to make software.

Source Code is Instructions for a Computer

1) To create a program, you need to write its source code — the instructions that tell the computer what to do.
2) Source code is written in a programming language, e.g. C++, BASIC, Java™, etc.
3) Programming languages make it easier to write programs — they can be easily understood by people. But they need to be translated to be understood by computers.
4) Source code editors are just text editors with a few fancy features that make it easier to write source code, e.g. autocomplete (which suggests a complete word based on a few characters that have been typed in).
5) A program is usually written in chunks — the whole thing is assembled at the end (see below).

Interpreters let you Run the Source Code

1) Interpreters can run (execute) the instructions in the source code by translating it, one line at a time, into machine code (see below) that can be understood by a computer's CPU.
2) The program will then run — but there might be some errors...

Debuggers Identify Problems with the Source Code

1) Source code has to be written precisely, otherwise the instructions can't be followed. If there's a problem, the program might crash (stop executing).
2) Debuggers tell programmers where mistakes have been made in the source code by highlighting the code that's causing the error.
3) Most debuggers let you run through the source code step-by-step, to help you work out what's causing the problem.

Compilers and Linkers Create the Finished Program

1) A compiler translates high-level (i.e. easy for humans to understand) source code to low-level (i.e. hard for humans to understand) machine code.
2) Machine code is the language of a CPU.
3) Compiling is like interpreting, but all of the source code is translated at the same time, rather than line by line.
4) It can be a slow process, but the final machine code is executed more quickly than if it's interpreted line by line.

A linker joins together (links) the various parts of compiled code into one program that can be executed and understood by a CPU. On Windows computers, executable programs have a .exe extension.

Integrated Development Environments (IDEs) are single programs that contain most or all of the programs mentioned on this page. IDEs make it easier to create, test and compile programs.

Get with the program and learn all of this stuff...

This page might seem complicated, but it's a piece of cake. The basic order is write the source code, debug it, compile it and then link the compiled bits together. Nothing difficult at all.

Warm-Up and Worked Exam Questions

Get these questions right and you're done — get them wrong and you've still got some learning to do...

Warm-Up Questions

1) What feature of animation software plays an animation again after it's finished?
2) Give one advantage and one disadvantage of using animated adverts on websites.
3) Why are programming languages, and not machine code, used to write programs?

Worked Exam Questions

1 Richard scanned a photograph and is editing the bitmap with a graphics software package.

(a) The resolution of the bitmap is 150 pixels per inch.

(i) What is meant by the term 'resolution'?

It's a measure of the number of dots making up the image. ✔ [1 mark] *A higher resolution means more dots per square inch, and a better image quality.* ✔ [1 mark]

(2 marks)

(ii) Explain what would happen to the image quality of the bitmap if it was enlarged.

It would be reduced ✔ [1 mark] *because each of the original pixels is effectively made larger, so the picture can look 'blocky'.* ✔ [1 mark]

(2 marks)

(b) Richard creates a vector image to place on top of the photograph.

(i) Describe how vector images are different to bitmap images.

Vector images are saved as coordinates and mathematical equations rather than a series of pixels. ✔ [1 mark]

(1 mark)

(ii) Give two advantages of vector images over bitmap images.

Vector images can be resized without reducing image quality. ✔ [1 mark]

Vector images are made up of individual objects that can be easily manipulated. ✔ [1 mark]

(2 marks)

2 Which **one** of the following is a type of fill effect found in most graphics software packages?

	Tick **one** box
Slope fill	
Gradient fill	✔
Incline fill	
Descent fill	

✔ [1 mark]

(1 mark)

Exam Questions

1 A cartoon is being shown on a television at 24 frames per second.

(a) Explain how it appears that the images in the cartoon are moving smoothly.

....

....

....

....

(4 marks)

(b) The cartoon was created using a technique called key frame animation.

(i) Explain what is meant by the term 'key frame animation'.

....

....

(2 marks)

(ii) Describe two features of animation software that make creating animations easier.

....

....

....

....

(4 marks)

(iii) Name two other animation techniques, other than key frame animation.

....

....

(2 marks)

2 Five pieces of software are labelled with the letters **A**, **B**, **C**, **D** and **E**.
Write one letter in each row of the table that best matches the description.

A Linker **B** Interpreter **C** Compiler **D** Source code editor **E** Debugger

	Description	**Letter**
(i)	text editor with features to make it easier to write in a programming language	
(ii)	translates all of the source code into machine code at once	
(iii)	highlights errors in source code	
(iv)	joins together the compiled parts of a program	

(4 marks)

Revision Summary for Section Five

That section was quite a mixed bag, but hopefully you've not lost your way... because it's time to see just how much you really know. The same rules as always apply — try one of the following questions and if you get it right, give yourself a high five and then move on to the next one. If you get it wrong, make a sad face and then skip back to the page with the answer on — learn all of it again and then come back here for a rematch.

1) Describe one similarity between presentation software and DTP software.
2) Name two ways that presentation slides can be brought to life. Give an example of each.
3) Describe how "timings" could be used to automate a presentation.
4) Describe two features of a professional-looking presentation.
5) Why might you use hyperlinks in a presentation?
6) Name two ways that presentations can be viewed.
7) Describe one feature that's found in both web design software and word processors.
8) What is a hotspot?
9) How can you capture information from users of your website?
10) What is a navigation bar?
11) Give an example of a media player.
12) Name three basic features that are standard to most media players.
13) Describe one piece of software that you could use to create or edit sounds.
14) Describe the difference between streaming and downloading.
15) What is the difference between bitmap and vector images?
16) Describe three tools in graphics software that help you to create and edit images.
17) What is each separate 'picture' in an animation called?
18) Describe the phenomenon of 'persistence of vision'.
19) Describe two animation techniques.
20) Give one advantage and one disadvantage of using 3D animation in a film.
21) What is source code?
22) Name one feature of a source code editor.
23) How does an interpreter run source code?
24) What software features can help to fix problems with source code?
25) Describe the main advantage of compiling source code, rather than interpreting it.
26) What does a linker do?

Data Logging

The stuff in this section is about different ways of recording, responding to and controlling events, either in the real world or in a model of it. Even if you've not had much of a chance to carry out this sort of ICT in your school, learn it — because it's in the exam.

Data Logging means Recording Data Automatically

1) Data logging means capturing information using sensors.
2) Measurements are taken, and then converted to data and stored. They can then be downloaded into a computer for analysis.
3) Data logging is best used whenever large amounts of data need to be collected over very long or short periods of time, or from hostile environments.
4) Examples of data logging activities include collecting weather data via satellite, radioactivity data from nuclear power stations, and temperature data from inside a pizza oven.

Data Logging needs the Right Hardware and Software

1) Data is collected by an input sensor. Most sensors work by converting environmental signals into electrical energy — producing either an analogue or a digital signal.
2) A detector at a set of traffic lights produces a signal whenever a vehicle passes near it. This is a digital sensor — it's either on or off.
3) A thermistor is a resistor whose resistance changes with temperature — the hotter the thermistor, the more easily electricity flows through it. Output from a thermistor can take a range of values — it's an analogue signal.

Sensors are often used to measure...

Light: Light-dependent resistors are used to determine when to switch street lights on.

Radioactivity: Geiger counters measure the amount of radioactivity emitted by a source.

Temperature: Thermistors can be used to control an air-conditioning system.

Sound: Sensors can be used to check that aircraft noise keeps within agreed levels.

Pressure: Like pressure pads used in burglar alarm systems.

Infrared: A sensor can detect a break in an infrared beam.

Air pressure: Sensors can be used to control emergency oxygen masks on aircraft.

Data Logging

Analogue Signals need to be Converted to Digital Signals

1) Before an analogue signal can be stored and downloaded onto a computer system, it needs to be converted into a digital signal — using an analogue-to-digital converter (ADC).

Digital v Analogue
Analogue: An analogue signal can take any value in a certain range. Digital: A digital signal can only take certain values.

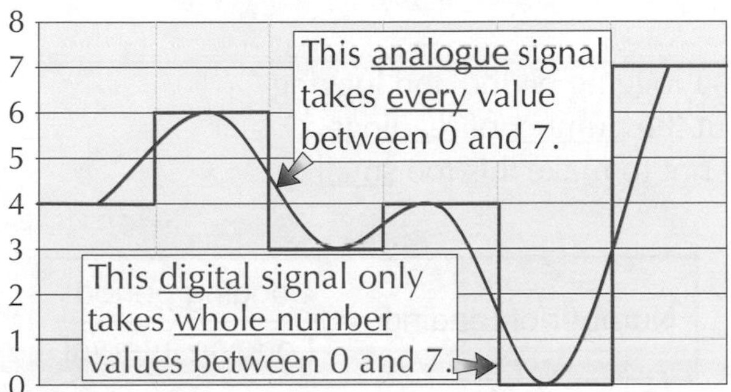

2) An ADC is often part of the interface board (the device that lets you connect the sensor to the computer).

3) Once the output's been converted into digital data, it's often stored in CSV (comma-separated value) format. This means that it can be imported into a spreadsheet for data analysis. The output from this analysis can be screen-based or paper-based, and will probably include graphs.

Choose an Appropriate Logging Period...

1) The logging period is just the total length of time you're going to collect data for. If this is too long, you can waste valuable time. But if it's too short, you might miss some important data.

2) The logging period depends on the thing that's being monitored. For example, an experiment to investigate the cooling of a cup of coffee should not take measurements over a two-year period — one hour would be better.

3) If you're not sure what logging period to use, do some preliminary research — for example, leave a cup of coffee and see roughly how long it takes.

Converting analogue to digital — easy as ADC

Make sure you learn what data logging is, what hardware and software is needed, the difference between analogue and digital signals, and what sensors can measure. That'll keep you busy...

Data Logging

This stuff's just common sense — but that doesn't mean you don't have to bother learning it.

You also Need a Decent **Logging Interval**

1) The logging interval is the time between one measurement and the next.
2) As a general rule, the longer the logging period, the longer the logging interval can be.

Use a long logging interval...	Use a short logging interval...
If you're measuring the growth of a tree over a two-year period, you could probably have a logging interval of a month.	On the other hand, measuring the temperature of a chemical reaction which lasts only a couple of seconds might require a logging interval of a fraction of a second.

3) Once you've decided on a logging period and logging interval, you can work out the number of readings you'll have — be careful not to make this too small.

$$\text{Number of readings} = \frac{\text{Logging period}}{\text{Logging interval}}$$

Data Logging has **Advantages** and **Disadvantages**

Advantages

1) Data logging can record information in places where humans find it hard to operate — e.g. the bottom of the sea, outer space, and inside nuclear reactors or pizza ovens.
2) Data can be collected over very long or very short periods — you could record the growth rate of a tree, or the rapidly changing temperature inside a nuclear explosion.
3) Intervals between measurements can be more accurate than when a human's doing the measuring — for example a temperature reading taken every 27 seconds will be exactly that.
4) Data loggers don't need tea breaks, lunch breaks or sleep.

Disadvantages

1) The hardware used for data logging can be very expensive and you may have to buy specialist software.
2) People will need training so they can use the data-logging equipment correctly. This will take time and it could cost money.
3) If the logging equipment malfunctions, you'll lose data — you'll need to back up your data from time to time.

Data loggers can collect data from dangerous environments

There are a few advantages to using data loggers rather than people to collect data, but they have their disadvantages too — make sure you know a few examples of both. You also need to know how to choose a sensible logging interval — it's usually based on how long the logging period is.

Control Systems

Control Systems are **Dedicated** or **Computer-Controlled**

A control system is a system of hardware and software that's used to control the operation of a piece of equipment. There are two main types of control system:

1) Dedicated control systems are basic systems that carry out a pre-programmed set of instructions, e.g. a traffic-light system where the lights change at fixed time intervals.
2) Computer-controlled systems use a computer to control the output device, and this computer can be connected to a sensor — making the system more flexible. These are used in traffic-light systems where the time between changes needs to alter depending on the volume of traffic.

Most **Computer Control Systems** use **Feedback Loops**

1) A feedback loop is when information from a sensor is used to control the output of a device. The sensor is often in a different place from the output device. For example, in central heating systems, input from a thermostat (the sensor) is used to control the output of the radiators.
2) Sometimes the feedback data comes from a sensor attached to the output device itself. For example, a robot used to check for leaks inside a sewerage system will send data about its position inside the sewer to a computer, which then uses it to guide the robot's forward movement.

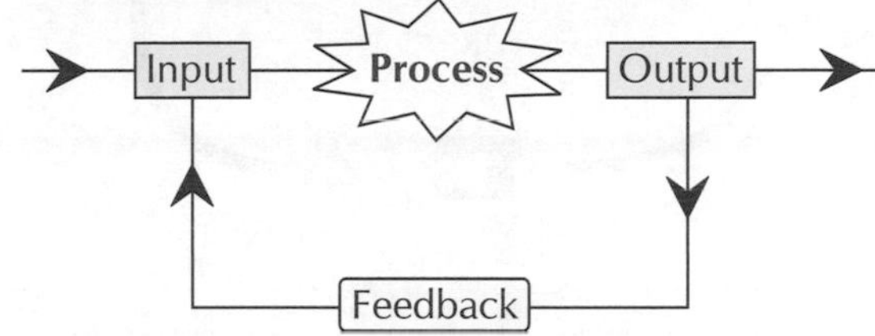

Computer Control Systems need Hardware and Software

1) Sensors are connected to the computer via an interface such as an analogue-to-digital converter (an ADC), or an interface board (also called a control board). This allows the two devices to communicate with each other.
2) The computer then processes the data according to a set of instructions.
3) The output signal from the computer is then sent to the output device. The output will be a digital signal but the output device might only operate using analogue signals — so an output interface containing a digital-to-analogue converter (DAC) might be needed.
4) The output device used will depend on the specific task — but could include a switch or a motor.

Example: Making a lamp brighter or dimmer depending on how much natural light there is.

1) A light-dependent resistor is used as the sensor.
2) As less and less light falls on it, its resistance increases.
3) The changing resistance affects the current running through it, which is an analogue signal.

4) An ADC converts this analogue signal into a digital signal, which is processed by a computer.

5) The computer's digital output passes through a DAC.
6) The DAC converts the digital output to an analogue voltage.
7) This analogue voltage determines the brightness of the lights.

Sensors need to be learnt

When you've passed your exam you can forget lots of these things — but for now, get it all revised.

Control Systems — Two Examples

These examples of control systems should prepare you for the questions you might get in the exam.

Greenhouses Control Environmental Conditions

1) In this diagram of a control system, a heater is controlled by the computer in response to readings from a temperature sensor.

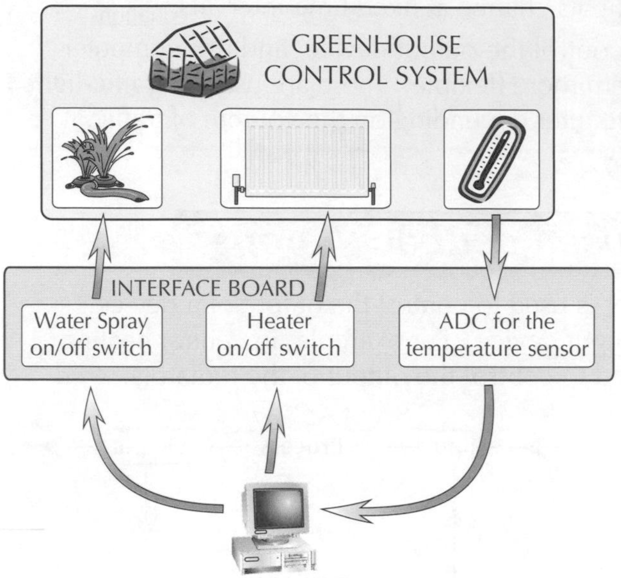

2) When the temperature falls below a certain level, the computer sends a signal to the interface board to switch on the heater. When the desired temperature is reached, the heater's switched off — this is an example of a feedback loop. (Central heating works in the same way.)

3) The water spray is controlled by a simple timer — once the timings have been programmed into the computer, the water spray will be switched on and off at regular intervals.

4) The water spray could be controlled using a feedback loop from a humidity sensor in the soil — but this would make the system more expensive. Other things that could be controlled include opening and closing windows, and the feeding of nutrients to the plants.

5) Fully automated systems are very expensive, so only large greenhouses will have them.

Burglar Alarms Alert People to Intruders

1) Burglar alarms are another good example of a computer control system that uses feedback. Basically the system constantly collects data from input sensors, and when the data suggests that an intruder is present the system sends a signal to an output device.

2) The input sensor might be an infrared beam, a noise sensor, pressure sensors on the floor or whatever. When the data from one or more sensors exceeds a preprogrammed limit, a signal is sent to an output device, such as a loudspeaker or siren.

3) Automatic doors work in a very similar way. Only the output device is different — it's a motor which opens a door.

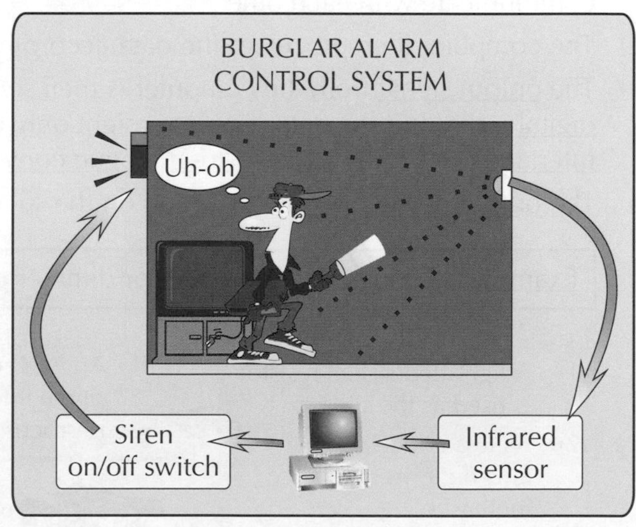

Input, process, output — that's the pattern you need to remember

There are loads of other examples of control systems, and all share the same idea — there's an input, which is processed, and then there's an output. Think of a video game — the input comes from the controller, it's processed by the console, then there's an output, e.g. a character moving.

Simulations

Flight simulators aim to recreate as closely as possible the experience of flying a real aircraft.

A Simulation is carried out Using a Model

1) A model is an artificial re-creation of an object or phenomenon, and should behave in the same way as the real thing — e.g. a model of a sports car built for testing in a wind tunnel.
2) A simulation is when the model is used to carry out an activity that mimics real life — like when bridge designers use a model to simulate what'll happen when the bridge is actually used.
3) A computer model is created using programmed instructions and equations. An example would be a computer model of the way an aircraft behaves when in flight.

Limitations of Modelling

1) Any model or simulation is only as good as the rules, programs and equations it's based on.
2) It's important to test the model, using situations where the actual results are known.
3) In this way the model and simulation can be improved.

Flight Simulators are Just Like the Real Thing

1) Flight simulators were developed to simulate the experience of flying a large jet aircraft — without the risk of a real plane crash. They're used to train pilots, and are built around a full-scale model of a cockpit.
2) Flight simulators are much safer than teaching a pilot to fly in a real plane. After a 'crash landing', the pilot can simply begin again.
3) Instead of windows there are high resolution computer screens that display computer-generated images. The images work in real time — meaning they respond exactly to the cockpit controls.
4) The cockpit is mounted on a number of hydraulic arms, which respond to the actions of the pilot and to preprogrammed environmental conditions. For example, the effects of flying through an electrical storm can be simulated.

5) The cockpit can be a closed environment — allowing things like cabin pressure and light levels to be as they would in reality. This means that some of the effects of a cabin fire can be simulated.
6) The system makes use of feedback loops. When the pilot alters the controls, signals are input into the computer, which then changes the output of the simulation, e.g. the image screens, hydraulic arms and cockpit environment controls.
7) The next step might be to have virtual-reality flight simulators. The image of the cockpit would be projected onto the inside of a visor, while the pilot's chair would shake about, simulating the movement of the cockpit.

Flight simulators are complex, but the idea behind them is simple

There are four main features to a flight simulator — real-time images, hydraulic arms, a closed environment and feedback loops — so learn these, and the effect they have on the final experience.

Robots and Control Language

Not all syllabuses need you to know LOGO commands, so check before you start learning them.

Robots *are Usually Computer-Controlled*

1) A robot is an automated piece of equipment designed to carry out routine repetitive tasks.
2) Simple robots are designed to carry out a preprogrammed set of operations — like spraying paint onto the bonnet of a car on an assembly line. There are two different ways to develop these instructions:

The Teach-And-Learn Method

a) The programmer writes a set of instructions.
b) The robot is observed as it carries these instructions out.
c) The instructions are improved if necessary.

The Do-It-Once-And-Remember-It Method

a) Some robots just need to be guided through the correct movements.
b) They then automatically produce the correct programming instructions to carry out the task.

3) Robots can be programmed to carry out a number of different tasks. For example, a robot could be programmed with different instructions so it can spray different-shaped car bonnets.
4) They usually have some sort of feedback system too, otherwise they're a potential safety hazard — if a robot can't detect that someone's walked in front of the bonnet, the person ends up getting sprayed, not the bonnet.

Robots

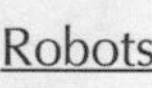

a) are cheaper to operate than paying people wages,
b) don't get tired or make mistakes,
c) carry out tasks that humans can't or won't perform.

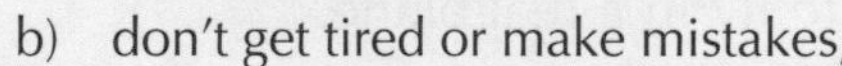

Robots

a) can't think for themselves, and so can't respond to new situations as well as humans can,
b) are very expensive to buy.

The Simplest ***Control Language*** *is* ***LOGO***

1) Devices are controlled using special programming languages.
2) A simple example of this kind of language is LOGO, which is sometimes used in schools to introduce the idea of control programs. You can use LOGO to move a turtle on a computer screen — and the trace of the turtle's movements is used to draw an object such as a shape or a letter.
3) You might get asked in the exam to list some of the simple commands used in LOGO, or to write a simple program. So have a look at this lot...

PROGRAMS AND LANGUAGES

A program is a sequence of instructions that a computer can carry out.

A programming language is basically the list of commands that the computer will accept.

Programs are eventually translated into machine code — the sequence of 0s and 1s that the computer understands. This is usually done automatically.

Some LOGO commands:

FORWARD X Move turtle forward X units
BACK X Move turtle backward X units
LEFT X Rotate turtle X degrees to the left
RIGHT X Rotate turtle X degrees to the right
REPEAT n [Y] Repeat instruction Y, n times
PENUP Stop drawing a trace
PENDOWN Start drawing a trace

A simple sample LOGO Program:

```
PENDOWN
FORWARD 40
REPEAT 3 [RIGHT 90 FORWARD 20]
LEFT 45
FORWARD 14
PENUP
```

Don't Teach-and-Learn, just Learn...

You need to know the pros and cons of robots, and maybe even how to program them. Get learning.

Warm-Up and Worked Exam Questions

Another few pages of questions for you to have a go at — you should know what to do by now...

Warm-Up Questions

1) Name three types of sensors used for data logging.
2) What is the difference between an analogue signal and a digital signal?
3) What is meant by the term 'logging interval'?
4) Give one benefit of using a flight simulator rather than real planes to train pilots.

Worked Exam Questions

1 Wheels and Co is a company that makes cars. At the moment, all the work is done with manually-operated machines, but the management are thinking of using robots instead.

(a) Give four advantages of using robots.

i) Robots are cheaper to operate than paying people wages; ✔ [1 mark]

ii) robots don't make mistakes; ✔ [1 mark] *iii) robots can carry out tasks that humans can't perform;* ✔ [1 mark] *iv) robots can work continuously.* ✔ [1 mark]

(4 marks)

(b) Give two disadvantages of using robots.

i) robots are very expensive to buy; ✔ [1 mark]

ii) robots can't think for themselves and respond to new situations. ✔ [1 mark]

(2 marks)

2 A simple LOGO program is shown below. The units for forward movements are the grid squares shown. Sketch the trace in the box below, starting from the circle.

```
PENDOWN
FORWARD 5
REPEAT 3 [LEFT 90 FORWARD 3]
PENUP
```

You might get a more complex program in your exam, but don't panic — all you have to do is follow the instructions really carefully.

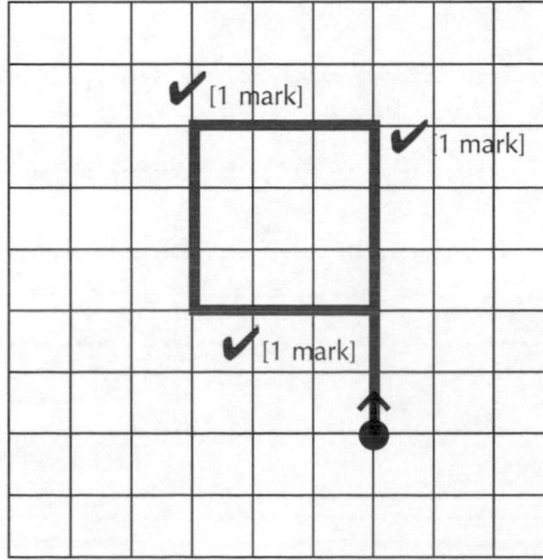

Some exam questions might have a modified version of the LOGO language, but you'll be told what the new commands mean.

(3 marks)

Exam Questions

1 A garden centre uses a computer-controlled heating system in its greenhouses.

(a) Name a sensor that could be used in this system.

....

(1 mark)

(b) Explain how this system could work.

....

....

....

(3 marks)

2 A weather station records the temperature at regular intervals using a data logging system.

(a) (i) Name two items of hardware that could be used in this system.

....

....

(2 marks)

(ii) The data will be analysed weekly by one of the weather station employees. Suggest a suitable logging interval for the system.

....

(1 mark)

(b) Give two advantages of using data logging equipment rather than people to record data.

....

....

(2 marks)

3 A flight simulator is used to train pilots to fly. Give three of the main features of this type of simulator and explain why they are important.

....

....

....

....

....

....

(6 marks)

Revision Summary for Section Six

That's another section under your belt. Let's see if everything is under control by simulating a test. Get all these questions right and you'll be a model student. If you make any errors, go over the stuff you got wrong and then try the questions again.

1) Give a definition of data logging.
2) Explain how a thermistor works.
3) What does CSV stand for? Why is it useful?
4) Explain the difference between a logging period and a logging interval.
5) Give three advantages of using data logging.
6) Give two disadvantages of using data logging.
7) Explain the difference between a dedicated control system and a computer-controlled one.
8) What is a feedback loop? Explain how a feedback loop might work in a smoke alarm.
9) What do the initials ADC and DAC stand for and why are these things needed?
10) Name three sensors you might find in a greenhouse and explain what they might be used for.
11) Describe how a burglar alarm works, using an input and output of your choice.
12) Some buildings have automatic sprinkler systems that spray water in the event of a fire. Explain how sensors and output devices could be used in such a system.
13) Explain the difference between a model and a simulation.
14) What is the main limitation of modelling?
15) Explain fully how a flight simulator works.
16) Describe the teach-and-learn method of programming a robot.
17) Describe the do-it-once-and-remember-it method of programming a robot.
18) Give three reasons why robots might be preferred to human workers.
19) Give two problems with robots.
20) Explain the difference between a programming language and machine code.
21) List four commands used in LOGO and explain what they mean.

LAN and WAN

A network is two or more computers connected together. Computers in a network can communicate with each other. The Internet is also a type of network — that's covered in this section too.

LANs are Small, Local Networks

LANs (Local Area Networks) are the networks that you see in most offices and schools.
They have the following hardware:

1) A Network File Server is a computer that runs the software needed by the network, and stores the files that users have created.
2) Individual workstations (basically desktop computers) give users access to the network. They can make use of the network's software and files. Some may need a network interface card to connect to the network, but most now have network hardware built in.
3) If a group of workstations share a printer then the system needs a print server. If two or more documents are sent to the printer at the same time, the print server will put them into a queue. Users can then carry on with other work whilst waiting for the documents to be printed.
4) For the network to operate, data needs to be sent to and from all parts of the network. This can be done using wire cables, fibre optic cables, or via radio signals.

   Note — a LAN doesn't have to include a server. LANs can be as simple as two or three computers linked together for sharing of files or software.

WANs are Long Range Networks

1) WAN is short for Wide Area Network. They are used when the computers that need to be connected together are in different places.
2) WANs need servers to operate the network. Users connect up to the network from a distance, often using telephone lines. Wireless systems such as microwave links or satellite links can also be used.
3) WANs are used by companies who have employees working away from the firm's main site. A good example would be oil exploration engineers who work in remote parts of the world. They're also used by firms who have a lot of teleworkers (see page 134).

Networks have Advantages and Disadvantages

Advantages of using networks:

1) Peripherals such as printers can be shared amongst many different users.
2) Software can be shared amongst different users.
3) Storing files centrally makes them less vulnerable to loss as a result of workstation failure.
4) Communication across the network is cheap and fast.

Disadvantages of using networks:

1) Cabling can be expensive to install and replace.
2) A fault with a server can prevent the whole network from working.
3) Security measures are needed to restrict access to the network.
4) Viruses could disable the entire network.

Networks make sharing things between people a lot easier

All this server talk might be confusing you — a server is just a computer that provides a service to other computers. There are many types of servers, each with a specific function. They might be referred to by their proper name, e.g. 'web server', or just 'server'. Make sure you know that.

Network Topologies

Network topologies — some of this stuff is a bit tricky at first glance. But if you give it a bit of thought, the pros and cons of each type are pretty obvious.

Star Networks Give Access to a Central Computer

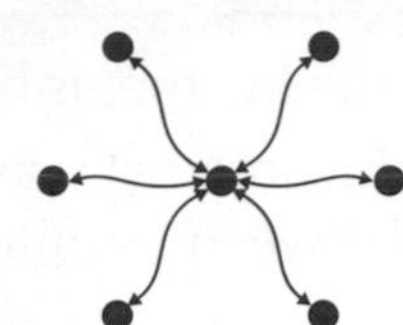

1) Star networks are used when a large number of workstations need to be connected to a central computer such as a mainframe or server.
2) Each workstation is connected directly to the central computer.

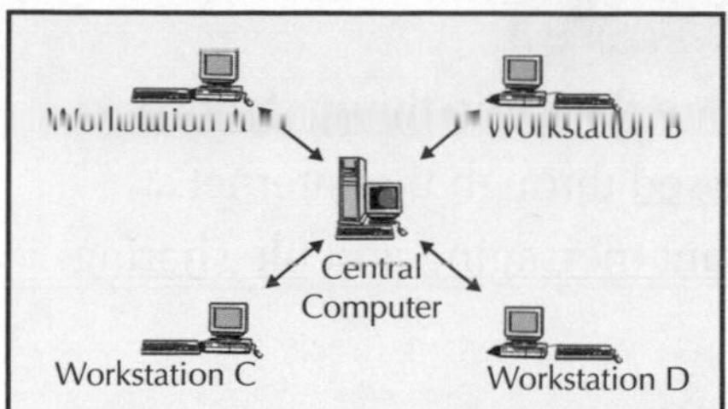

Pros
1) Performance in one part of the network is unaffected by events elsewhere.
2) It's easy to add more computers to the network.

Cons
1) Failure in the central computer causes the whole network to break down.
2) Uses a lot of cabling, so it's expensive.

Line Networks are the Cheapest

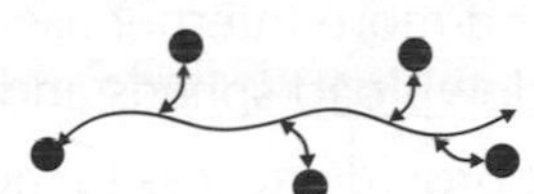

1) In line networks (bus networks) data is sent to and from the file server along a line of cable.
2) All terminals are connected to this central line.

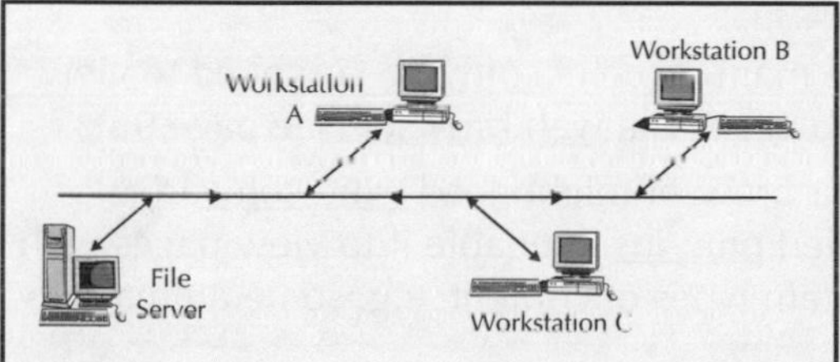

Pros
1) Cheap — because it uses less cabling.

Cons
1) With lots of users the system becomes very slow, as all data goes along a central line.
2) Failure of the central cable will bring the whole network down.

Ring Networks are Faster than Line Networks

1) Ring networks are a bit like line networks, except that all the equipment is linked in a ring.
2) Data flows around the network in one direction only.

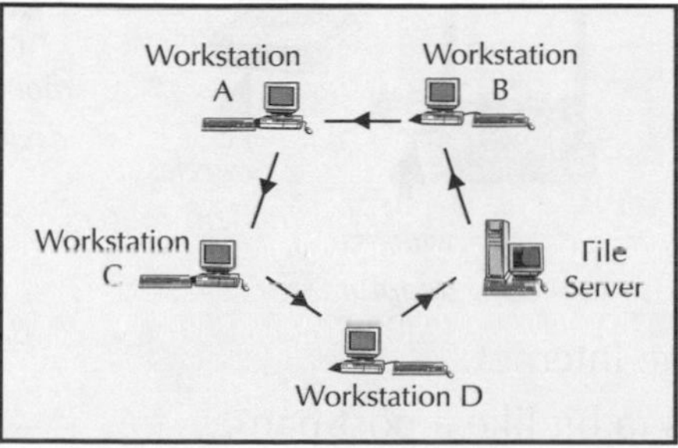

Pros
1) Cheap to expand.
2) Fast — as data flows in one direction only.

Cons
1) With lots of users the system becomes slower, as all the data is sent along a single line.
2) Failure of the ring cable brings the whole network down.

Don't be put off by these network diagrams...

... all you need to know are the three most common network topologies, and their pros and cons.

The Internet

The Internet — you might have heard of this before...

The Internet is an International Network of Computers

1) The Internet is basically a very big Wide Area Network (WAN) (see page 92 for more).
2) The Internet was originally developed by the US government to improve communication between its military computers. But it's since grown into what we all know today.

The World Wide Web is only Part of the Internet

1) A lot of people think that the World Wide Web and the Internet are the same thing. Not so.
2) The Web is a system of interlinked documents (web pages) accessed through the Internet.
3) Some of the other major uses of the Internet include e-mail, instant messaging and file sharing.

Getting Connected to the Internet

1) In the early days of home Internet everyone used dial-up connections, which were very slow and meant you couldn't use the phone while connected to the Internet.
2) These days, more and more Internet users have broadband connections, which give much greater download speeds and mean you can still use the phone.
3) The companies that provide access to the Internet are called ISPs (Internet Service Providers).
4) You need special hardware and software to connect to the Internet and the Web:

Hardware

1) Data from your ISP is sent through a modem (modulator / demodulator) to convert it into a form that can be transmitted, e.g. along telephone lines. A modem connected to your computer converts the data back into a form your computer can understand.
2) If you want a wireless system at home, you can get a wireless modem router (modem and radio transmitter in one). The router connects to the ISP via a phone line, and computers with wireless adaptors connect to the router using radio signals (this is Wi-Fi™).
3) Many mobile devices can access the Internet from anywhere using mobile broadband. Mobile broadband uses mobile phone networks to transfer data to and from the Internet.
4) Most mobile phones can use mobile broadband. You can also buy modems that provide broadband by connecting computers to mobile networks. A device that plugs into a computer's USB port and provides mobile broadband is called a dongle.

Software

1) The main piece of software you need to view web pages is a web browser (see page 96).
2) Your browser might need extra software called plug-ins to enable it to view pages with certain types of content, e.g. some animations.

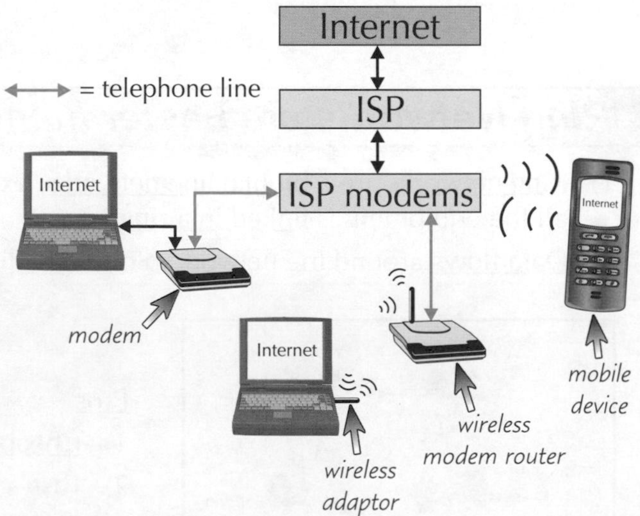

5) File servers and print servers (see page 92) can be connected to the Internet.
6) E-mail servers are another type of server — they distribute e-mails (a bit like a postman).

The Internet is just a WAN that spans the world

All you need to remember is that the Internet is a massive network and it's not the same as the World Wide Web. Make sure you know about the stuff you need to connect to the Internet, too.

Internet Security

A big problem with the Internet is that data can be intercepted relatively easily by unauthorised users. Exchanging information via phone or digital lines still isn't totally secure.

On-Line Shopping uses **Encryption Software**

1) Some people don't like on-line shopping because they're worried that their credit card details might be intercepted and used to make unauthorised purchases. Encryption software can reduce this risk.
2) Sensitive information (e.g. credit card details) is encrypted by the website into a code using an algorithm (a set of rules). This code can only be decoded with the right software and a password called a key.
3) In theory, only the retailer's website knows the key, so even if someone intercepts the information, they won't be able to use it.

Websites that encrypt details like this are called 'secure', and display a padlock icon in the browser.

Passwords give **Restricted Access** to some Websites

An intranet is like a private mini-Internet that can only be viewed by people connected to a particular organisation. An extranet is basically an intranet that's connected to the Internet.

1) Some websites restrict access to authorised users only.
2) Schools allowing pupils and parents to access material on their extranet might do this to prevent other people accessing the information.
3) On-line magazines also do this, so they can charge people for access.
4) The usual way to restrict access is to issue user names and passwords.

Get Protection from **Hackers** and **Viruses**

1) Hacking means accessing a computer system and its files without permission. It's totally illegal, and once inside a system, the hacker might be able to view, edit, copy or delete important files, or plant a virus.
2) Organisations can protect themselves by using passwords, encrypting files, and using firewalls and hacking-detection software (see page 129).
3) A virus is a program deliberately written to infect a computer, and make copies of itself. They often corrupt other files — and even operating systems. They move between computer systems by attaching themselves to harmless computer files and e-mails (see below).
4) The main way to reduce the risk of viruses is to use anti-virus software — but it's important to use an up-to-date version because new viruses are detected every day.

Take Care Opening E-mail **Attachments**

1) It's possible to send files via e-mail — these are called attachments. For example, you could e-mail a picture or a video file to a friend.
2) Unless you're expecting to receive an attachment, treat any you receive with suspicion — it's easy to get a virus from an infected attachment.
3) Some e-mail software lets you view an attachment without downloading it, or use virus-checking software to scan it before opening it. Both help to reduce the risk of getting a virus.

It's always better to be cautious about things on the Internet...

It's a pretty scary world out there. So make sure you know how to protect yourself. Learning the different ways on this page will help you in the exam as well as on the Internet.

Web-Browsing

Even if you think this is all second nature to you, read it carefully...

A Web Browser Displays Web Pages

1) The World Wide Web (see page 94) is made up of a lot of pages — billions and billions.
2) To get your hands on all this information, you need a web browser.
3) It's a piece of software that can understand the code that web pages are made up of, and display the pages in the right way.

A URL is the Address of a Web Page

1) URL stands for Uniform Resource Locator — in other words, the address of a web page (or any other resource on the Internet). For example: http://www.cgpbooks.co.uk
2) You can type a URL directly into a web browser — but some URLs can be extremely long or complicated, so there are other ways to access web pages.

Search Engines and Portals Find Pages

1) Search engines are websites that help you find other websites, without having to know their URL.
2) The basic type of search is a keyword search — you type in a keyword and the search engine lists a load of websites containing that keyword.
3) Or you can do a complex search, using things like AND and OR.
4) Portals are websites offering many services in one place, e.g. search engines, e-mail and on-line shopping.

Most search engines work by storing details or keywords of different websites, but no single search engine will have data on every website — so it's worth using more than one.

Web Browsers have Features to Help You Browse

BOOKMARKS

Browsers can save URLs you use often as 'bookmarks' or 'favourites', so you don't have to keep typing them or searching for them.

STOP and REFRESH buttons

To prevent your browser from loading the web page it's accessing, you can hit the stop button. To reload a page, use the refresh button.

HOME PAGE

You can set a URL to be accessed as soon as you open a browser — this is the browser's home page. Browsers have a home button that takes you back to the home page.

PHISHING FILTER

Phishing is when people try to get user names, passwords, bank details, etc. by using a web page that looks official. Some browsers look for signs of phishing and prevent you from entering details if a web page is dodgy.

NAVIGATION buttons

You can flick through the pages that you've already looked at by using the back and forward buttons in your browser.

POP-UP BLOCKER

Some browsers automatically block pop-ups — adverts that appear in a new window when you're looking at some web pages.

Browsing the Internet is a bit like wandering through a huge library...

This stuff isn't complicated or difficult, but you need to know all of it. Oh, and it's easy to think that you're an expert because you've used a search engine before, but that might not be the case...

E-Mail

That's right, it's time to learn the basics of something that you probably use on a daily basis.

E-Mail is Electronic Mail

1) E-mail is a way of sending messages (and files) from one computer to another.
2) You need an e-mail account to send and receive e-mails — you can usually get one from your ISP or from a web-based e-mail service.
3) Your account is identified by its e-mail address, e.g. cgpbooks@cgpbooks.co.uk. The bit before the @ sign is personalised — the bit after tells you the e-mail account provider.
4) An e-mail address is like a postal address, so people can direct a message to you by sending it to your e-mail address. Messages are collected in the inbox of your account.
5) After you've read an email, you can reply to it, forward it on to someone else, store it away in a folder (see below) or delete it.

Creating and Sending an E-Mail is Simple

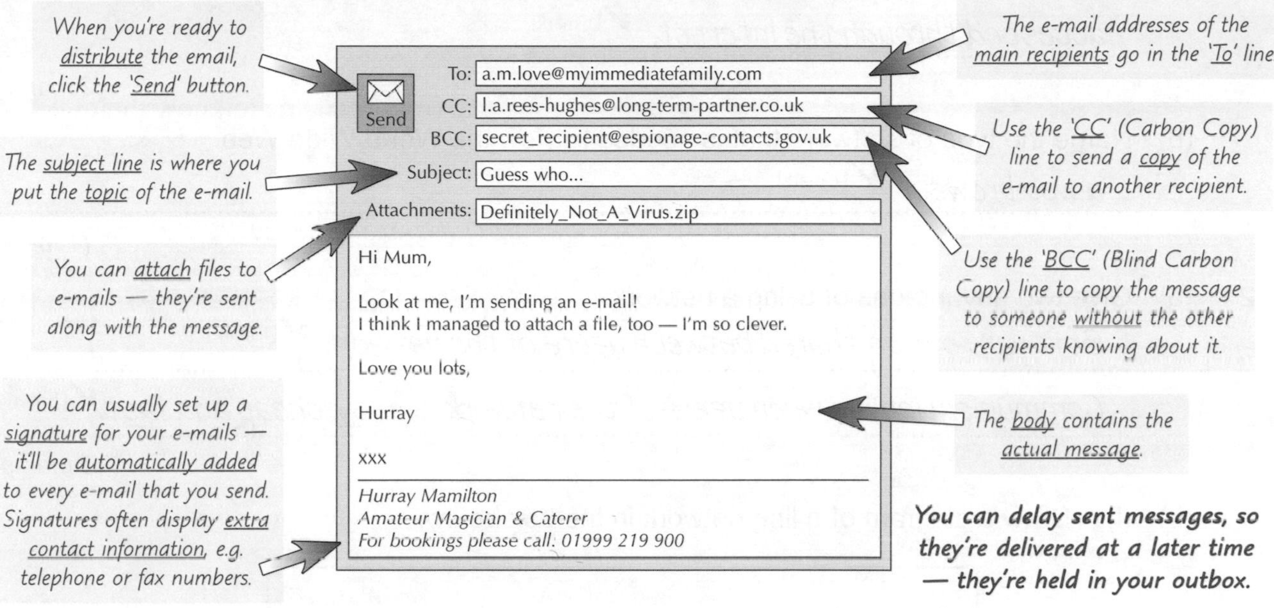

You can delay sent messages, so they're delivered at a later time — they're held in your outbox.

1) When you're writing an e-mail, you need to make sure it's appropriate for the recipients.
2) For example, if it's a business e-mail you should use a formal style and formal language.
3) E-mails to friends and family can be light-hearted, e.g. use different font colours and silly pictures.

E-Mail Software can Manage Messages and Contacts

1) Nearly all e-mail software lets you create different folders to store e-mails in.
2) Some software will automatically filter junk e-mails out of your inbox.
3) Junk mail (or spam) is unsolicited (not asked for) and usually advertises things, e.g. pharmaceuticals — but the sellers are often pretty dodgy.
4) Most e-mail software lets you manage your contacts, so you can store the e-mail addresses of people that you e-mail regularly. You can also create mailing lists, which are groups of e-mail addresses — useful when you're sending out regular messages to lots of people.

Make sure you learn this page just as thoroughly as the others

Even if you've sent an e-mail before, don't assume you can answer any question about this stuff.

Warm-Up and Worked Exam Questions

You're about halfway through this section — the ideal time to see how much you've actually learnt.

Warm-Up Questions

1) Give one advantage and one disadvantage of star networks.
2) What is the Internet?
3) Describe the difference between a search engine and a portal.
4) What is a phishing filter?
5) If you're writing an e-mail for your boss, what sort of language should you use?

Worked Exam Questions

1 (a) Describe what the World Wide Web is.

It's a system of interlinked web pages that are ✔ [1 mark]

accessed through the Internet. ✔ [1 mark]

(2 marks)

(b) Name the type of software that is needed to view the World Wide Web.

a web browser ✔ [1 mark]

(1 mark)

2 (a) Give two advantages of using a network.

Software can be shared between users of the network. ✔ [1 mark]

Communication between users of the network is easy, cheap and fast. ✔ [1 mark]

(2 marks)

(b) (i) Draw a diagram of a line network in the box below.

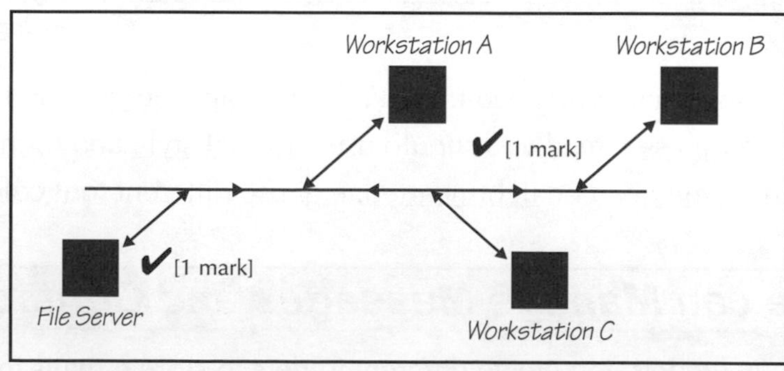

(2 marks)

(ii) Give one advantage and one disadvantage of line networks.

Advantage: *They're fairly cheap as they use less cabling than other network topologies.* ✔ [1 mark]

Disadvantage: *If the central cable fails, the whole network is brought down.* ✔ [1 mark]

(2 marks)

Another con is that line networks become very slow with a lot of users — this is because all of the data is passed along the central line.

Exam Questions

1 People are often concerned about their computers being infected by a virus.

(a) (i) What is a computer virus?

....

(1 mark)

(ii) Give one effect that viruses can have on computers.

....

(1 mark)

(iii) Suggest one way in which a computer could become infected with a virus.

....

(1 mark)

(b) Suggest two ways of preventing viruses from infecting a computer.

....

....

(2 marks)

(c) Some people do not shop on-line because they are concerned that personal details might be intercepted. What can on-line shops do to reduce the risk of this happening?

....

....

(2 marks)

2 Five web browser features are labelled with the letters **A**, **B**, **C**, **D** and **E**.
Write one letter in each row of the table that best matches the description.

A Stop button

B Phishing filter

C Bookmark

D Popup blocker

E Home page

	Description	**Letter**
(i)	A URL that is saved in the web browser	
(ii)	The URL that is accessed automatically after a web browser is opened	
(iii)	Halts a web browser as it's loading a web page	
(iv)	Prevents new web browser windows from opening without permission	

(4 marks)

Modern Communication Methods

You need to know about a few of the hi-tech ways that you can communicate with other people.

Mobile Phones Can Send Text Messages Using SMS

1) Mobile phones can be used to send SMS text messages (SMS stands for Short Message Service).
2) Single messages can be up to 160 characters long, but you can string multiple messages together.
3) They're fiddly to type, and people often abbreviate words using textspeak. This makes them most useful for short, informal messages.

Instant Messaging is like Texting over the Internet

Typing messages in real time over the Internet is called instant messaging.

1) As long as both users are connected to the Internet, they can receive messages from the other instantaneously.
2) You can make it even more personal by using webcams or by sending and receiving audio in real time like a phone call.
3) Instant messaging services let you add or remove people from a personal contacts list so you're in control of who can contact you.

Chat rooms are a sort of open instant messaging conversation — anyone can enter a chat room and talk to people who are connected to the same room. It's hard to control who talks to who in chat rooms — which raises concerns about children's safety.

Forums are like Places for Discussion

Lots of websites have forums, where people usually discuss topics related to the website's content. Forums are made up of individual threads (a question or comment and all its posted responses).

1) Forums are run by administrators and moderators. They're responsible for keeping messages appropriate, and for monitoring users.
2) Users normally have to register to post (leave) comments — some sites ask for a lot of details, some only a username and password. On most you have to accept some terms and conditions before posting anything.
3) Forums usually display all the previous comments on the topic in order, with any new contributions appearing at the bottom of the thread.

Bulletin boards are like forums, but they're usually used for announcements, e.g. adverts and details of events.

VoIP lets you Call People Using the Internet

1) VoIP stands for Voice over Internet Protocol — it sounds complicated, but it's just a way of having a voice conversation with someone over the Internet.
2) A traditional phone call involves sending and receiving voices through a telephone system — a VoIP call just sends everything via the Internet.
3) VoIP calls are generally cheaper than traditional phone calls, or even 'free' (after you've taken into account how much it costs you to access the Internet).

It has never been easier to talk to people all around the world

All these technologies are marvellous, but it makes it harder to avoid talking to people you really don't want to. My advice — find a quiet corner, stick your head in this book and get learning...

Social Networking

If you use forums and instant messaging services you can be quite anonymous and not share much personal information — but social networking websites rely on customised web pages.

Networking Websites Combine Interactive Features

Social networks are big business in the Internet world.
Most social network websites contain a mixture of:

1) An e-mail service.
2) Instant messaging.
3) A way to publish original material like blogs.
4) Forums or groups designed for people with a certain interest.
5) Facilities for sharing files (like music or videos) or website links with other members.
6) Ways to chat over webcams or make voice calls over the Internet.

Blog is short for web log — a blog is just a collection of messages over time on a certain subject, e.g. a person's day or world news. Blogs can be read and commented on by other people.

Some Websites Let You Create an Entire Profile

When you've registered with certain websites, you can create a profile.

1) Users upload a photo or picture of themselves to be their profile photo.
2) You can add personal details, e.g. age, town of birth, schools, etc.
3) You can also add lots of other information about yourself, e.g. hobbies, music tastes, sports, pets, shoe size, favourite herb or spice... anything.

Social networks also have search facilities so you can find other users to link your profile to. You can search a number of different fields — the most common is someone's name, but you can search by e-mail or username, as well as by location or by an interest you might share. A link is only established when both users have confirmed they are happy to do so.

Social Networks have Advantages and Disadvantages

Advantages
(mainly social)

1) Social networks are country and world-wide. You can keep up with friends all over the place, and even make new ones.
2) They can be a good place for people to be creative and get pieces of their own work noticed.
3) Large networks are brilliant for raising awareness about charity appeals, sponsored events, and other good causes.

Disadvantages
(mainly security or privacy)

Most social networking websites let you change privacy settings, but:

1) You can still share too much information and put yourself at risk from things like identity theft.
2) Friends made through the website might lie about themselves.
3) Employers have been accused of letting the profiles become a factor in their eventual decision about job applications.

Some information you should definitely keep to yourself...

Social networks are mainly for interacting with friends, but it's best to be careful — don't give nasty people any opportunities... and make sure you know about the different features on social network sites.

Digital TV Systems

TV has come a long way since it was first invented — you need to know what it's like now.

Digital TV is the New Standard of Broadcasting

1) Digital TV has a few advantages over old analogue TV broadcasts — the quality of pictures and sounds is higher, more channels can be broadcast and programmes can be interactive (e.g. different camera angles, commentary, etc.).
2) Another feature of digital TV is an Electronic Programme Guide (EPG) — it's basically an interactive TV guide showing what's on over the next week or two.
3) Digital TV is delivered to people's homes in one of three main ways:

Terrestrial — the signal is broadcast over the air and received by aerials on houses.

Cable — the signal is sent through a cable, e.g. an optical fibre, to people's homes.

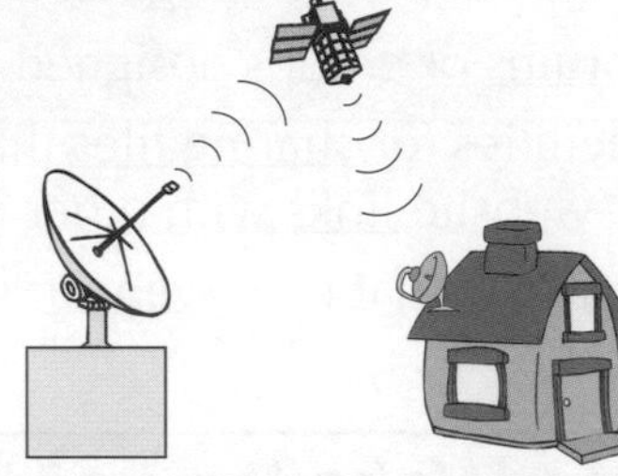

Satellite — the signal is transmitted to a satellite in space, which then relays the signal back to Earth, where it's picked up by satellite dishes on people's houses.

4) Some TV services (usually cable or satellite) have monthly subscription charges — this payment gets you more channels and other features:
   - Video on demand — you can pick what programmes you want to watch, and when you want to watch them.
   - Parental control — parents can disable channels to prevent their children from being corrupted.
   - Pay-per-view events — subscribers can view sports events and films... for an extra fee.

Personal Video Recorders let you Record TV Digitally

1) Satellite and cable TV providers often give subscribers a Personal Video Recorder, or PVR.
2) Programmes are recorded to a hard disk in the PVR, rather than a video cassette or DVD. They can then be watched at a later time (this is called time shifting).
3) PVRs can also pause live TV programmes. When you hit pause, the programme is recorded. Then when you hit play, you watch from the start of the recording — and as you watch it, the PVR still records the live feed:

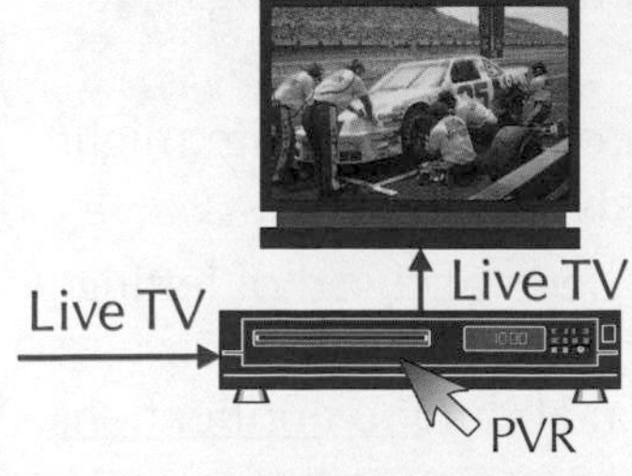

This is what happens when you watch TV normally.

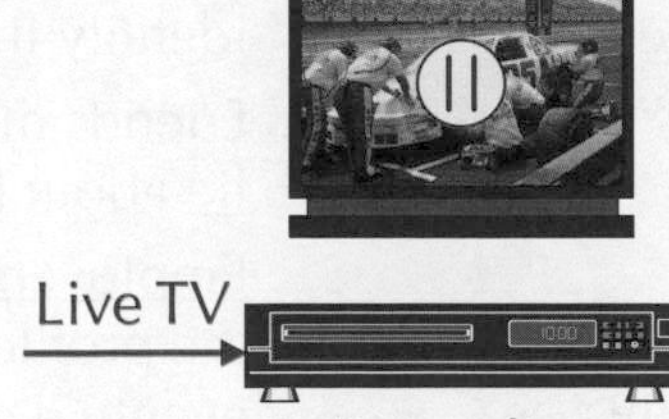

When the TV broadcast is paused, the PVR starts to record the live feed.

PVRs are also called digital video recorders.

Live TV

Recorded TV

Recording

When play is pressed, recorded footage is played back — the PVR still records the live feed (and plays it back) so the viewer doesn't miss anything.

Home Entertainment Systems

Entertainment systems have also changed — media centres are the fashionable thing to have now...

Integrated Home Entertainment Systems are the Future

1) A traditional home entertainment system would have separate hardware for different tasks, e.g. a hi-fi for music, a DVD player for films, a set-top box for digital TV, etc.
2) An integrated home entertainment system (or media centre) is all of those pieces of hardware, and more, in one — it's possible thanks to advanced home computers and digital media.
3) Media centres are basically computers designed for watching media — they're usually smaller, quieter and simpler to operate than a normal computer.

Media Centres have Lots of Inputs and Outputs

1) Media centres, like normal computers, have a hard disk — this means they have similar functions to PVRs (see the previous page).
2) Like normal computers, media centres can play audio CDs, DVDs, and a variety of audio, video and picture files, e.g. MP3s and JPEGs.
3) Files can be played from the hard disk, or a removable USB drive, or they can be streamed (sent) from another computer — using cables or a wireless connection.
4) Media centres have a TV tuner inside of them, so they can receive broadcasts delivered by one of the methods on the previous page. Media centres can often receive radio broadcasts.
5) Many media centres can be connected to the Internet — this lets users access Internet TV services like the BBC iPlayer (a video on demand service) and their e-mail accounts.
6) Media centres are usually controlled by one remote control, which lets the user navigate around a simple GUI (see page 28). A TV or monitor is connected to the media centre to view all the media, and sometimes separate speakers and an amplifier are used for audio.

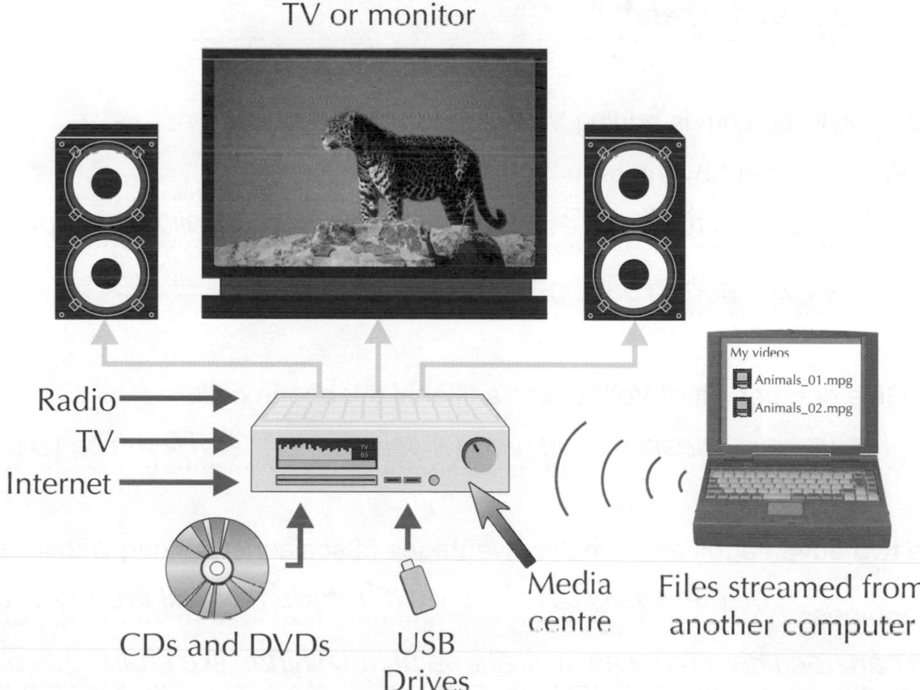

Media centres are basically media-focused home computers

In the good old days, you'd have loads of hardware scattered about your living room — each with a different function. With the advent of integrated home entertainment systems, all you need is one box.

Warm-Up and Worked Exam Questions

Congratulations, you've nearly finished another section. As you should expect by now, there are few questions for you to answer — if you get any wrong, make sure you re-learn the stuff before moving on.

Warm-Up Questions

1) What does SMS stand for?
2) Describe what a chat room is.
3) What is a bulletin board?
4) Give two ways in which the content on forums can be controlled.
5) Name three things that you might find on someone's social networking website profile.

Worked Exam Questions

1 ContactMyFace.com is a social networking website.

(a) Describe each of the following features that are present on ContactMyFace.com and other social networking websites.

(i) Forums

They are areas for discussion of particular topics. ✔ [1 mark] *Forums are made up of threads, which are comments/questions and people's responses to them.* ✔ [1 mark]

(2 marks)

(ii) Instant messaging

This is when people type messages to each other in real time ✔ [1 mark] *over the Internet.* ✔ [1 mark]

(2 marks)

(b) ContactMyFace.com is adding VoIP support to its website.

(i) What is meant by the term 'VoIP'?

VoIP stands for Voice over Internet Protocol. ✔ [1 mark] *It allows people to have voice conversations over the Internet.* ✔ [1 mark]

(2 marks)

(ii) Give one benefit of VoIP over traditional telephone calls.

It's usually cheaper than using a telephone/it's often free to use. ✔ [1 mark]

(1 mark)

(c) Give two advantages and two disadvantages of social networking websites.

Advantages *You can easily catch up with friends from all around the world.* ✔ [1 mark]

You can use them to raise awareness about things like charity events. ✔ [1 mark]

Disadvantages *It's really hard to tell if someone is lying about who they are.* ✔ [1 mark]

Putting personal information on them means you're at risk from identity theft. ✔ [1 mark]

(4 marks)

Exam Questions

1 Tick **two** boxes to show which of the following features would **not** be found in an integrated home entertainment system.

	Tick **two** boxes
TV tuner	
Floppy disk drive	
Hard disk drive	
Internet connection	
Command-line interface	

(2 marks)

2 Alice is thinking about switching to a digital TV service. She has been looking at cable and terrestrial TV packages.

(a) Give one advantage of digital TV over analogue TV.

....

(1 mark)

(b) (i) Describe the different ways in which cable and terrestrial TV are transmitted.

....

....

(2 marks)

(ii) Describe one other way in which TV is transmitted.

....

....

(2 mark)

(c) The cable TV package comes with a Personal Video Recorder (PVR).

(i) Give two common features of a PVR.

....

....

(2 marks)

(ii) Describe two other features that could form part of a cable TV package.

....

....

....

....

(4 marks)

Revision Summary for Section Seven

Well, you knew it was coming, so don't try to act all surprised. Like with all the other sets of questions, try your hardest to answer each question — if you get it right, you will be granted access to the next question. If you don't know the answer, retrace your steps back to the page in question and learn it all like you've never learned before. Right then, here we go...

1) What do the letters LAN and WAN stand for?
2) What's the difference between a LAN and a WAN?
3) Explain two advantages and two disadvantages of connecting computers in a network.
4) Sketch a diagram of a star network, a line network and a ring network.
5) Which of these types of network uses the most cable?
6) Which two types of network are the slowest?
7) Explain the difference between the Internet and the World Wide Web.
8) Name the old-fashioned and modern ways of connecting to the Internet.
9) What does ISP stand for?
10) Explain what a modem does.
11) Describe two types of server that are connected to the Internet.
12) Describe how on-line shopping can be made less risky.
13) What is an intranet and how can you restrict access to one?
14) Explain what hacking is and describe one way that a company can protect itself from hacking.
15) How can you reduce the risk of getting a virus from an e-mail attachment?
16) What kind of software is needed to view web pages?
17) What does URL stand for?
18) How can you access web pages without knowing their URL?
19) Describe three features of a web browser that help you to navigate the Web.
20) What do you need before you can start to send and receive e-mails?
21) What do CC and BCC stand for?
22) Describe one use of an e-mail signature.
23) What is junk mail?
24) What is a mailing list?
25) Describe three modern methods of communication.
26) Name three things that you might find on a social networking website.
27) Describe one advantage and one disadvantage of social networking websites.
28) Give two advantages of digital TV over analogue TV.
29) Explain three common features of satellite and cable TV services.
30) Describe what's going on inside a PVR when you pause and resume live TV programmes.
31) Describe four features of an integrated home entertainment system.

Systems Life Cycle and Systems Analysis

This is perhaps the scariest bit of ICT — changing existing information systems into new and improved ones. A brief overview first... specifics later on.

A System Life Cycle Shows How a System Changes

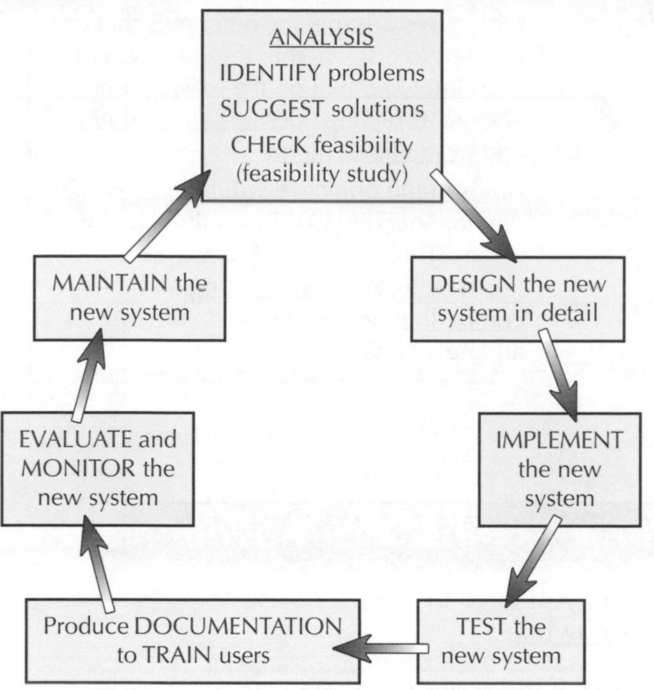

The diagram on the left is a system life cycle — the different stages that you go through when developing a new ICT system.

Familiarise yourself with it — it'll help you to see how all the bits in this section fit together.

It also makes the important point that the job isn't finished when the new system has been implemented — the new system will eventually become less useful, and the whole cycle begins again.

An information system is just a way of inputting, storing, processing and outputting data.

The term systems analysis is often used to describe the analysis and design stages.

Systems Analysis Involves Identifying Problems

1) There are two main types of problems with existing systems.
   - Firstly, there might be problems with a manual system where introducing a computerised system would make things better.
   - Secondly, there might be problems because the existing computer system is unable to cope with the information processing demanded of it.
2) In order to identify the problems the systems analyst needs to:
   - interview users of the system to find out their experiences;
   - analyse the results of questionnaires given to the users;
   - observe people using the system;
   - study documents such as user guides, printouts and error reports.
3) From this research the systems analyst should understand how the present system works and what the problems are.
4) This information is then used to work out how a new system could be put together that would solve these problems. There's more about this side of systems analysis on the next page.

It all starts with identifying problems in the current systems

Learn that circle diagram above. It's a really good summary of what this whole section's about — which is really useful because it's easy to get lost in the world of ICT systems.

More Systems Analysis

OK, so you've found out that your existing system isn't that brilliant any more.
In that case you'll need to come up with a new system to solve the problems.

Systems Analysis Also Involves Suggesting Solutions

1) The other side of systems analysis means coming up with a new system that solves the problems in the existing system.

2) The systems analyst will set several objectives for the new system, and then come up with a design to achieve those objectives.

3) At this stage in the life cycle, the systems analyst has a rough idea of how to make the new system, but nothing concrete. All the details will follow later, once a feasibility study has been carried out.

Objectives are specific outcomes that can be used to test whether the new system is an improvement on the existing one. They're also called performance criteria and evaluation criteria.

An example objective would be, "reduce the time needed to process the data by 25%". This is a good objective because it can be tested by measuring and then comparing the time taken on the old and new systems

A Feasibility Study Checks the New System is Worthwhile

1) When you've got the basics of the new system down, you need to work out if making it will be (i) possible and (ii) worthwhile...

2) This is where a feasibility study comes in (the last part of the analysis stage):

(i) Is it possible to make the new system?

A systems analyst has to look at and compare all of the hardware, software and trained people available to them, and then decide if the new system can actually be made.

(ii) Will the benefits of making and operating the new system be greater than the costs?

This is known as a cost-benefit analysis — it takes into account things like the cost of new equipment and the increase in overall efficiency, as well as the less obvious things, e.g. the cost of redundancies and retraining.

3) A feasibility study is usually based on 'best guesses' — it's very hard to be certain about everything without actually building the new system. But without some guesses at this stage you won't be able to estimate the likely cost of the new system.

The Feasibility Study is Presented to the Decision-Makers

1) The feasibility study needs to be presented to the people who will have to decide whether or not to proceed with the new system. These are often company directors or senior managers.

2) Sometimes a number of different solutions will be recommended.

Can it be done and should it be done — two important questions

So, that's the analysis stage polished off. Make sure you know about both systems analysis and feasibility studies — they're both important, as their outcomes decide if a new system goes ahead.

Design — Input, Process and Output

Once you've been given the go-ahead by the head honchos, it's time to start fleshing out the new system. The next few pages are all about the design stage of the system life cycle.

Input — How the Data is Captured

1) This involves thinking about methods of data capture (page 121).
2) It also means thinking about the format of that data. For example, the input data might need to be organised into fields of fixed or variable length.
3) The use of codes can reduce the file size. For example, a person's gender can be entered as M or F — reducing the number of bytes needed to store the data.
4) Forms should be sketched showing what the user will see whilst they input the data.

Input Checklist

- Decide where the data will come from. ☐
- Design the data capture forms. ☐
- Decide how the data needs to be structured. ☐
- Decide how the data will be input. ☐
- Design the input screen. ☐
- Decide how the data will be validated. ☐

Process — What Happens to It

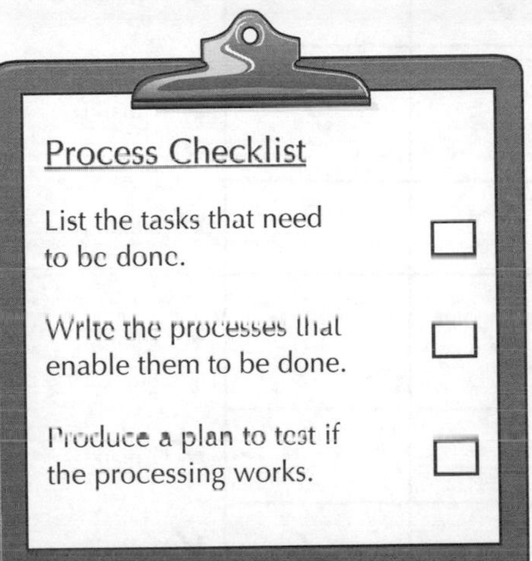

1) The tasks that the system needs to perform should be based on the original problem and objectives.
2) The processes needed to carry out each task might include spreadsheet formulas, database searches, desktop publishing page design, and word-processing mail-merge routines.
3) The processes could also include exchanging data between different applications. For example, importing a spreadsheet and using it to create a table in a word-processing package.
4) Test plans check that things work as expected. A test plan for the field 'month of birth' might include using normal data such as 6, extreme data such as 12 and invalid data such as Boris (see page 114). This will test whether the data validation works.

Output — Let it Out

1) The Golden Rule is to be user-friendly. This means that the output must be appropriate for the needs of the audience.
2) Users should only be shown the information that they need — and it should be communicated in a way they will easily understand. Layout is as important as content.
3) The layout of output screens and printouts should first be sketched in rough. They should then be shown to the user to check they're OK.

Output Checklist

- Decide what data needs to be output. ☐
- Decide how to present the information. ☐
- Decide which output devices to use. ☐
- Design output screens. ☐

A thorough design can save you lots of problems later on

There might only be three stages, but don't let that fool you — there's a lot of stuff to consider when you're talking about inputs, processes and outputs. Only move on when you know the lot.

Warm-Up and Worked Exam Questions

It seems like now is a good time to see how you've got on with the first couple of stages of the system life cycle. Like with all the other questions you've done — if you get one wrong, learn the stuff again.

Warm-Up Questions

1) What is an information system?
2) Give two typical reasons for updating an existing information system.
3) What three main things are worked out at the design stage of a new system?

Worked Exam Questions

1 A clothes shop is updating its sales system. The new system is in the design stage.

(a) Tick **one** box in each row of the following table to show whether each action would take place during the **input**, **process** or **output** stage of the new system.

Action	Input	Process	Output	
Item database is searched for a product code		✓		✓ [1 mark]
Transaction details are shown on a sales assistant's computer monitor			✓	✓ [1 mark]
Sales assistant types a product code into a computer	✓			✓ [1 mark]
Product details are exchanged between the item database and the stock level database		✓		✓ [1 mark]
Sales assistant scans a product's bar code	✓			✓ [1 mark]
A copy of the receipt is printed for the customer			✓	✓ [1 mark]

(6 marks)

(b) Two of the systems analysts who are designing the new system have different opinions on what data should be shown on a customer's receipt:

1) All of the available product data should be shown on the receipt, e.g. price, product name, product number, product range, size and stock level.

2) Only the data appropriate for the customer should be shown, e.g. price, product name and size.

Which of the two opinions is more appropriate? Give reasons for your answer.

Opinion 2 is more appropriate because customers should only be shown the information that they ✓ [1 mark] *need. Things like stock level are not useful to them, and would make the output of the system less user-friendly.* ✓ [1 mark]

(2 marks)

Exam Questions

1 A company has hired a team of systems analysts to create a new order system for them.

(a) Suggest two ways that the systems analysts could find out what problems there are with the old system.

....

....

(2 marks)

(b) The systems analysts are working with the managers of the company to decide on the objectives of the new system.

(i) What is an objective?

....

....

(2 marks)

(ii) Tick **two** boxes to show which of the following are suitable objectives.

	Tick **two** boxes
Increase the time taken to process an order by 30%	
Decrease the cost of processing an order by 5p	
Decrease the time taken to process an order	
Improve the productivity of the company	
Decrease the time taken to process an order by 30%	

(2 marks)

(c) After deciding on the new system's objectives, the systems analysts will conduct a feasibility study.

(i) Describe what is meant by the term 'feasibility study'.

....

....

....

....

(4 marks)

(ii) Feasibility studies are often based on 'best guesses'. Explain why this is the case.

....

....

(2 marks)

Design — Top-Down and Data-Flow

It's really important to know how all the bits of the system fit together. The three types of diagram on the next two pages show how this can be done. Make sure you know the differences between them.

Top-Down Diagrams Set Out the *Main Tasks*

1) Top-down design looks at the whole system by identifying the main tasks to be done and then breaking them down into smaller tasks.
2) If you read a top-down design from top to bottom each big task is broken down into smaller tasks. Reading it from left to right tells you the order in which they happen.
3) Top-down diagrams show what has to happen — but they don't always show how they'll happen.
4) The example below shows the tasks needed to create and print a copy of a new database record.

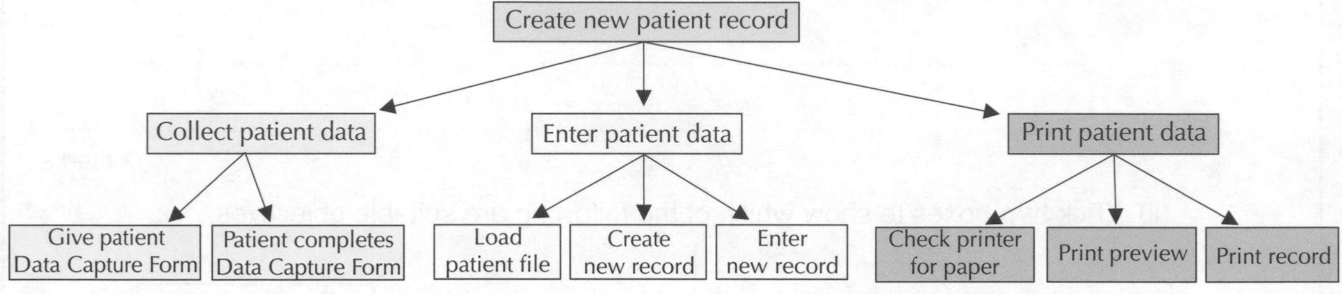

Data-Flow Diagrams Show *What Happens* to the Data

1) Data-flow diagrams show how data moves around the system — and what happens to it at each stage. There are three main symbols used.
2) The rectangle shows where data has come from. The sausage shows a process such as a search. The square shows where the data is stored — this can include a manual store of a hard copy.
3) Data-flow diagrams show what happens to the data — but they don't show what hardware and software are needed to make this happen.
4) The example shows how an optician can send reminder letters to people who have not had an eye test within the past year.
5) This is a data-flow diagram for just one task. A whole system could be shown by linking together the separate diagrams for each task — rather like linking up different people's family trees.

Customer data file
Produce list of patients overdue for an appointment
Standard letters file
Merge fields into appointment reminder letter
Copy kept in filing cabinet

You need to learn these charts, even if they are a bit dull...

It's unlikely you'll be asked to draw one of these in the exam. However you might get shown one and asked questions about it. So make sure you can turn these diagrams into written instructions.

Design — System Flowcharts

Most people find these incredibly scary. But they're pretty straightforward really. Once you know what the symbols mean all you've got to do is practise drawing them.

Learn the Symbols...

System flowcharts show exactly how the data will move through the system.

The symbol for stored data is sometimes replaced by one of the other green symbols if the analyst wants to specify the type of storage medium to be used.
(The colours used here aren't standard — they're just to make it easier to follow.)

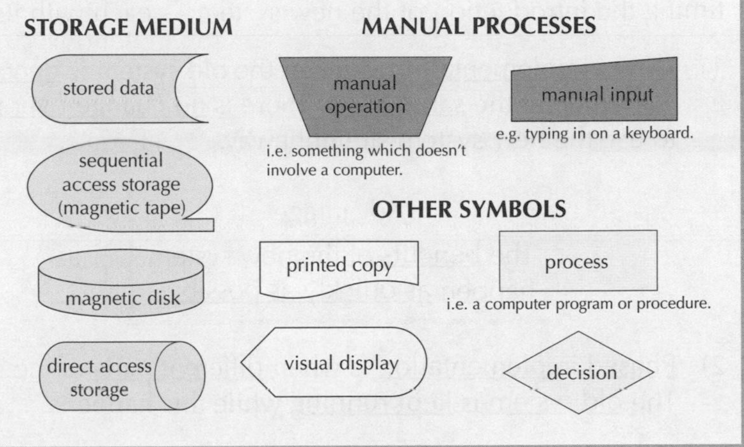

...so you can Use Them

1) Here's an example of a system flowchart for creating a new patient record at a dentist's surgery.
2) The customer completes a data-capture form. This information is then entered onto the patient record file by the receptionist.
3) The new patient record is then used to create a mail-merged letter welcoming the new patient to the surgery.
4) The decision box is an example of an algorithm. If the input data is invalid the receptionist must verify whether the input data is the same as the data on the original data-capture form.
5) If it's the same then the patient needs to be contacted to check the correct details. If it's different there has been an input error and the receptionist must re-enter the data.
6) Once the flowchart's been drawn, the programmer will be able to write the commands that will create the system.

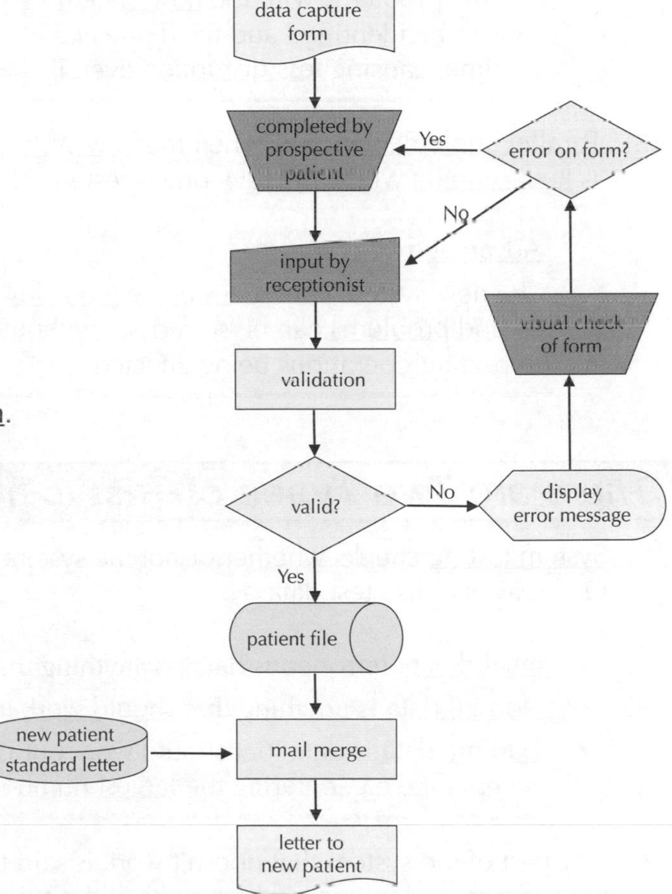

Recognise these symbols by their shapes

You really need to practise drawing these charts. Step one — memorise and copy out all the symbols. Step two — memorise and copy out the flowchart on this page. Step three — draw a system flowchart for the diagrams on the previous page. Step four — go on to the next page...

Implementation and Testing

When you've got your new system ready to go, it's time to implement it. But you'll need to keep testing it, to make sure that you uncover any problems that might stop the software from working.

There are Three Different Ways to Implement the System

Implementation happens when data from the old system is loaded onto the new system, and the new system is used to carry out the task it was designed for. There are three different ways of timing the introduction of the new system — each with its benefits and problems:

1) Direct implementation is when the old system is decommissioned and the new system started up at the same time. There is no change-over period, so the users need to be able to use the new system straight away.

Advantage	Disadvantage
The benefits of the new system happen as quickly as possible.	Any bugs not picked up during testing could have disastrous effects.

2) Phased implementation is when different parts of the system are introduced one at a time. The old system is kept running while this happens.

Advantage	Disadvantage
Any problems with the new system can be identified and fixed one at a time, causing less disruption overall.	It can take a long time to introduce the new system this way — so the benefits take a long time to come through.

3) Parallel implementation is when the new system is introduced all in one go — but the old system is kept running whilst the new one is tested. This means that for a while there are two systems.

Advantage	Disadvantage
The new system can be tested very quickly — and problems can be sorted out without important operations being affected.	All tasks need to be done twice.

There are Two Types of Test to be Done...

1) System testing checks whether or not the system will work. One way is to use test data.

- Invalid data (erroneous data) is anything that the system should reject.
- Normal data is anything that should work in the system.
- Extreme data is data that should work but is at the edge of what is acceptable, e.g. entering the largest numbers that a field can accept.

2) Any part of the system that doesn't work is said to have a bug — testing enables the programmer to know which parts of the system need to be debugged.
3) Acceptance testing checks whether the system meets the needs of the users. This might involve a trial run with real users — which can help the programmers make the system more user-friendly.

Learn all the pros and cons of the different implementation methods

Why not try writing a mini-essay about implementing and testing a new piece of software...

Documentation, Evaluation and Maintenance

People need training to use a new system effectively. This is where the user documentation steps in.

User Documentation Explains How to Operate the System

As the name suggests, user documents are written to help the people who will use the system. There are three types of guide — depending on when they might be needed:

1) Installation guides explain how the system should be installed and programs loaded — as well as which peripherals are needed and how they should be installed.
2) User guides give instructions on how to perform tasks using the system — for example how to carry out searches and print data from a database.
3) Tutorials are short training manuals explaining how the system works. They might include exercises which help the user to practise operating the software.

User documentation can be hard to write. This is because it needs to be written in simple language so the users can understand what they have to do — but at the same time it needs to use the same technical terms that are used in the software.

Evaluation Checks if the System Still Meets its Objectives

1) Once the system is installed its performance will be monitored to see whether it's working properly. From time to time it'll be evaluated. This is a check to see if the system still meets its objectives — in other words whether it still does what it was designed to do.

2) Evaluation is basically repeating the research carried out at the start of the system life cycle. In other words observing and interviewing users and studying printouts.

3) One reason why the system might not meet its objectives is if the workload increases. The demands on the system may become greater than its ability to cope. In other words it becomes obsolete. This brings the system life cycle full circle and the analyst is brought back to begin work on a new system.

Technical Documentation Explains How to Maintain it

Technical documentation is written for the computer engineers and programmers who will maintain the system after it's been installed. Since they're computer experts, the guides can be full of technical language and complex system diagrams. There are two times when it's needed:

1) When something goes wrong and the system needs to be repaired. The technical manual should enable fault finding to take place — in other words, tell the engineer what's wrong. It should then explain how to fix it.

2) When the system needs upgrading — for example, installing a better user interface. The computer engineer needs to know how this can be done.

Documentation is vital so you can learn how to fix problems

Make sure you learn everything properly. Try memorising each section, covering it up and then writing down as much as you can remember — keep doing this until you've learnt it all by heart.

Warm-Up and Worked Exam Questions

You'll be glad to know that you've just about finished this section on ICT systems. But I've not forgotten about testing your knowledge — have a go at these questions before you leap to the next section.

Warm-Up Questions

1) What does a top-down diagram show?
2) What does a data-flow diagram show?
3) Describe what happens at the implementation stage of a system life cycle.
4) How is a computer system evaluated?

Worked Exam Questions

1 A library has installed a new computer system. A systems analyst is running an acceptance test with a few of the library staff members.

(a) (i) What is the aim of an acceptance test?

To find out if the system meets the needs of the users. ✔ [1 mark]

(1 mark)

(ii) The analyst also performs her own tests on the system. Describe two types of test data that are used during system testing.

Erroneous data ✔ [1 mark] *— this is data that should be rejected by the system.* ✔ [1 mark]

Extreme data ✔ [1 mark] *— this is data that works but is at the upper or lower limit of what is acceptable.* ✔ [1 mark]

(4 marks)

Normal data is the other type of test data — it should work fine in the system.

(b) The systems analyst has written technical and user documentation for the new system.

(i) Describe one type of user documentation.

User guides ✔ [1 mark] *contain instructions that explain how to perform tasks using a system.* ✔ [1 mark]

(2 marks)

(ii) Explain one difference between technical and user documentation.

Technical documentation is written for computer engineers or programmers so contains a lot of technical language. ✔ [1 mark]

User documentation is written in less technical language. ✔ [1 mark]

(2 marks)

(iii) When might technical documentation be needed?

When a system needs to be repaired. ✔ [1 mark]

(1 mark)

Exam Questions

1 A theatre is installing a new computer system using phased implementation.

(a) (i) What is meant by the term 'phased implementation'?

....

....

(2 marks)

(ii) Give one advantage and one disadvantage of phased implementation.

Advantage ....

Disadvantage ....

(2 marks)

(b) Describe one other method of implementing a new computer system.

....

....

(2 marks)

(c) The new system will be evaluated again three years after its implementation.
Explain why it is necessary to evaluate computer systems after their implementation.

....

....

(2 marks)

2 There are five stages involved in introducing a new computer system —
analysis, **design**, **implementation**, **testing** and **evaluation**.
For each of the tasks below, say which stage they occur in:

(a) Interviewing users about how well the new system is working.

....

(b) Carrying out a cost-benefit analysis.

....

(c) Deciding how information about new patients will be entered onto the system.

....

(d) Interviewing users of the old system.

....

(e) Checking what happens when you create two new records with the same name.

....

(f) Transferring data from the existing records onto the new computer database.

....

(6 marks)

Revision Summary for Section Eight

Well done, you made it to the end of Section Eight. Now you know all about making new systems — or do you? This stuff's really important in the world of ICT, so it's pretty likely that you'll get asked some questions about it in your exam. So, roll up your sleeves, grasp the nettle and take the bull by the horns — there are some tough questions coming up.

1) What comes between analysing and implementing a new computer system?
2) List three ways of gathering information about the problems of an old system.
3) As well as finding problems with old systems, what else does a systems analyst do?
4) What is the difference between objectives, performance criteria and evaluation criteria?
5) What is a feasibility study for?
6) What question does a cost-benefit analysis try to answer?
7) List three things that should be done when designing a system's input.
8) List three things that should be done when designing a system's processes.
9) List three things that should be done when designing a system's output.
10) In which two ways do you read a top-down diagram?
11) What does it mean if you see a sausage on a data-flow diagram?
    a) Input b) Process c) Data store.
12) Correctly label each symbol in the box.

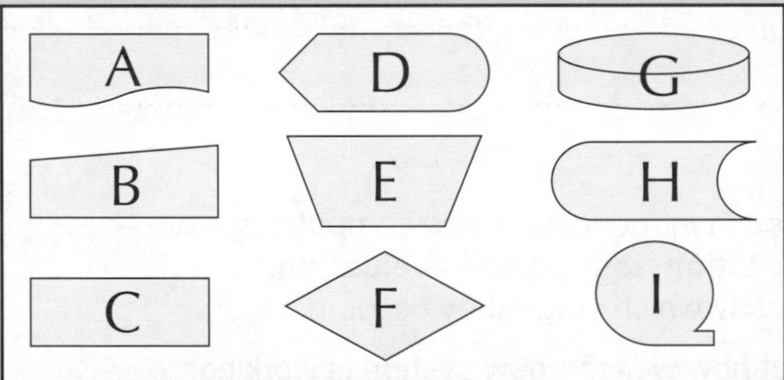

13) Which would be the correct symbol for each of the following events?
    a) Displaying a screen prompt to log on
    b) Keying in your user name
    c) The computer checking that your user name is on its list
    d) Making a hard copy of a document
14) Explain how parallel implementation is different from direct implementation.
15) Explain how phased implementation is different from parallel implementation.
16) Give one benefit and one problem of each type of implementation.
17) What are the three types of test data needed? Give an example for each if testing the validation of data entries for the field "Day of month born".
18) What is the difference between system testing and acceptance testing?
19) List three different types of user documentation — and explain when each one should be used.
20) What is the difference between monitoring and evaluation?
21) Describe two occasions when the technical documentation of a system will be needed.

Information and Data

You already know that computers are machines for processing data.
But for that to make complete sense, you need to know exactly what data is.

Data has **No Meaning**

Data is information that has no meaning. For example, take the number 120987.
The number could mean absolutely anything. It could be a birthday, an amount of money, a phone number, or about a billion other things. But one thing it isn't is information.

Data only becomes information when you know the context of the data.

Information = Data + Meaning

Computers are machines that process data — but they don't understand the data they process.

Learn the **Input**, **Process**, **Output** Cycle

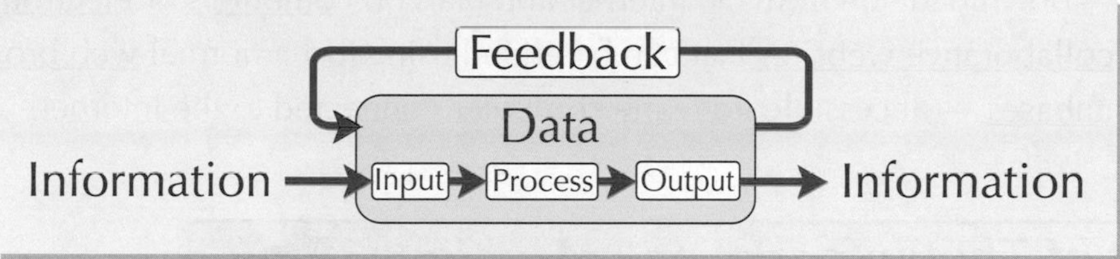

(A) Data is Entered at the **Input** Stage

1) Information is converted into data when it's entered into the computer.
2) This might mean having to convert information into a code.
   For example the date 26th September 1964 might be converted into 260964.
3) The data should then be validated (checked to make sure it's of the right type, e.g. a number), and verified (checked to make sure it's actually correct).

(B) The Computer then **Processes** the Data

1) Processing involves turning the input data into something else.
2) For example, a set of examination results could be put into a computer which then calculates the average score.

(C) The Results are then **Shown** at the **Output** Stage

1) Output is when the computer communicates the results of the data processing to the user.
2) The two most common ways are a screen display and printed paper.
3) At this point the data becomes information again.
4) The information obtained at this stage might then be used as feedback to input more data.
   This turns the system into a cycle.

Take the meaning away from information and you're left with data

If you get a computer to process incorrect data, the results will be meaningless. This is called Garbage In, Garbage Out (GIGO). Some people call this 'computer error', but they're wrong — it's human error. Computers hardly ever make mistakes. They just do what they're programmed to do.

Searching for Information

We can access more useless information now than at any time in history. That's progress.

We Live in an **Information Age**...

1) Even now, a lot of our information comes from fairly traditional sources — for example, newspapers, magazines, books, maps, conversations... and so on and so on.
2) But digital technology means we can now process and store data more easily and cheaply than ever before. Communications technology has also improved massively over the last decades. The result is that more information is now communicated to more people than ever before.
3) For example, we now have CDs and DVD-ROMs (so cheap that newspapers often give them away), text messages, and probably most importantly, the Internet.
4) The Internet means we now have access to:
   - blogs (short for "web logs") — these are a bit like online diaries.
   - podcasts — downloadable media files that are often syndicated (made available for download on other sites). People can subscribe to receive new "episodes" as they're released.
   - e-books — downloadable from the Internet and read on computers or electronic readers.
   - wikis — collaborative websites that can be edited using just a normal web browser.
   - online databases — accessible from any computer connected to the Internet.

There's more about collaborative working on page 138.

...but a **Lot** of That Information is **Useless Junk**

One word of warning... "quality control" on the Internet isn't everything it could be.

1) Not everything on the Internet is true... but it's often hard to tell the good stuff from the bad.
2) There's also the problem of security. Information can be accessed illegally and so potentially changed. Also, any data you download may bring with it unwanted stuff like viruses.
3) And security problems don't just affect businesses and organisations. Even information you send is vulnerable (e.g. your address or credit card details)... so beware.

DO CRAB to Help Find the **Information Gems**

Following this "DO CRAB" advice means you're more likely to find useful info than junk.

Date	When was the information put on the Internet? (It could be out of date.)
Oh dear	I can't actually think of anything for "O".
Clear	Don't use information you don't understand — you might get the wrong end of the stick.
Relevant	Make sure the information is relevant to your needs.
Authors	Who wrote the information? Would you expect them to be experts on the subject? (E.g. I might not totally believe an essay on quantum physics written by the Chuckle Brothers. Or at least... I'd double-check that they had actually studied quantum physics.)
Bias	Ask whether the authors are definitely objective. Or could they be biased for some reason? (E.g. a business might exaggerate the usefulness of one of its products.)

Don't assume that everything on the Internet is true

Data can be vulnerable when it's stored (e.g. if it's stored on a computer connected to a network). And it's especially vulnerable while it's being transmitted from one place to another. So take care of your data, and don't let baddies get it. Okay, lecture over. Now get on and learn this stuff.

Data Collection

Data capture is the way that information's first gathered and put on a computer system. It's the input part of the 'input — process — output' cycle.

Data Capture turns Information into Data

Data capture is sometimes called data collection. It's a two-part process.

1) The information has to be obtained.
2) The data has to be entered onto the computer using an input device.

First you have to Capture your Data...

1) Manual methods of capturing data involve a person — usually to key in information that someone else has supplied on a paper-based data-capture form or questionnaire.
2) Automatic methods of data capture don't require a person to key in data supplied by someone else. All sorts of automatic data capture methods exist these days, such as...

- Online Forms — users can type information into a form on a website. This info can then be used to automatically update a database or place an order, for example.
- Card readers — credit card numbers are read automatically, from either a microchip (as in "Chip and PIN") on the front of the card or the magnetic stripe on the back.
- Bar-code readers — e.g. in supermarkets, product codes can be quickly scanned.
- Voice-recognition devices — like the ones used in security entry systems.
- Biometrics — like when a scanner reads the fingerprint info stored on a passport (which can then be checked against a person's actual fingerprint to check that the passport is really theirs).
- RFID tags — contain information that can be read by radio receivers. They're often found in vehicles (to automatically pay tolls for tunnels, bridges and so on) or products (so shops and delivery companies can track individual items).
- OMR devices (Optical Mark Recognition — see page 6). Forms sometimes need to be filled in by making marks in particular places. These marks are then read using a scanner. Examples include computerised school registers and multiple-choice answer sheets.

Each Method has its Advantages

Automatic Data Capture Systems

Faster and more accurate than manual systems.

Humans don't have to be present — so it's useful in dangerous/inaccessible places (e.g. nuclear reactors).

Manual Data Capture Systems

Cheaper — less hardware and software needed, so the system will be less expensive.

Data capture systems can be manual or automatic

OK, loads of words, but not really that much to learn. Just concentrate on learning one example each of manual and automatic data capture. Then for each example check you can explain both why that method's good, and why the other methods wouldn't be so good.

Checking Data

Here are the two main methods of making sure that the data entered is accurate...

Data Validation Checks the Data is of the **Correct Type**

Data validation checks that the data is of the right type (e.g. percentages should be numbers from 0 to 100). Validation can be performed automatically by the computer whilst data is entered.

1) Range Check: This checks that the data is within a specified range. For example, a person's month of birth should be a number from 1 to 12.
2) Presence Check: This makes sure that important information has actually been entered. For example, a customer record might have to contain their date of birth, so the software won't allow the date of birth field to be left empty.
3) Check Digit: This helps to check that numerical data has been entered accurately. The final digit of a number is determined by a formula that uses all the previous digits. So if the number's been entered incorrectly, the check digit will probably be wrong. A good example is the ISBN number on a book — the last digit is a check digit.
4) Data Type Check: This checks that text hasn't been put where numbers are needed, for example.
5) Look-up Lists: These allow the user to enter just the first few characters of an entry. The computer then presents a list of all "legal" entries that start with those characters, and the user can select one.
6) Length Check: This makes sure that the entry is the right length. For example, a date of birth has to be exactly 8 digits long (DDMMYYYY).

The main benefit of data validation is that it's automatic — so it is quick and easy to spot errors.

Data Verification Ensures the Data is **Accurate**

Data verification is different — it means making sure the data which has been input is the same as the original data. There are two main verification techniques.

1) Proofreading is when a person reads the data that has been entered onto the system and compares it with the original. Any incorrectly entered data will be edited.
2) Double entry is when the data is entered twice by two different people. The computer then compares the two versions. Any errors found are then corrected.

Validation and Verification **Both** have their **Problems**

Sadly, nothing's perfect and these checks are no exception — they both have their problems.

Problems with Data Validation

1) Any problems with the validation program could mean mistakes are allowed.
2) It only makes sure that the data is the right type — not that it is accurate.

Problems with Data Verification

1) Double entry is time-consuming — and so it can be very expensive.
2) Proofreading is also time-consuming — and doesn't eliminate human error.

Learn the difference between validation and verification

Validation, verification — two fun new ways to say 'checking'. The main thing here is to know the difference between them and the pros and cons of each method. It might help to draw a table...

IKBS and Expert Systems

Expert systems sound pretty exciting. But IKBS sounds as dull as any other four-letter acronym.

Expert Systems *Ask a Series of* ***Questions***

1) Information Knowledge-Based Systems (IKBS) are also known as expert systems.
2) They're intended to model the knowledge of a human expert — meaning that the expert system should be able to replace the human.
3) They contain a 'knowledge bank' of data about a particular subject, as well as a set of instructions for processing the knowledge.
4) The idea is that the computer asks the user a series of questions, with the answer to each question helping to determine what the next question should be. Eventually the computer has enough information to suggest a solution to the problem.
5) Expert systems can be used to give advice about illnesses that match certain symptoms, or advice on tax/welfare benefits etc.

Expert Systems Can Help Solve ***Technical Problems***

Some computer operating systems use expert systems to help sort out technical difficulties.

1) The expert system asks a question, which the user answers.
2) Depending on the answer, the expert system might suggest a possible fix to the problem. If it does, the user can try the fix. If not, the system asks another question.
3) The system asks a series of questions and can suggest a series of possible fixes. The expert system helps find the correct solution as quickly as possible without having to try them all.

Advantages

1) Common problems can be solved relatively quickly.
2) It's efficient — one expert system can be used in many different places to solve loads of different problems at the same time.
3) Even quite obscure problems can often be fixed — if the "knowledge bank" and the supply of questions are detailed enough.
4) The knowledge bank and questions can easily be updated so that more problems can be solved.

Disadvantages

1) It needs the user to have a certain amount of technical knowledge — it might not work if the person with the problem knows absolutely nothing about computers (they might not be able to answer the questions, or try the suggested fixes).
2) Some people might prefer to have a human talk to them to help solve the problem.
3) It's only as good as the knowledge and questions that have been programmed into it, so it's possible that the system won't be able to suggest a fix for every problem that people might have.

Sadly, you can't take an expert system into your ICT exam...

Well... not an automated one, anyway — you're going to be totally reliant on the expert system in your brain. So update the knowledge bank by revising this page very very carefully. And then test yourself by writing down all you can remember. Have another go if you get anything wrong.

Warm-Up and Worked Exam Questions

That was a brief but information-packed section — which is good because it means there's plenty of stuff to test you on. Have a go at these questions and (as always) go over any topics you get stuck on.

Warm-Up Questions

1) What is information?
2) Give three examples of automatic data capture methods.
3) What data validation method can check if a number between 1 and 12 has been entered?
4) What is a check digit?
5) Name the two parts of an expert system.

Worked Exam Questions

1 Which **one** of the following is **not** used to capture data automatically?

	Tick **one** box
Magnetic card reader	
RFID tags	
Paper application form	✓
Fingerprint scanner	

✓[1 mark]

(1 mark)

2 A computer operating system uses an expert system to provide its users with help.

(a) Briefly describe how an expert system works.

The system contains a knowledge bank of data about a particular subject ✓[1 mark] *and a set of instructions for processing the knowledge.* ✓[1 mark] *The expert system asks the user a series of questions and each answer helps to determine what the next question should be.* ✓[1 mark] *When the system has enough information it suggests a solution to the problem.* ✓[1 mark]

(4 marks)

(b) Suggest one reason why people may not like using an expert system.

They might prefer to speak to a human about their problem. ✓[1 mark]

(1 mark)

(c) Expert systems are easy to update. Give two other advantages of expert systems.

Common problems can be solved quite quickly. ✓[1 mark]

They're efficient, as one expert system can be used in many different places to solve loads of different problems at the same time. ✓[1 mark]

(2 marks)

Exam Questions

1 Roger is writing a report on the popularity of football. He is researching the sport on a wiki.

(a) Explain what is meant by the term 'wiki'.

....

....

(2 marks)

(b) Describe three ways in which Roger could evaluate the information he finds to see if it is suitable for his report.

....

....

....

....

....

....

(6 marks)

2 A teacher enters a class's test results into a spreadsheet. The test was in a multiple-choice format and a maximum of 60 marks were available. The spreadsheet calculates the percentage scored by each pupil.

(a) (i) Give two suitable data validation methods that the teacher could use.

....

....

(2 marks)

(ii) Explain one reason why data validation will not guarantee that the correct test scores are entered into the spreadsheet.

....

....

(2 marks)

(b) Describe one method of data verification the teacher could use to check the accuracy of the data.

....

....

(2 marks)

(c) What method of automatic data capture could be used to collect the test data?

....

(1 mark)

Revision Summary for Section Nine

Well that's another section over and done with — not. You know the score by now — you've read the stuff, you think you've learnt it — but have you really? Get all these questions right first time and you can call yourself a genius. Get some wrong and you can go back and learn the stuff properly.

1) What's the difference between data and information?
2) Describe the input–process–output cycle of data processing.
3) Describe what's meant by the following:
   a) a blog
   b) a podcast
   c) syndication
   d) e-book
   e) wiki
4) Why should you be careful about believing everything you read on the Internet?
5) How can you tell a reliable source of information on the Internet from a dodgy one?
6) What is meant by data capture? What two things does it involve?
7) What's the difference between automatic and manual data capture? Give two examples of each.
8) Give one advantage each of manual and automatic data capture systems.
9) How should instructions be written on a data capture form?
   a) Using complex syntax and vocabulary to communicate elementary linguistic structures.
   b) In plain English.
   c) In binary.
10) What's the difference between data validation and data verification?
11) Explain any four methods of data validation.
12) Explain any two methods of data verification.
13) Describe two problems each with data validation and data verification.
14) What does IKBS stand for?
15) What does an expert system do? How does it work?
16) Give three possible uses for an expert system.
17) Give four advantages and two disadvantages of an expert system.

Computers and the Law

Computers are used to store and process important data — so there are laws to control their use.

The Data Protection Act Controls the Use of Personal Data

1) The Data Protection Act was introduced in the UK in 1984. It gives rights to data subjects (i.e. people who have data about them stored on computer systems). The Act was updated in 1998 to take the increasing use of computers, and changes in European Union law, into account.
2) The Act mainly consists of eight data protection principles — summarised here:

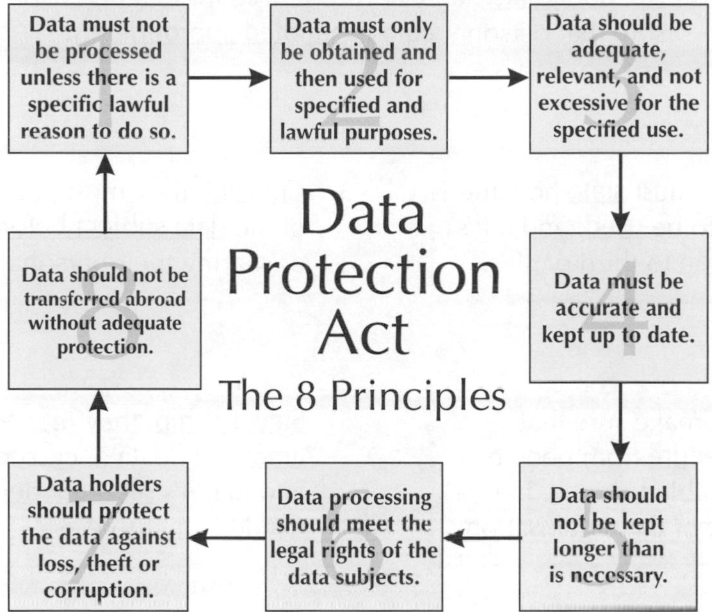

3) The law requires that most organisations that plan to retain data register with the government.
4) It also entitles data subjects to see the personal data about them that's held by an organisation. If an organisation breaks the law, they can be fined and made to pay compensation to the data subject.
5) However, some data is exempt from access by data subjects. This includes data that might:

- affect a tax assessment
- affect a criminal investigation
- affect the outcome of a court case
- identify another person (unless that other person has given their consent)

All organisations that deal with personal data must follow this act

There's quite a lot to learn on this page — first make sure you know each of the eight principles of the Data Protection Act. Then memorise the four reasons why some data is exempt from access.

Computers and the Law

The Personal Data Guardianship Code is for Data Handlers

1) The Personal Data Guardianship Code was created to help people follow the Data Protection Act.
2) It suggests that organisations have one senior person who is responsible for data handling.
3) The responsible person has five main duties (the principles of the code):

1) Accountability: they're responsible for making sure that personal data is handled appropriately.

2) Visibility: they must state how the data is going to be used, and if it's being passed on to third parties.

3) Consent: they must get the consent of the data subject before accessing or sharing their personal data.

4) Access: they must make sure that personal data is secure from people who shouldn't be able to see it, both inside and outside of the organisation.

5) Stewardship: they must make sure that the amount of data accessed is not excessive, and that it's securely deleted when it's not needed any more.

The Computer Misuse Act Prevents Illegal Access to Files

This law was introduced in 1990 to cope with the problems of computer hackers and viruses. The Act made the following three things illegal:

1) Unauthorised access to computer material (e.g. hacking). This includes viewing parts of a network you're not permitted to see, and the illegal copying of programs — software piracy.

2) Gaining unauthorised access to a computer to carry out serious crimes like fraud and blackmail.

3) Unauthorised changing of computer files — including planting viruses, and deleting files.

If convicted, an offender can face an unlimited fine and a five-year prison sentence.

These guidelines and acts make your personal data and files safer

It's nice to know that these laws and guidelines exist. It's a bit of a shame that you need to know about each one in some detail... make sure you know their full names and what they do.

Hardware and Data Security

Now you know the legal stuff, it's time to find out about protecting computer hardware and data.

Physical Security Protects the *Hardware*

Hardware is expensive — follow these 7 rules to keep it safe:

1) Serial numbers — Keep a record of all serial numbers, and mark the organisation's name and postcode on all equipment — this helps police to identify stolen property.
2) Alarms — Computer rooms should be protected by burglar alarms.
3) Fire protection — Use fireproof doors and smoke alarms. Also, automatic gas-flooding systems could be used to put out any fires to prevent water damaging the equipment.
4) Lock windows and doors to prevent access.
5) Avoid putting computers on the ground floor of buildings, where they can be easily seen from outside.
6) Blinds or curtains should be closed at night, and monitors should be switched off, so the computers are less visible.
7) Surveillance — security cameras can be installed to put off would-be thieves, or to help identify anyone who has stolen something.

Access Security Limits a Person's Use of the *Network*

1) All authorised users should be given user names and create their own passwords. This will limit unauthorised access to the network.
2) Individual users can be assigned access rights. For example, network managers can be given access to the software that controls how the network is run, while other users can be limited to certain types of application software such as word processors.
3) A firewall increases the protection of a network from external threats (like hackers). They offer some security, but can't provide total protection.
4) Intrusion detection flags up attempts to hack into a network as they happen. Some intrusion detectors automatically limit network access when they think a hack is taking place.

Be Careful with your *Data* when Using the *Internet*

1) Phishing is when a not-so-nice person sends you an e-mail, pretending to be from your bank or another organisation that holds your personal details.
2) You're usually asked to enter your personal details on a website linked to in the e-mail.
3) The website often looks like a real website — it might fool people into believing it's the real deal.
4) The not-so-nice person hopes you'll put in your details so they can steal your identity.
5) A common policy of banks and other organisations is that they'll never ask for your details in an e-mail (or over the phone) — so you can just delete e-mails that do ask for this info.
6) Banks have a number of procedures to protect your data when you're doing online banking.
7) Many require accounts to have multiple passwords and secret answers.
8) Some banks send out card readers to their customers — like the Chip & PIN devices in shops.

Protecting your hardware and data is essential

This page isn't too difficult, and you've probably heard of most of this security stuff before. Make sure you understand what phishing is — it could come in handy for your exam, and in real life too.

Health and Safety Issues

Computers weren't originally designed to be used all day. Make sure you know about the health and safety risks of continuous computer use and what can be done to reduce them.

Computer Use can Cause *Three Main Health Problems...*

There are three main problems — connected either with poor design of the equipment, or from not using the equipment properly. In each case the risk is small, but the effects can be serious.

1) Repetitive strain injury (RSI) is a general term for aches, pains and muscle or tendon damage resulting from overuse of a keyboard or mouse. Many medical conditions have been linked to RSI, such as carpal tunnel syndrome which causes finger pain and numbness.

2) Spending too long in front of a monitor can cause eye strain and headaches. Screen glare and poor-quality images on older monitors can make it hard for the eyes to focus properly.

3) Circulation, fitness and back problems might result from sitting all day in front of a computer rather than walking around. This is more of a long-term health problem.

...Which Have *Three Main Solutions*

1) Take regular breaks from computer work. Looking away from the screen, walking around and exercising your fingers and hands can also help to reduce the health risks.

2) Use the correct equipment. You should have:

   a) a proper computer chair with backrest,
   b) an ergonomically-designed keyboard that makes it easier to touch-type without straining fingers,
   c) good background lighting and a screen filter to reduce monitor glare.

3) Arrange equipment properly. Adjust the chair and monitor to find the most comfortable position.

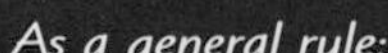

As a general rule:
- *Your forearms should be roughly horizontal.*
- *Your eyes should be level with the top of the monitor.*

You need to be comfortable at your computer to work effectively

But surely no one expected sitting down all day to be as healthy as running around in the fresh air... Cover the page, make a table with one column for problems and another for solutions, then fill it in.

Health and Safety Issues

Employers Need to **Follow the Law**

The main law covering computer use at work is the Health and Safety (Display Screen Equipment) Regulations 1992. The law says that employers need to do five main things:

1) Analyse workstations, and assess and reduce risks:
Employers need to check that computer equipment (and the area around it) is safe, e.g. there are no overloaded sockets, no trailing wires and malfunctioning equipment is replaced.

2) Ensure workstations meet minimum requirements:
Lighting needs to be correct, e.g. enough ambient light, and direct sunlight blocked using blinds. Workstations shouldn't be at an extreme temperature, i.e. too hot or too cold — air conditioning can control this.

3) Plan work so there are breaks or changes of activity:
Employers mustn't expect workers to work at a computer all day. They must provide regular breaks or allow them to do non-computer work.

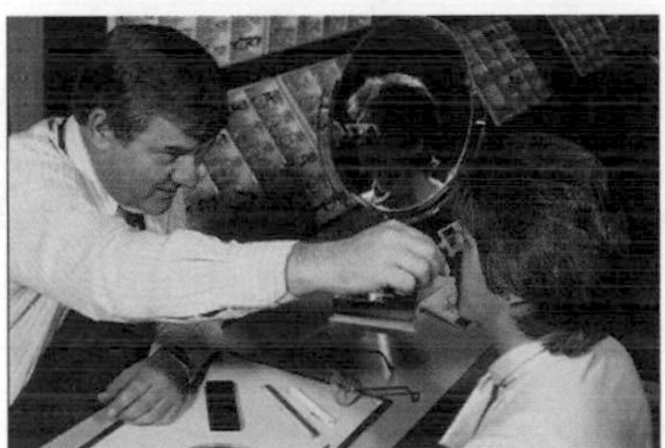

4) Provide free eye-tests:
to all staff who regularly use monitors as part of their job.

5) Provide health and safety training and information:
So employees can take action themselves to reduce the health risks, e.g. no eating or drinking at desks — this improves hygiene.

If working conditions aren't ideal, get your employer to sort them out

Only five things for you to remember about health and safety regulations and they're all just common sense — the rules are designed to make working with a computer as comfortable as possible.

Computers and the Workplace

All these fancy computers have had quite a big impact on the world of business.

ICT has Replaced Some Jobs but Created Others

1) Computers have completely replaced humans in performing some jobs, and reduced the number of people needed to do others.
2) These have mainly been repetitive jobs, or those that involve applying rules in a logical way — this is what computers do best.
3) However, computers aren't that good at social skills — so jobs that need a human touch won't be taken over by computers for a while yet.
4) Computers and technology help to create jobs too — there are jobs and industries that only exist because of computers.

Jobs replaced by computers

1) Manual jobs replaced by robots, e.g. some car-assembly jobs.
2) Many office jobs replaced by computers, e.g. many accountancy/finance tasks can be performed by computers.

Industries created by computers

1) Network management.
2) Data management.
3) Systems analysis and management.
4) Hardware and software manufacturing.

ICT Enables Completely New Ways of Working

Here are a few examples of how ICT has changed the workplace:

1) Automated stock control is the process of managing stock levels (e.g. in a shop) without human input.
2) When an item is sold, the sale information is passed on to a stock-control system that monitors stock levels.
3) If the number of any item in stock has fallen below a certain level, the system will automatically order more.

1) In recent years it has become increasingly popular for people to shop on the Internet (e-commerce), rather than in actual shops.
2) This has reduced the need for some businesses to have a 'high-street presence' — they can sell just as much but without the costs of renting and running a building.

1) Just-in-time (JIT) stock control is often used by manufacturers now.
2) The just-in-time method aims to keep stock levels to the bare minimum — ideally zero. Stock is used immediately as it arrives, so there's no cost for storing it.
3) JIT wouldn't be possible without excellent communications and constant monitoring of stock levels and rates of usage — things computers and improvements in ICT have made much easier.

Computers aren't always better than humans

Unfortunately you're not allowed to employ a computer to sit your exams for you. But don't worry, the good old-fashioned method of learning this page until you know it backwards will see you right.

Computers and the Workplace

All of these technological advances have helped the world become a smaller place — not literally, mind, but you can communicate with people thousands of miles away as if they were right next to you.

Globalisation has been Partly Caused by ICT

1) Globalisation is the process of all the world's systems and cultures becoming more integrated — it's the whole world coming together like a single community.
2) This has become possible because of developments in communications (and transport) technology.
3) Important developments include e-mail, the Internet and mobile phones, as well as technology to transfer more information more quickly.
4) This allows businesses to operate all over the world. For example, a company can have its offices in one country and easily communicate with manufacturing plants and markets on the other side of the world — nowadays people don't need face-to-face meetings in order to communicate effectively.
5) Some industries have been completely transformed. For example, stock markets (where shares in companies are bought and sold) used to involve people making deals face to face with other people. Nowadays everything is done on computers — you can buy shares in a foreign company without leaving your seat.

A company that operates in more than one country is called a multinational corporation (MNC).

Emerging Technologies are Changing Things for the Future

New technologies have always had a big effect on businesses — e.g. steam engines and the telephone were new technologies once. More recently, computers and the Internet changed things forever. "Emerging technologies" could transform businesses in the future. Here are a few examples:

Biometrics: this is all about identifying a person from their bodily features — e.g. their fingerprints, irises (the coloured bit in your eyes) or face. Biometric data is generally unique to an individual, so it's a good way of making sure someone is who they say they are — this means biometrics are useful for things like ID cards, passports, and logging on to computers.

3D printing: this is when three-dimensional objects are made by printing layers of material on top of each other. It's useful for making prototypes of products quickly and cheaply. In the olden days (a few years ago) the only way to get a prototype was by using skilled people to make models — 3D printing will mean this process is as easily done by an office worker as an engineer.

Computer-assisted translation: before computers, translations were done by skilled linguists. Nowadays, computer-assisted translation allows anyone to translate more or less anything.

Computer-assisted translation isn't 100% accurate yet, but it keeps getting better.

New technologies emerge all the time, and the effects on business and people's everyday lives can be hard to predict.

The world of ICT is constantly changing

Globalisation is a funny word that's bandied about a lot, but make sure you understand what it means and why ICT is helping to increase it. Then learn the rest of the page as a treat...

Computers and People

As you'd expect — if computers have an impact on businesses, they have an impact on the people working for the businesses too. This page is all about that, so have a read...

ICT enables **Flexible Working**

1) Rather than travel to an office, Internet technology makes it possible for employees to telework (i.e. work from home), uploading and downloading work as necessary. It has advantages and disadvantages:

Teleworking is useful for people doing collaborative work (see page 138).

Advantages	Disadvantages
Less time is spent on commuting. It means you can spend more time on doing your work (or relaxing). It also cuts down on travel costs.	You won't have as much face-to-face contact with your colleagues, so it's easy to feel isolated. Sometimes it's easier to communicate with people in person (plus it's always nice to have a chat with someone).
Working conditions can be tailored in your own home. You can have the radio on, open a window, eat food — anything to make you more comfortable while you work.	You might get distracted at home, e.g. you could nip to the shops, do the washing-up, watch a film... and there'll be no one to tell you to get on with your work.

2) Mobile computing has allowed people to work on the move — they're not tied down to a desk in an office. Modern mobile computers, e.g. laptops and PDAs, can be as powerful as desktop computers, although their battery life can restrict just how mobile they actually are.
3) Hot-desking is another buzzword that's all about flexible working — employees sit at any free desk in an office, rather than having their own designated place. It could be in one of their employer's offices, or in a work-centre shared by people who work for different organisations. This is made possible because many employees don't need to use physical objects (e.g. tools or books) to carry out their jobs — they just need access to computer files (e.g. software or data stored on a network).

ICT can **Increase Job Satisfaction** but it **Requires Training**

1) Advances in ICT have made it much easier for workers to carry out tasks that in the past would have been too specialised to do themselves. For example, thanks to 3D printing (see page 133), designers can actually create scale models of their designs. And small-business owners can create professional-looking brochures to show their products.
2) This has increased productivity (which is good for the business) and improved job satisfaction (which is good for workers).
3) However, in order to use all this technology effectively, people have to be trained — which can cost a business time and money.
4) And since technology improves all the time, keeping up to date with the latest developments can be expensive — there's the obvious cost of buying the technology, but there's also the cost of retraining people.

ICT has changed the way that many people do their jobs

Flexible working is only possible because of the advances in ICT in recent years — it would have been difficult for people to imagine things like teleworking and mobile computing a few decades ago.

Warm-Up and Worked Exam Questions

That was a big chunk of revision. Here are three pages of questions to make sure you took it all in...

Warm-Up Questions

1) Describe two ways that network managers can control access to their network.
2) Explain why some retail businesses now prefer not to have a high-street presence.
3) Name two emerging technologies that might affect businesses in the future.

Worked Exam Questions

1 A company is investing in new technology so its employees can work flexibly.

(a) (i) Give one advantage of improvements in ICT to workers.

They can easily carry out tasks that were previously too specialist, ✔[1 mark] *making their jobs more varied and satisfying.*

(1 mark)

(ii) Give one disadvantage of improvements in ICT to companies.

Workers need to be trained to use new technology, which can be expensive. ✔[1 mark]

(1 mark)

(b) Describe the difference between teleworking and hot-desking.

Teleworking is where people work from home, often using the Internet to transfer work to and from their office. ✔[1 mark]

Hot-desking is where employees sit at any free desk in an office, rather than having their own designated place. ✔[1 mark]

(2 marks)

(c) The company is producing a leaflet to make its employees aware of the new ways they can work. Describe two advantages of teleworking that could be included in the leaflet.

i) Less time and money ✔[1 mark] *will be spent commuting.* ✔[1 mark]

ii) Working conditions can be tailored ✔[1 mark] *to make you more comfortable while you work, e.g. you can have the radio on, open a window, etc.* ✔[1 mark]

(4 marks)

(d) A few senior managers at the company are worried that teleworking might cause some problems. Describe two disadvantages of teleworking.

i) People who telework won't have as much face-to-face contact ✔[1 mark] *with their colleagues, so it's easier for them to feel isolated.* ✔[1 mark]

ii) People who telework might get distracted at home, ✔[1 mark] *e.g. they could go to the shops and their productivity might suffer.* ✔[1 mark]

(4 marks)

Exam Questions

1 Tick **two** boxes to show which of the following statements about the Data Protection Act are **true**.

	Tick **two** boxes
Companies must never transfer data outside the United Kingdom	
Companies must protect data from damage or theft	
If data is accidentally destroyed, companies must pay compensation	
People can ask to see the personal data held about them	
Companies must destroy personal data after it has been used once	

(2 marks)

2 (a) Describe three principles of the Personal Data Guardianship Code.

1 ....

....

2 ....

....

3 ....

....

(6 marks)

(b) Give two things that are illegal under the Computer Misuse Act.

....

....

(2 marks)

(c) Give two types of data that are exempt from the Data Protection Act act.

....

....

(2 marks)

3 Mrs Musson works as a school secretary. She sometimes suffers from back pain, eye strain and unsteadiness in her hands at the end of the working day. Suggest three pieces of advice for Mrs Musson to help her avoid these problems in the future.

....

....

....

(3 marks)

Exam Questions

4 Delene is worried about the computers in her laboratory being stolen or hacked.

(a) Suggest four methods of security that could protect Delene's computers from theft.

....

....

....

(4 marks)

(b) Give two ways that Delene could protect her computers from hackers.

....

....

(2 marks)

(c) Delene is also concerned about phishing. Explain what is meant by the term 'phishing'.

....

....

(2 marks)

5 (a) (i) Explain what is meant by the term 'globalisation'.

....

....

(2 marks)

(ii) Describe the effect of globalisation on the location of businesses.

....

....

(2 marks)

(b) Describe the effects of improvements in ICT on the type and availability of jobs.

....

....

....

....

....

....

(6 marks)

Collaborative Working

If you find revising a bit lonely then the next three pages have been created with you in mind — they are all about working with other people.

Collaborative Working is Basically Team Work

1) Collaborative working is where people work together to reach a common goal.
2) The people could be individuals, part of an official group or team within a business, a whole organisation, or even entire countries.
3) Collaboration is often a recursive process (e.g. if Abe and Bob are working on the same document, then Abe might do a little bit of work, then Bob might do something to it, then Abe does a bit more, and so on).

A Group Plan can Reduce Conflict and Increase Consistency

1) Lots of people working together always has the potential for disaster — everyone has their own opinion on how to do something, which can cause conflicts.
2) People working on a project should have a plan of the best way to achieve the common goal — it should take everyone's opinion into account (but not everyone will think it's perfect).
3) As work on the project begins, individuals should be checking that their work follows the plan.
4) One part of the plan might be a description of the layout for any documents produced during the project, e.g. reports and presentations — this is the house style.
5) House styles are good for collaborative work, otherwise the finished project could be a bit of a dog's breakfast — an ugly mix of clashing colours and fonts.

Project Management is Vital to Collaborative Working

1) Project management is all about making sure a project is completed on time, on budget, and that it meets the required objectives.
2) Balancing all of these things is not easy — they may change after the project has been started, e.g. it might need to be completed in three weeks not five, or the project might have to solve world hunger as well as the original objective of world peace.
3) All of the work towards a project has to be scheduled — each bit must be planned to take place at a certain time. The fewer unknowns there are about a project, the easier it is to manage.
4) Each individual working on a project has to be aware that their key role is to finish their work by the given deadline. If they don't, they'll slow down the project or even prevent it from achieving its objectives.
5) Good communication between individuals in the collaboration is also vital — people should be aware of other people's work schedules, and meetings could be synchronised (happen at the same time), so that more than one thing can be discussed and more people's opinions can be heard.

Collaborative work has to be carefully managed

All this collaborative working stuff seems obvious, but don't fall into the trap of assuming you know it all. You need to be able to describe things like group plans and project management.

Collaborative Working and Software

You need to know when collaboration is used and the stuff that can help make the whole thing easier...

Collaboration Happens in Different Situations

1) An obvious place for collaboration is in businesses — it can be more efficient than people working on their own (as long as communication is good), which saves businesses time and money.
2) It's also found in education — students can work together to achieve a goal, e.g. completing a homework project. It helps them to develop their communication and organisation skills.
3) Many leisure activities involve collaboration. For example, online games sometimes require players to work together to achieve their objectives.

Software can Make Collaborative Work Easier

Shared workspaces are areas on the Web used for storing things like documents, to-do lists and calendars. Members of a collaboration can log on to the workspace to view and edit documents, add things to the calendar and so on. It's a bit like a shared computer that exists on the Web.

Workflow is basically the sequence of steps something has to go through before it's finished. Some software can automate these steps, e.g. after a document has been edited, it's automatically sent to someone to proofread it.

Project management tools help to plan a project efficiently, e.g. schedule tasks, assign people to complete those tasks and show how much of a project has been completed.

Communication tools that help collaborative work include VoIP (Voice over Internet Protocol — transmitting speech via the Internet), instant messaging, telephones, e-mail... I could go on. You might not be too familiar with teleconferencing though...

Teleconferencing Links People in Different Places

1) Teleconferencing uses ICT to connect people in different locations using sound and/or video.
2) Locations are connected by a telecommunications system (e.g. a phone line, the Internet, or a satellite link) so that several people can communicate as though they're in the same room.
3) There are two main types of teleconferencing:

Audio conferencing

- Allows oral communication only.
- Each person has a microphone to talk into, and a speaker that outputs what other people are saying.
- Audio conferences can be held using fairly basic telephones, so it's not too expensive.
- On the downside, you can't see people's body language, so messages are easier to misunderstand.

Video conferencing

- Allows oral and visual communication.
- It uses speakers, microphones, video cameras and monitors to transmit sound and images.
- You can see people during the meeting, so it's more human and personal.
- But the equipment is more expensive than normal telephones.

4) Teleconferencing saves time and money on travelling to a meeting place — people can hold meetings without leaving their offices.
5) But teleconferencing is not perfect — there's always the risk of technical failure — if the machinery breaks down, then the meeting's over.
6) There can also be delays as messages are transmitted — this can make conversation difficult.

Collaborative Working — Sharing Info

All this collaborative working isn't much use if the different parts of a project aren't brought together. Fortunately the Internet has made sharing stuff much easier, but there are things to be aware of...

Naming Conventions and Version Control are Important

1) To manage files effectively, filenames and different versions of files need to be controlled.
2) Naming conventions for files mean everyone on a project names documents the same way. It avoids confusion when lots of people are working with similar files. A naming convention might include the following:

- File description — a brief explanation of what the file contains.
- Date of creation — in a specific format e.g. YYYY-MM-DD.
- No spaces or special characters — these can cause errors, or make the filename look weird, e.g. spaces are converted to '%20' by web browsers.

You've got to make sure that everyone is using the same naming convention and version control method — otherwise it's all pointless...

3) Version control helps if you have lots of files that are different versions of the same thing.
4) One way of distinguishing between versions is to put a lowercase 'v' (for 'version') and a number at the end of the filename — start at 1 and go upwards. So if someone wants to open the most recent version they just look for the highest number.

Data needs to be Securely Accessed and Transferred

1) With some collaborative work there may be documents that should only be accessed or edited by certain people, e.g. personal information or results data.
2) Some operating systems let you change the access rights of files so you can control what people can and can't do with them — this kind of security helps to reduce accidents and increase confidentiality.
3) The transfer of data also needs to be done securely — especially when using the Internet.
4) Loads of files are transferred using the Internet — they're uploaded to a file server (see page 92), and someone else can download them at a later time.
5) User names, passwords and encryption (converting the data into a code) help to protect the data as it's being transferred — the chances of a thief being able to read it are reduced.
6) Files can also be transferred physically, e.g. on a USB drive or a DVD. Password-protecting or encrypting them can prevent the files from being used if they fall into the wrong hands.

Compressing Files can Reduce Transfer Times

1) The bigger a file's size, the longer it takes to transfer it to another computer.
2) File-compression software can compress (zip) files using algorithms, which makes transferring them quicker. The programs can also decompress (unzip) zipped files, so they have the same file size as the original files.
3) A file's data isn't changed when it's zipped up — it's just stored in a different way. It's a bit like scrunching up a sponge — it gets smaller, but it'll pop back to how it was when you let it go.

Work out things like file naming conventions before a project starts

Naming conventions and version control sound really geeky, but they're both extremely useful when it comes to file management. The same thing goes for passwords, encryption and file compression.

Online Behaviour

Here are some words of wisdom about the online kingdom. Yes, it's boring — but it's important.

The Internet is Great — but is Not Without Problems

The beauty of the Internet is that it lets you access almost everything you could ever want. But its simplicity and global scale has allowed people to use it for evil...

Getting your mitts on things like programs, music, and films is incredibly easy thanks to the Internet — a lot of people download things without a second thought. But unless the person or organisation that owns the stuff gives permission to download it, it's illegal. Online theft is a crime, as much as it is in the 'real world'.

Information on the Web isn't always reliable. People can either accidentally or intentionally upload incorrect information, which can then be passed quickly around the world without anybody realising it's untrue.

Spam e-mail (see page 97) is a major problem. It's possible for spammers to send millions and millions of e-mails to people without even breaking a sweat — great for them, not so great for everyone else.

Plagiarism is when someone tries to pass off another person's work as their own. It's an issue that's magnified by the Internet — because there's so much information available on the Web, many people think they can copy some of it and it'll go unnoticed.

It's Not OK to be Nasty to People

1) Some people feel that the online world is separate from the rest of society. This is not true.
2) For example, people use different methods of online communication to upset other people — 'cyber bullying' is a real problem and the consequences are just as awful as normal bullying.
3) Defamation is another problem — some people make up things about other people on websites and blogs because 'it's only the Internet'. But if you get caught, you could be in big trouble.

The online and offline worlds are both populated by people

It's easy to forget that Internet users are people, especially when they're represented by a picture or some text. But you should always treat people online as you would if you were in a room with them.

Online Behaviour

Staying Safe Online *just needs a Little Bit of* **Common Sense**

You're probably more than aware of all the horrid stuff that goes on over the Internet. That's not a reason to stop using it — you just have to use your head to avoid getting in trouble:

Protect *your* **Personal Details**

When you're communicating with someone over the Internet you should never give anyone your personal details — especially your full name, address or bank details. Don't even give this info over the Internet to people you know — it could be someone pretending to be them, or there could be someone 'listening in', intercepting everything.

It's best to keep this information off social networking sites, too.

Ignore **Unwanted E-mails**

If you get a dodgy-looking e-mail from someone you don't know, delete it — don't open it, or forward it on to other people. If you've accidentally opened the e-mail, don't open any files attached to it. The same thing goes for any hyperlinks — they might look legitimate but they could be very dodgy.

Think Twice *Before* **Meeting Online Friends**

If you've met someone online, say through a chat room or social networking site, it's always safer not to meet up with them in real life. It's unbelievably easy for someone to lie about themselves over the Internet, so you can never be sure that you're being told the whole story...

Be Careful *when Using* **Webcams**

When you're using a webcam, don't assume that it's just you and them — there could be people watching you that you can't see. It's also pretty easy to record a webcam feed, so anything silly that you do might come back to haunt you.

Avoid Pornographic Websites

A lot of pornographic websites are breeding grounds for viruses and other unpleasant computer programs. The best advice is to steer clear of them — if you do somehow end up on one, never, ever download or install any programs that the website asks you to.

Don't be afraid of the Internet, but you need to know how to stay safe

This stuff probably seems like a big wodge of common sense — and you'd be right to think that. But it's really important, not just for your exam, that you stay safe online — so learn this page.

Inequality and Disability

You need to know about the social implications of ICT too.

Different Levels of Access to ICT Affects Individuals...

1) Not everyone has access to a computer and the Internet, or knows how to use them. This creates the potential for a two-tier society — those who are computer-literate (and "information rich"), and those without easy access to computers and the Internet ("information poor").
2) Even now, people without computer skills can find it harder to get a job because a lot of employers have basic computer literacy as a minimum requirement for new staff.
3) And if you're not connected to the Internet, you can miss out on a lot of stuff, for example:

Online deals, e.g. cheaper car insurance and money-off vouchers.

Educational resources, e.g. revision websites and online encyclopedias.

Cultural things, e.g. new music, funny videos and world news.

...as well as Cultures and Communities

1) There are loads of different languages used around the world, but most of the stuff on the Web is written in just a few of them — this creates a culture inequality, where people can't access information because it's not in their language.
2) However, because the Web reaches across the world, it's now easier than ever to explore different cultures — all from the comfort of your own home.
3) The Internet can allow people living in countries where contact with the outside world is controlled by the government to get their opinions heard.
4) Some countries don't like the fact that the Internet lets people get any information they want — so they attempt to censor some of it.

- The most famous example of this is in China. The Golden Shield Project, or 'Great Firewall of China', filters out websites that the Chinese government doesn't want people to see.
- This includes websites about foreign news, blogging, and violent or pornographic websites.
- It's a huge project but it angers a lot of people, not just in China, as it prevents people from accessing the information they want to — something which we take for granted.

There's Hardware and Software for People with Disabilities

Some disabilities prevent people from using the usual mouse and keyboard to operate a computer — but there's hardware and software that can overcome this issue:

1) Braille keyboards make it easier for blind computer users to type.
2) Microphones can be used to operate a computer — voice-recognition software is needed to convert the sound into commands. It's useful for things like word processing.
3) Some software converts text to a voice. So if a person can't read, the computer will read it to them.
4) Some operating systems let you customise your desktop to make it easier to use. For example, increasing the text and icon size, and increasing the contrast so things stand out more.

A literate computer — one that reads stuff back to you...

It's quite easy to assume that everyone knows how to use a computer, especially in this 'digital age'. But you need to know that ICT inequality exists and the effects it's having on people.

Political and Environmental Issues

Recording, processing and storing vast amounts of data certainly has benefits. But there are potential ethical problems too. Have a read of all this...

Technology can Help **Protect** the **Environment**

1) Data logging techniques (page 82) can help monitor the environment — for example:

- concentrations of various gases in the atmosphere (e.g. carbon dioxide),
- temperatures in different regions and oceans (e.g. using sensors on satellites),
- loads of other things (e.g. rainfall, soil water content, snow depth, cloud cover...).

2) The hope is that this data can be used to understand atmospheric processes better, which should make it easier to decide the best way to deal with climate change.

Technology Brings **Political** and **Ethical** Dilemmas

1) Laptops, CDs, memory sticks and hard drives can store lots of data and are extremely portable. This is great... until the laptop or the memory stick gets accidentally left somewhere, stolen or lost in the post. It's happened a few times in recent years, sometimes with very sensitive data.
2) Identity theft has become more common over the years too, and in some ways is made easier by advances in technology (e.g. phishing scams — page 129).
3) Britain now has loads of CCTV (closed circuit TV) cameras. They make many people feel safer, the police can sometimes identify crime suspects from the footage, and they're claimed to deter crime. However, some people raise fears of a Big Brother style "surveillance society", where your every move is monitored and recorded. It's also not clear whether cameras really do deter crime.
4) National government databases, containing details of everyone in a country's population, are also controversial. In theory, it's even possible to record and store everyone's DNA profile. Supporters claim crimes would be easier to solve, and there'd be less identity theft, for example. Others feel governments would have access to private data about citizens that they don't really need. Such databases are also expensive, and there's also the risk of data loss.

Technology Can Monitor All Sorts of **Everyday Activities**

1) Technology can be used to encourage recycling — e.g. "Pay-as-You-Throw" schemes.
2) Microchips (RFID tags, see page 121) are attached to people's wheelie bins. These can identify which house each bin belongs to.
3) When the bins are emptied, each bin is weighed by a set of scales built into the bin lorry.
4) People who throw away lots of rubbish would then be charged more for their rubbish to be collected.
5) The idea is that those people probably aren't recycling as much as they could. Having to pay to throw away recyclable rubbish might make them consider actually recycling it.

6) But this approach isn't popular with everyone.

- Some people dislike the intrusion — they feel it's like having "spies in their bins", keeping an eye on what they throw away.
- Others feel it's just an excuse to bring in another tax.

Warm-Up and Worked Exam Questions

Here we go, nearly the last two pages of questions in the book — try your best to get these right...

Warm-Up Questions

1) Give one situation where collaborative working might be used.
2) Describe how the problem of plagiarism has been increased by the Internet.
3) Explain why some people think ICT has led to a 'two-tier society'.

Worked Exam Questions

1 A team is working on a project. Each member of the team is working at a different site. The team transfers work files using a file server that is connected to the Internet.

(a) One member of the team has complained about the time it takes to transfer large files. Give one way of reducing the time taken to transfer files.

By compressing (zipping) the files. ✔ [1 mark]

Increasing the speed of each team member's Internet connection would also make file transfers quicker.

(1 mark)

(b) Suggest two ways of protecting the team's data.

The data could be encrypted. ✔ [1 mark]

Access to the file server could be limited using user names and passwords. ✔ [1 mark]

(2 marks)

(c) At the end of the project, the team noticed a lack of a consistent style across their work. Describe how the team could achieve a consistent style on their next project.

They could use a plan that included details on the project's house style. ✔ [1 mark] *The house style defines how documents produced during the project should look.* ✔ [1 mark] *The members of the team could refer to the plan to make sure they were being consistent.* ✔ [1 mark]

(3 marks)

2 Discuss two controversial uses of new technology.

Some people are concerned about the increasing number of CCTV cameras ✔ [1 mark] *because they feel that everything they do is being monitored and recorded.* ✔ [1 mark] *However, other people feel safer because of the presence of CCTV cameras.* ✔ [1 mark] *National databases also cause people concern — a national database would hold the information, e.g. DNA profiles, of every person in a country.* ✔ [1 mark] *Some people are worried about what governments would use the data for and the cost of the technology needed.* ✔ [1 mark] *Other people think they would make crimes easier to solve.* ✔ [1 mark]

(6 marks)

Exam Questions

1 (a) What is teleconferencing?

....

....

(2 marks)

(b) Give two advantages and two disadvantages of using a teleconferencing system.

Advantages ....

....

Disadvantages ....

....

(4 marks)

(c) Describe one piece of software that is designed to make collaborative working easier.

....

....

(2 marks)

2 Tick **two** boxes to show which of the following will help you to stay safe online.

	Tick **two** boxes
Only check e-mails during the day	
Always use a webcam when you talk to strangers online	
Don't give anyone your personal details	
Download every file that you are asked to	
Delete e-mails from people you do not trust	

(2 marks)

3 Eric owns an Internet café.

(a) Name two features that Eric could use to make his computers more accessible to disabled people.

....

....

(2 marks)

(b) Explain why it's increasingly important for people to have access to ICT.

....

....

....

....

(4 marks)

Revision Summary for Section Ten

Fantastic — you've reached the end of the book... nearly. But you're not going anywhere until you've done this last lot of questions. If you're not sure about an answer, look it up, then try the question again. This section's all about getting you to think about the overall impact of computers, so some of these questions won't have a right or wrong answer, just a good or bad one.

1) What data is covered by the Data Protection Act?
2) Explain the eight principles covered in the Act.
3) What is the Personal Data Guardianship Code designed for?
4) Describe the five principles of the Code.
5) What three things are illegal under the Computer Misuse Act?
6) Explain three measures that can be taken to reduce the risk of damage to hardware.
7) How does intrusion detection help to protect networks?
8) Describe one procedure that banks use to protect your data online.
9) Identify two health problems from the overuse of computers, and explain their causes.
10) Explain three ways that the risks associated with computer use can be reduced.
11) Explain three things that are covered by the Health and Safety (Display Screen Equipment) Regulations 1992.
12) What sorts of jobs have computers replaced humans in performing? Give two examples of such jobs.
13) Name three industries that have been created by the increased use of computers.
14) Describe how ICT can be used to automatically control stock levels.
15) Explain the effect of improvements in ICT on the location of businesses.
16) Describe two emerging technologies that may affect businesses and other organisations in the future.
17) What is teleworking? Describe one advantage and one disadvantage of teleworking.
18) How have improvements in ICT increased some people's job satisfaction?
19) Describe what collaborative working is.
20) Explain how a group plan and project management helps collaborative working.
21) Describe two situations where collaborative working might be used.
22) Name three pieces of software that make collaborative work easier.
23) Name two things that need to be controlled for effective file management.
24) In your own words, describe what's meant by: a) spam, b) plagiarism.
25) Describe four ways of increasing online safety.
26) Describe one way that technology can help to protect the environment.
27) Explain one political and one ethical problem that technology has caused.
28) Describe how technology can be used to encourage recycling.

Practice Exam

Once you've been through all the questions in this book you should feel pretty confident about the exam. As final preparation, here is a practice exam to really get you set for the real thing. You need to keep an eye on how long it takes you to finish this paper — you've got 75 minutes to try and get all 100 marks. You'll be expected to get through your real exam at a similar rate (you have longer, but there are more questions). Good luck...

General Certificate of Secondary Education

GCSE Information and Communication Technology (ICT)

Centre name					
Centre number					
Candidate number					

Surname	
Other names	
Candidate signature	

Time allowed: 75 minutes.

Instructions to candidates
- Write your name and other details in the spaces provided above.
- Answer **all** questions in the spaces provided.
- Do all rough work on this question paper.
- Write your answers in black or blue ink or ball-point pen.

Information for candidates
- The marks available are given in brackets at the end of each question or part-question.
- There are 11 questions in this paper.
- The maximum mark for this paper is 100.

Advice to candidates
- Work steadily through the paper.
- Don't spend too long on one question.
- If you have time at the end, go back and check your answers.

Answer **all** questions in the spaces provided.

1 (a) Four types of operating system are labelled with the letters **A**, **B**, **C** and **D**. Write one letter in each row of the table that best matches the description.

A Multi-user operating system

B Real time operating system

C Online operating system

D Multi-tasking operating system

	Description	**Letter**
(i)	Managing a computer's resources so programs aren't interrupted and can meet a deadline for their response	
(ii)	Can run many programs at the same time by sharing out a computer's resources	
(iii)	Allows multiple people to log into a computer and use it at the same time	

(3 marks)

(b) Operating systems are designed to organise files.

(i) What is a file?

....

(1 mark)

(ii) Describe what is meant by the term 'file extension'.

....

....

(2 marks)

(c) Many operating systems are controlled through a graphical user interface (GUI). Which **one** of the following statements about GUIs is **false**?

	Tick **one** box
GUIs are more accessible than command-line interfaces	
GUIs can be customised to suit a user's tastes	
GUIs can only receive typed commands	
GUIs make use of windows, icons, menus and pointers	

(1 mark)

7

Turn over for the next question

2 (a) Which **one** of the following does **not** describe a method of transmitting digital TV?

	Tick **one** box
Terrestrial	
Microwave	
Cable	
Satellite	

(1 mark)

(b) In each row of the table below, write one communication technology from the following list that best matches the description.

- Integrated home entertainment system
- Short message service (SMS)
- Instant messaging
- Voice over Internet protocol (VoIP)

	Description	**Communication technology that best matches the description**
(i)	A computer with a simple GUI that is designed to play a variety of media	
(ii)	A method for sending audio conversations through the Internet	
(iii)	Sending and receiving text messages through the Internet in real time	

(3 marks)

(c) Hundreds of billions of e-mails are sent every day. A lot of these messages are spam. Explain what is meant by the term 'spam e-mail'.

....

....

(2 marks)

(d) Describe the following features of e-mail software.

(i) BCC

....

....

(2 marks)

(ii) Signatures

....

....

(2 marks)

10

3 (a) Four features of presentation software are labelled with the letters **A**, **B**, **C** and **D**. Write one letter in each row of the table that best matches the description.

A Handouts

B Timings

C Animations

D Frames

	Description	**Letter**
(i)	Options to automatically control when animations and slide transitions happen	
(ii)	Printed hard copies of a presentation	
(iii)	Different ways of making a slide's frames appear on the screen	

(3 marks)

(b) Hyperlinks can be used in presentations. What is a hyperlink?

....

(1 mark)

4

4 (a) What is meant by the term 'persistence of vision'?

....

(1 mark)

(b) In each row of the table below, write one animation technique from the following list that best matches the description.

- Flip book animation
- 3D animation
- Key frame animation
- Stop-motion animation

	Description	**Animation technique that best matches the description**
(i)	Physical objects are posed and photographed to create frames	
(ii)	Animation software is used to pose computer-created models in each frame and the animator can change viewing angles easily	
(iii)	Pictures are drawn onto sheets of paper and each sheet makes up one frame of the animation	

(3 marks)

4

Turn over for the next question

5 (a) Which **two** of the following are types of computer software?

	Tick **two** boxes
Operating system	
RAM	
Central processing unit	
Word processor	
Video card	

(2 marks)

(b) Describe two differences between a DVD-RW and a CD-ROM.

....

....

....

....

(4 marks)

6

6 Look at the following text.

> There are three main objectives which we need to meet:
> Increase awareness of our products by 20%. Ensure that query response times are less than one day. Reduce spending by £14 000.
>
> Please contact the manager of each department to discuss any strategies:
>
> Advertising manager: Debbie Harris, extension 229, dharris@sondrick.com,
> Support manager: Mark Rowland, extension 256, mrowland@sondrick.com,
> Purchasing manager: Kelly Skye, extension 214, kskye@sondrick.com.

(a) Suggest two ways of formatting the text above to maximise its clarity.

....

....

(2 marks)

(b) (i) Give one difference between word processors and desktop publishing software.

....

(1 mark)

(ii) Name one type of document that is most suitably produced with:

- a word processor
- desktop publishing software

Word processor ....

Desktop publishing software ....

(2 marks)

5

7 Becky is using data-logging equipment to investigate noise levels outside her house.

(a) What is meant by the term ‘data logging’?

....

(1 mark)

(b) Becky is setting up the equipment. She has set the logging period to 7 days.

(i) Describe what is meant by the term ‘logging period’.

....

(1 mark)

(ii) Give one other thing that Becky needs to set before data collection can start.

....

(1 mark)

(c) Becky uses a spreadsheet to analyse the noise level data.
Part of the spreadsheet is shown below.

	1	2	3
A	Reading number	Noise level (dB)	Above 65 dB?
B	1	58	No
C	2	52	
D	3	60	
E	4	65	
F	5	80	Yes
G	6	72	
H	7	43	
I	8	00	
J	9	91	

Becky has to find out whether each reading is greater than **65 dB**. Write a formula that could be entered in cell C3 to give the output “Yes” or “No” as appropriate.

....

....

(2 marks)

(d) Discuss the advantages and disadvantages of using data-logging equipment compared to manual data collection.

....

....

....

....

....

(5 marks)

10

Turn over for the next question

8 Max is setting up his office's Internet connection with an Internet service provider (ISP).

(a) (i) The Internet is a WAN. Describe the difference between a WAN and a LAN.

....

....

(2 marks)

(ii) Give one advantage and one disadvantage of using networks.

Advantage ....

Disadvantage ....

(2 marks)

(b) The computers in Max's office will be connected using a star network topology.

(i) Describe a star network topology.

....

(1 mark)

(ii) Give one advantage and one disadvantage of a star network topology.

Advantage ....

Disadvantage ....

(2 marks)

(iii) Name one other type of network topology.

....

(1 mark)

(c) The staff in Max's office will use the Internet to view websites.

(i) What type of software is used to view websites?

....

(1 mark)

(ii) Other than text and pictures, give two features that can be used to make a website more appealing.

....

....

(2 marks)

(d) Describe the security risk of using bank cards to make purchases over the Internet and explain how this risk can be minimised.

....

....

....

....

(4 marks)

15

9 Malwell & Sons is a window-cleaning company that operates in Burnhart and Otterfields. It stores its customer account details in a database. Part of the database is shown below.

Account ID	Title	Initial	Surname	Number	Address1	Address2	Postcode	Balance
00256	Mr	F	Torr	18	Tulip Lane	Burnhart	BH2 1LP	-15.12
00542	Mrs	G	Ready	22	Peacock Street	Otterfields	OF6 1LE	-36.41
00262	Ms	T	Alton	5	Reel Street	Burnhart	BH1 2BW	0.00
00579	Mr	M	Hamilton	21	Otter Way	Otterfields	OF8 2PB	0.00
00652	Miss	T	Price	16	Pennell Lane	Burnhart	BH6 8YO	-6.76
00257	Mr	A	Park	114	Peacock Street	Otterfields	OF6 2LE	2.80
00676	Mr	R	Sallow	33	Turner Street	Otterfields	OF1 1HR	-32.30
00354	Mrs	S	Peterson	66	Tulip Lane	Burnhart	BH2 4LP	-25.60
00111	Miss	K	Bourne	42	Cross Street	Burnhart	BH3 9HR	0.00

(a) Paul Malwell, the owner of the company, has created the following query:

Address2 = "Burnhart" AND Balance < 0

Describe what this query will search for.

....

....

(2 marks)

(b) Paul runs the query on the whole database and gets 38 results. Paul wants to write to each of the 38 customers and ask them to settle their account balance. Describe how Paul could use mail merge to create these letters.

....

....

....

....

(4 marks)

(c) Discuss the potential advantages and disadvantages of storing people's details on national government databases.

....

....

....

....

....

(5 marks)

11

Turn over for the next question

10 A school wants to update the system it uses to collect and process registration data. This flowchart shows the current system:

Teachers complete a paper register

↓

Secretary checks registers for missing data and manually adds up the number of children present and absent

↓

Secretary writes up a daily absence report for the whole school

(a) The new system should use an automatic data-capture method to transfer the data from the register into a computer. Describe one method that could be used.

....

....

(2 marks)

(b) Suggest software applications that could calculate the number of pupils present and absent, and create a weekly absence report. Give reasons for your answer. (You may suggest either one application to carry out both tasks, or two different applications.)

....

....

....

....

(4 marks)

(c) Name the type of data validation that checks for missing data.

....

(1 mark)

(d) Describe two types of data that should be used when testing the new system.

....

....

(2 marks)

(e) Describe the difference between user documentation and technical documentation for a system.

....

....

....

....

(4 marks)

Question 10 continues on the next page

(f) Describe a method that could be used to implement the new system. Give one advantage and one disadvantage of the method

....

....

....

....

....

(5 marks)

18

11 Describe ways of using the Internet safely and ethically.

You will be marked on your use of English and appropriate technical vocabulary, and your ability to organise information.

....

....

....

....

....

....

....

....

....

....

....

....

(10 marks)

10

Continue your answer on a separate sheet of paper

END OF TEST

Section One — Computers and Hardware

Page 9
Warm-Up Questions

1 It's a fast PC without things like a monitor or keyboard. It's designed to process a lot of data.

2 Each key on a keyboard is connected to a switch which closes when the key is pressed. This sends a signal to the CPU based on the key's location.

3 They are input devices that record environmental information and convert it into digital data.

Pages 10-11
Exam Questions

1 (i) B ***(1 mark)***
(ii) C ***(1 mark)***
(iii) A ***(1 mark)***

2 (a) E.g. motherboard / video/graphics card / sound card / RAM/memory / wireless card ***(1 mark for each, up to a maximum of 3 marks)***
(b) (i) It's a computer's main processor/a microprocessor ***(1 mark)***.
(ii) It processes all of the data in a computer system ***(1 mark)***, e.g. for running applications/ responding to user inputs ***(1 mark)***.

3 (a) Hardware is all the parts of a computer system that you can physically touch ***(1 mark)***. Software is the programs that a computer runs ***(1 mark)***.
(b) Hardware: e.g. monitor / mouse / keyboard / CPU / motherboard / hard drive / RAM / video/graphics card / sound card
(1 mark for each, up to a maximum of 2 marks)
Software: e.g. operating system ***(1 mark)***, applications software ***(1 mark)***
There are loads of answers you could put here — for examples of hardware, just make sure that both of your answers could be physically touched. As for software — you could have also named a specific piece of applications software, e.g. spreadsheet software, graphics software, database software, etc.

4 (a) A concept keyboard is made up of keys that have symbols or words on them ***(1 mark)*** that represent a piece of data, e.g. an item on a menu ***(1 mark)***.
(b) E.g. it's easier/quicker to enter data / fewer errors are likely to be made ***(1 mark)***.

5 Tick next to 'LCD monitor' ***(1 mark)***
Tick next to 'laser printer' ***(1 mark)***

6 (a) (i) The user moves a ball around with their hand or finger ***(1 mark)*** and the direction and speed of the ball's movement moves the pointer on a computer screen ***(1 mark)***.
(ii) Graphics tablet / mouse / touchpad ***(1 mark)***
(b) (i) e.g. the image is ready to edit as soon as it has been taken / the digital photo can be e-mailed as an attachment ***(1 mark)***
(ii) a scanner ***(1 mark)***

Page 21
Warm-Up Questions

1 Read-Only Memory

2 1024 B

3 It's a cheap way to back up large amounts of data.

Pages 22-23
Exam Questions

1 (a) Advantages: e.g. good quality printing/fairly high resolution / cheap to buy / small enough to use on a desk ***(1 mark for each, up to a maximum of 2 marks)***
Disadvantages: e.g. quite slow at printing / replacement cartridges can be very expensive ***(1 mark for each, up to a maximum of 2 marks)***
(b) Advantages: e.g. print at a very high resolution / very fast printing / very quiet ***(1 mark for each, up to a maximum of 2 marks)***
Disadvantages: e.g. expensive to buy / expensive to repair ***(1 mark for each, up to a maximum of 2 marks)***
(c) (i) Buffering is when pages are stored in a buffer (memory) in the printer before printing ***(1 mark)***. Spooling is when the printed document is stored on the hard disk before being held in a print queue ***(1 mark)***.
(ii) They allow the user to get on with other tasks while printing takes place ***(1 mark)***.
(d) E.g. because his printing needs to be really accurate / because he prints out documents on large sizes of paper ***(1 mark)***.

2 (a) An output device that can move and perform simple mechanical tasks ***(1 mark)***.
(b) 1) Motors are powered by electricity. Stepper-motors move in a series of small but accurate steps, e.g. in a flatbed scanner / servo-motors move continuously, e.g. in a drill. 2) Hydraulic actuators are powered by liquid pressure. They're quite slow and used for heavy lifting equipment.
3) Pneumatic actuators are powered by air pressure. They are quite responsive and used on things like automated production lines ***(Up to 2 marks for each description, up to a maximum of 4 marks)***.

3 Advantage: e.g. flash memory is very stable / very reliable / compact ***(1 mark)***
Disadvantage: e.g. it can be easily lost/stolen / it wears out eventually ***(1 mark)***

4 (i) D *(1 mark)*
(ii) B *(1 mark)*
(iii) A *(1 mark)*

5 (a) (i) 1024 MB *(1 mark)*
(ii) fewer bytes *(1 mark)*

(b) (i) It's temporary memory that can be read from or written to *(1 mark)*.
(ii) When a computer doesn't have enough RAM for what it's doing it uses the hard drive as a memory overflow *(1 mark)*. However, it takes longer to access data on the hard drive than RAM *(1 mark)*. Adding more RAM to a computer means more data can be stored in RAM *(1 mark)*, so more data can be processed more quickly, improving performance *(1 mark)*.

(c) ROM is permanent memory *(1 mark)* that contains data/instructions that are never changed, e.g. the instructions to load the operating system of a computer *(1 mark)*.

Section Two — Operating Systems and Applications

Page 33
Warm-Up Questions

1) It means it can run many programs at the same time.
2) E.g. the operating system is stored on a server that's not owned by the user. The operating system can be accessed from any Internet-enabled computer.
3) It's a file that tells OSs how to communicate with computer hardware.
4) Windows, Icons, Menus, Pointers
5) E.g. calculating/analysing data

Page 34
Exam Questions

1 (a) E.g. it's a user interface that allows the user to communicate with the computer *(1 mark)* using windows, icons, menus and pointers *(1 mark)*.

(b) Advantage: can be easier to use/more intuitive than a command-line interface / can be customised to personal tastes *(1 mark)*.
Disadvantage: can be slower to use than command-line interfaces / menus might not be laid out logically *(1 mark)*.

2 Tick next to 'find and replace' *(1 mark)*
Tick next to 'change page orientation' *(1 mark)*

3 (a) use the shut down menu *(1 mark)*
(b) E.g. restart his computer / reinstall the software / install patches for the software / check that his hardware is connected properly / update his drivers ***(1 mark for each, up to a maximum of 2 marks)***

The question was about a software problem but the problem might have been caused by a hardware malfunction — so it's right to mention ways of checking hardware.

Section Three — Spreadsheets and Databases

Page 45
Warm-Up Questions

1) numerical data, text/alphanumeric data, formulas
2) It's an instruction to the computer to process data held in specific cells.
3) line graph
4) A relative cell reference refers to the cell in a certain position relative to the formula cell (e.g. 2 cells left). If the formula cell is copied to another location, the reference changes. An absolute cell reference is one that is fixed, so if the formula cell is copied to somewhere else, it still refers to the same cell.

Pages 46-47
Exam Questions

1 (a) (i) The formula uses relative cell references *(1 mark)*, so when it's pasted into cell C6 the formula becomes =B6*B3 *(1 mark)*. B3 is empty, so the formula gives a value of £0.00 *(1 mark)*.
(ii) =B5*B2 *(1 mark)*

(b) A bar chart is most suitable *(1 mark)* because each category is discrete/separate *(1 mark)*.

2 (a) =IF(B4>=50,"pass","fail") *or* =IF(B4<50,"fail","pass") *(1 mark)*
(b) =IF(B4>=B2, "pass", "fail") *or* =IF(B4<B2, "fail", "pass") ***(1 mark for using cell B2 and 1 mark for using absolute referencing)***

3 (i) C *(1 mark)*
(ii) B *(1 mark)*
(iii) D *(1 mark)*

4 (a) (i) =B10–B9 *(1 mark)*
(ii) e.g. =(B10–B9)*B3 *or* =B11*B3 ***(2 marks for the correct answer, 1 mark only for multiplying cell B3 by any other value)***

(b) The band could increase/decrease the cost of making a T-shirt in cell B9 and see how the total profit column decreases/increases *(1 mark)*.

Page 53
Warm-Up Questions

1) It's a store of data.
2) The design view is where you create the table. The datasheet view is where you enter data.

3) record-format and column-format

Page 54
Exam Questions

1 (a) It's a field of a database table ***(1 mark)*** that can uniquely identify any record in the table ***(1 mark)***.

(b) (i) It's a database where data is stored in separate tables ***(1 mark)***.

(ii) The tables in the database are linked together ***(1 mark)***, which means that information only needs to be stored in the database once ***(1 mark)***.

(c) Method 1: e.g. range check ***(1 mark)*** — if the data falls outside of a certain range then it can't be entered ***(1 mark)***.

Method 2: e.g. input mask ***(1 mark)*** — this forces data to be entered in a certain format, e.g. DD/MM/YYYY ***(1 mark)***.

2 (i) C ***(1 mark)***

(ii) D ***(1 mark)***

(iii) E ***(1 mark)***

Section Four — Word Processing and Desktop Publishing

Page 63
Warm-Up Questions

1) desktop publishing
2) the point where a new page starts
3) word count
4) First you organise your data source, e.g. a spreadsheet or database. The first row should be the field names. Next, create a document and add the merge fields to the document. Then merge the data with the document.

Page 64
Exam Questions

1 Tick next to posters ***(1 mark)***

Tick next to magazines ***(1 mark)***

2 (i) B ***(1 mark)***

(ii) C ***(1 mark)***

(iii) A ***(1 mark)***

(iv) D ***(1 mark)***

3 E.g. spelling checkers only recognise misspelt words ***(1 mark)***, so words like 'were' and 'where' might be wrong in their context, but the spelling checker won't find a problem ***(1 mark)***.

A spelling checker can usually work in different languages ***(1 mark)***, so if it's set to the wrong language it might not pick up errors in the document ***(1 mark)***.

Section Five — Presentation and Web Software

Page 72
Warm-Up Questions

1) e.g. video / music
2) The audience might find it easier to follow the presentation / the audience can write their own notes on a handout.
3) They save time and effort because they contain everything needed for a new page. They help to give web pages a consistent look.
4) text that scrolls across the screen
5) It needs to be converted into a digital format.

Page 73
Exam Questions

1 (i) E ***(1 mark)***

(ii) C ***(1 mark)***

(iii) D ***(1 mark)***

(iv) A ***(1 mark)***

2 Tick next to 'mute' ***(1 mark)***

Tick next to 'fast forward' ***(1 mark)***

3 (a) It's a series of media/audio/video files ***(1 mark)*** that are downloaded as episodes ***(1 mark)***.

(b) Streamed media is played through a media player without being stored ***(1 mark)***, but podcasts are usually saved before being played ***(1 mark)***.

(c) People can view/listen to a podcast whenever they want / people can use any suitable media player to view/listen to the podcast ***(1 mark)***.

Page 79
Warm-Up Questions

1) looping
2) Advantage: e.g. they attract people's attention

   Disadvantage: e.g. they can be annoying
3) Because programming languages are easier for humans to understand than machine code.

Page 80
Exam Questions

1 (a) Each frame of the cartoon is an individual image that is shown and hidden in turn ***(1 mark)***. Each image lingers in your eye for a fraction of a second, and this is called persistence of vision ***(1 mark)***. The lingering image fills the gap between frames ***(1 mark)***, so it looks like you're watching an image moving smoothly ***(1 mark)***.

(b) (i) It's where an animator uses animation software to set up the key frames at the start and end of an action ***(1 mark)***. The software then works out the frames between the key frames ***(1 mark)***.

(ii) E.g. onion skinning ***(1 mark)*** is where a faint outline of the previous frame is shown to make it easier to draw the next frame ***(1 mark)***. Rotoscoping ***(1 mark)*** is where the frames of a live action video are shown so they can be traced over for a more natural-looking animation ***(1 mark)***.

(iii) flip book animation / stop-motion animation / 3D animation / Claymation™ ***(1 mark for each, up to a maximum of 2 marks)***

2 (i) D ***(1 mark)***

(ii) C ***(1 mark)***

(iii) E ***(1 mark)***

(iv) A ***(1 mark)***

Section Six — Measurement and Control

Page 89
Warm-Up Questions

1) Any three of: e.g. light / radioactivity/Geiger counter / temperature/heat / sound / pressure / infrared / air pressure

2) An analogue signal can take any value in a certain range. A digital signal can only take certain values.

3) The time between one measurement and the next.

4) E.g. it's safer than using a real plane / different environmental conditions can be simulated.

Page 90
Exam Questions

1 (a) temperature/heat sensor/thermistor ***(1 mark)***

(b) The temperature/heat sensor measures the temperature and sends a signal to the computer ***(1 mark)***. If the temperature is below a certain level, the computer turns a heater on ***(1 mark)***. When the temperature reaches the desired level, the computer turns the heater off ***(1 mark)***.

2 (a) (i) E.g. temperature/heat sensor / ADC / computer/ processor ***(1 mark for each, up to a maximum of 2 marks)***

(ii) e.g. three hours ***(1 mark)***

You have to use a bit of common sense here — you don't want to take a reading every minute because the temperature won't change that much and you'll have too much data at the end of a week. But taking the temperature once a day would be too infrequent — your answer should be between 30 minutes and 6 hours.

(b) Data-logging equipment can record information in places where humans find it hard to operate / data can be collected over very long or very short periods / logging intervals can be more accurate than when a human's doing the measuring / data loggers don't need to take breaks ***(1 mark for each, up to a maximum of 2 marks)***.

3 ***Maximum of 6 marks available:*** Real-time images ***(1 mark)***, which mean that the program reacts immediately to the pilot's actions ***(1 mark)*** / hydraulic arms ***(1 mark)***, which hold up the cockpit and move it according to the actions of the pilot and to simulated weather conditions ***(1 mark)*** / a closed environment ***(1 mark)***, so the cabin can be pressurised and lighting set to simulate reality ***(1 mark)*** / feedback loops ***(1 mark)***, so that when the pilot alters the controls, signals are sent to the computer, which changes the output of the simulation (e.g. image, position of the arms) ***(1 mark)***.

Section Seven — Networks and Communication

Page 98
Warm-Up Questions

1) Advantage: e.g. performance in one part of the network is independent of other parts / it's easy to add more computers to them.

Disadvantage: e.g. failure in the central computer causes the whole network to break down / they use a lot of cabling, so they're expensive.

2) It's a network/WAN that connects computers around the world.

3) A search engine is a website that lets people search for other websites using keywords. A portal is a website that offers lots of services, e.g. search engines, e-mail and on-line shopping.

4) It's a feature of some web browsers that alerts users if the website they're on might be trying to steal things like their user names, passwords and bank details.

5) formal language

Page 99
Exam Questions

1 (a) (i) It's a computer program that is written to infect computers and copy itself ***(1 mark)***.

(ii) E.g. they can corrupt computer files ***(1 mark)***.

(iii) E.g. the user opens an infected e-mail attachment ***(1 mark)***.

(b) E.g. by using up-to-date anti-virus software / by viewing e-mail attachments rather than downloading them / by not opening e-mail attachments unless you trust the source ***(1 mark for each, up to a maximum of 2 marks)***.

(c) They can encrypt personal data ***(1 mark)*** so it can only be decoded with special software and a key that only the on-line shop website knows ***(1 mark)***.

2 (i) C ***(1 mark)***

(ii) E ***(1 mark)***

(iii) A ***(1 mark)***

(iv) D ***(1 mark)***

Page 104
Warm-Up Questions

1) Short Messaging Service
2) It's like an open instant messaging conversation — people can enter the chat room and type messages to each other over the Internet in real time.
3) It's a place where people post and discuss announcements, e.g. adverts or events.
4) E.g. forums usually have moderators that monitor users and keep messages appropriate. Before somebody posts on a forum they could be asked to sign up and give their details/agree to some terms and conditions.
5) Any three of, e.g. name / age/date of birth / birthplace / address / education details / work details / hobbies / music/film/book tastes / profile picture

There are lots more things you could have answered with — just use your common sense and think of things you might have on your own profile.

Page 105
Exam Questions

1 Tick next to 'floppy disk drive' ***(1 mark)***

Tick next to 'command-line interface' ***(1 mark)***

2 (a) E.g. pictures/sounds are better quality / there are more channels / allows users to access interactive features / you can access an Electronic Programme Guide/EPG ***(1 mark)***

(b) (i) Terrestrial TV is broadcast over the air and received by aerials on people's homes ***(1 mark)***. Cable TV is sent through a cable/optical fibre directly to people's homes ***(1 mark)***.

(ii) E.g. satellite TV ***(1 mark)*** is where the signal is transmitted to a satellite and then relayed to satellite dishes on people's homes ***(1 mark)***.

You could have talked about IPTV (Internet Protocol Television) instead — it's basically TV that's broadcast over the Internet.

(c) (i) E.g. they can record programmes to a hard disk so they can be watched at a later time/time shifting ***(1 mark)***, the ability to pause live TV ***(1 mark)***

(ii) ***Maximum of 4 marks available***: E.g. video on demand ***(1 mark)*** — this allows you to pick what programmes you want to watch and when you want to watch them, without you having to record them first ***(1 mark)*** / parental control ***(1 mark)*** — this lets parents disable certain channels that they don't want their children to watch ***(1 mark)*** / pay-per-view events ***(1 mark)*** — these are special programmes, e.g. sports events and films, that can be watched for an extra fee ***(1 mark)***.

Section Eight — Making ICT Systems

Page 110
Warm-Up Questions

1) It's a way of inputting, processing and outputting data.
2) They're manually operated (when they could be automated/computerised); they can't cope with the information processing demanded of them.
3) The inputs, processes and outputs of the new system.

Page 111
Exam Questions

1 (a) They could: interview users of the system to find out their experiences / give questionnaires to the users and analyse the results / observe people using the system / study documents such as user guides, printouts and error reports ***(1 mark for each, up to a maximum of 2 marks)***.

(b) (i) A specific outcome that can be measured ***(1 mark)*** to test whether the new system is an improvement on the existing one ***(1 mark)***.

(ii) Tick next to 'decrease the cost of processing an order by 5p' ***(1 mark)***

Tick next to 'decrease the time taken to process an order by 30%' ***(1 mark)***

There were some similar options in the table, but only the two above were specific, measurable and test if the new system has made an improvement on the existing system.

(c) (i) A feasibility study is used to work out if it's possible to make the new system ***(1 mark)***, e.g. by looking at and comparing all of the hardware, software and trained people available ***(1 mark)***. A feasibility study also includes a cost-benefit analysis ***(1 mark)*** to work out if the benefits of making and operating the new system will be greater than the costs ***(1 mark)***.

(ii) It's difficult to be certain about everything, e.g. the hardware that will be needed, without actually building the new system ***(1 mark)***. But guesses need to be made at this stage otherwise you can't estimate the likely cost of the new system ***(1 mark)***.

Page 116
Warm-Up Questions

1) A whole system broken down into its main tasks which are then further broken down into smaller tasks.
2) How data moves around a system and what happens to the data at each stage.
3) Data from the existing system is loaded onto the new system and the new system starts to be used for its designed purpose.
4) By interviewing users of the system / analysing the results of questionnaires given to users of the system / observing people using the system / studying user guides/printouts/error reports.

It's basically the same things that are done when you identify problems with an existing system at the analysis stage.

Page 117
Exam Questions

1 (a) (i) It's when the different parts of a new system are introduced one at a time ***(1 mark)*** while the old system is kept running ***(1 mark)***.

(ii) Advantage: e.g. bugs in one part of the system can be fixed before implementing the next part of the system ***(1 mark)***.

Disadvantage: e.g. it might take a long time to completely implement the new system and see its benefits ***(1 mark)***.

(b) Direct implementation ***(1 mark)*** is when the old system is shut down and the new system is started at the same time ***(1 mark)*** / parallel implementation ***(1 mark)*** is when the new system is introduced in one go, but the old system is kept running while the new one is tested ***(1 mark)***.

(c) The demands on a system will change over time, e.g. its workload might increase ***(1 mark)***, so it's important to check if the system still does what it was designed to do/meets its objectives ***(1 mark)***.

2 (a) evaluation ***(1 mark)***

The question was about the new system — if users were interviewed about the existing system it would be the analysis stage (see part d).

(b) analysis ***(1 mark)***

(c) design ***(1 mark)***

(d) analysis ***(1 mark)***

(e) testing ***(1 mark)***

(f) implementation ***(1 mark)***

Section Nine — Processing Information

Page 124
Warm-Up Questions

1) It's data with a meaning/in a context.
2) Any three of, e.g. online forms / card readers / bar-code readers / voice-recognition devices / biometric/ fingerprint/retina scanners / RFID tags / OMR devices
3) range check
4) It's a number that can be used to help check that numerical data has been entered accurately. It's determined by a formula that uses all the other digits in the number. If the number has been entered incorrectly, the check digit will probably be wrong.
5) A knowledge bank of data about a particular subject and a set of instructions for processing the knowledge.

Page 125
Exam Questions

1 (a) Wikis are websites that can be edited using a normal web browser ***(1 mark)*** by anyone who has access to the website ***(1 mark)***.

(b) E.g. Roger could check that the information is relevant to his report ***(1 mark)***, for example that it's about the popularity of football and not other sports ***(1 mark)***. He could also check that the information is accurate ***(1 mark)***, for example by finding a different information source that agrees with the wiki ***(1 mark)***. Roger could also check that the author of the information is not biased ***(1 mark)***, for example if the author is involved in football then the information on the popularity of football might be exaggerated ***(1 mark)***.

2 (a) (i) E.g. range check / presence check / data type check ***(1 mark for each, up to a maximum of 2 marks)***

(ii) It only makes sure that the data is the right type and not that it is accurate ***(1 mark)***. For example, the teacher may incorrectly type in 45 instead of 54, but the data is still valid ***(1 mark)***.

(b) The teacher could proofread the spreadsheet ***(1 mark)*** by checking the entered data against the original data and editing any incorrect data ***(1 mark)***.

(c) OMR/Optical Mark Recognition ***(1 mark)***

The clue was in the question — the test was in a multiple-choice format and OMR could easily capture the data from the answer sheets.

Section Ten — Other ICT Issues

Page 135
Warm-Up Questions

1) E.g. they can give authorised users names and passwords to limit unauthorised access to the network. They can also assign access rights to individual users to limit users to certain types of application software, e.g. word processors.
2) Because they can sell just as much through an online shop but without the costs of renting and running a building.
3) Any two of, e.g. biometrics / 3D printing / computer-assisted translation

Page 136-137
Exam Questions

1 Tick next to 'companies must protect data from damage or theft' ***(1 mark)***

Tick next to 'people can ask to see the personal data held about them' ***(1 mark)***

2 (a) The person responsible for data handling in an organisation: is accountable for making sure that personal data is handled appropriately / must be open about data use by stating how the data is going to be used, and if it's being passed on to third parties / must get the consent of the data subject before accessing or sharing their personal data / must make sure that personal data is secure from people who shouldn't be able to access it, both inside and outside of the organisation / must make sure that the amount of data accessed is not excessive, and that it's securely deleted when it's not needed any more ***(1 mark for each, up to a maximum of 6 marks)***.

(b) gaining unauthorised access to computer material / gaining unauthorised access to a computer to carry out serious crimes / unauthorised changing of computer files ***(1 mark for each, up to a maximum of 2 marks)***

(c) data that can: affect a tax assessment / affect a criminal investigation / affect the outcome of a court case / identify another unconsenting person ***(1 mark for each, up to a maximum of 2 marks)***

3 E.g. Mrs Musson should: take regular breaks from her computer / make sure that her chair is at the correct height / make sure her monitor is at the correct height/distance from her face / ask her boss for an ergonomically-designed keyboard / ask her boss for a monitor filter / ask her boss to provide good background lighting ***(1 mark for each, up to a maximum of 3 marks)***.

4 (a) e.g. mark the laboratory's name and postcode on all the equipment / protect the laboratory with a burglar alarm / lock windows and doors to prevent access / close blinds or curtains/switch off monitors at night / install security cameras ***(1 mark for each, up to a maximum of 4 marks)***

(b) E.g. by using a firewall ***(1 mark)*** or intrusion detection software ***(1 mark)***.

(c) It's when someone sends you an e-mail and pretends to be from an organisation that holds your personal details ***(1 mark)***. The e-mail usually contains a link to a website that asks you to enter your personal details ***(1 mark)***.

5 (a) (i) It's the process by which the whole world is becoming integrated into one giant community ***(1 mark)***. It's being caused by improvements in ICT, such as e-mail, the Internet and mobile phones, because these allow more information to be transferred more quickly ***(1 mark)***.

(ii) It has allowed businesses to operate all over the world ***(1 mark)***. For example, companies can have their offices in one country and easily communicate with manufacturing plants and markets on the other side of the world ***(1 mark)***.

(b) E.g. as computers and technology have become more advanced, they have completely replaced humans in performing some jobs ***(1 mark)***, and reduced the number of people needed to do others ***(1 mark)***. These have mainly been jobs involving manual labour (e.g. car-assembly) or office jobs (e.g. some parts of accountancy) ***(1 mark)***. On the other hand, improvements in computers and technology have helped to create jobs ***(1 mark)***. For example, jobs for systems analysts ***(1 mark)*** and hardware and software manufacturing industries only exist because of computers and technology ***(1 mark)***.

Page 145
Warm-Up Questions

1) E.g. in businesses / in education / online games.
2) Because there's so much information available on the Web, people think they can use some of it as their own work and it'll go unnoticed.
3) There are two types of people in modern society — those who have access to ICT/are computer literate and those who don't have access to ICT. This means some people will miss out on certain opportunities, e.g. jobs that require ICT skills, or special offers that are only available on the Internet.

Page 146
Exam Questions

1 (a) It's where ICT is used to connect several people in various locations ***(1 mark)*** using sound and/or video ***(1 mark)***.

(b) Advantages: e.g. several people can communicate as though they're in the same room ***(1 mark)***. Teleconferencing saves time/money on travelling to a meeting place ***(1 mark)***.

Disadvantages: e.g. if there's a technical failure the meeting is over ***(1 mark)***. There can be delays as messages are transmitted, which can make conversations difficult ***(1 mark)***.

(c) E.g. software enabling shared workspaces, which are areas on the Web that store things like documents, to-do lists and calendars ***(1 mark)***. Members of a collaboration can log on to the workspace to view and edit documents, add things to the calendar and so on ***(1 mark)***.

You could have also talked about software that automates workflow, or project management software.

2 Tick next to 'don't give anyone your personal details' ***(1 mark)***

Tick next to 'delete e-mails from people you do not trust' ***(1 mark)***

3 (a) E.g. Braille keyboards / microphones and voice-recognition software / text-to-voice software / customisation options to enhance the computers' operating system desktops ***(1 mark for each, up to a maximum of 2 marks)***.

(b) E.g. People who haven't got access to ICT might find it difficult to get a job ***(1 mark)*** because many employers have basic computer literacy as a minimum requirement for new staff ***(1 mark)***. People who don't have access to the Internet could miss out on things ***(1 mark)***, for example educational resources or world news ***(1 mark)***.

Practice Exam Paper

Pages 149-157

1 (a) (i) B ***(1 mark)***

(ii) D ***(1 mark)***

(iii)A ***(1 mark)***

(b) (i) It's a block of data stored under a single name/filename ***(1 mark)***.

(ii) It's the information at the end of a file's name ***(1 mark)*** that tells the computer what type of file it is/what program should be used to open it ***(1 mark)***.

(c) Tick next to 'GUIs can only receive typed commands' ***(1 mark)***

2 (a) Tick next to 'microwave' ***(1 mark)***

(b) (i) integrated home entertainment system ***(1 mark)***

(ii) voice over Internet protocol ***(1 mark)***

(iii)instant messaging ***(1 mark)***

(c) Spam e-mail is unsolicited/unwanted e-mail ***(1 mark)*** that is sent to many people at the same time, usually to advertise a product ***(1 mark)***.

(d) (i) BCC stands for blind carbon copy ***(1 mark)***. It's used to send e-mails to people without other recipients of the message knowing that they received it ***(1 mark)***.

(ii) Signatures are customisable text messages and/or images ***(1 mark)*** that can be automatically added to the end of each e-mail that you send ***(1 mark)***.

3 (a) (i) B ***(1 mark)***

(ii) A ***(1 mark)***

(iii)C ***(1 mark)***

(b) It's a frame that takes you to another slide when it's clicked ***(1 mark)***.

4 (a) It's when an image lingers in your vision after it has been shown and hidden ***(1 mark)***.

(b) (i) stop-motion animation ***(1 mark)***

(ii) 3D animation ***(1 mark)***

(iii)flip book animation ***(1 mark)***

5 (a) Tick next to 'operating system' ***(1 mark)***

Tick next to 'word processor' ***(1 mark)***

(b) E.g. DVD-RWs are blank discs that can have data written to them, which can then be deleted and new data can be written to them ***(1 mark)***. CD-ROMs come with data on them that can't be deleted and the disc can't be written to ***(1 mark)***. DVD-RWs can hold over 4 GB of data ***(1 mark)*** whereas CD-ROMs can only hold around 650 MB of data ***(1 mark)***.

6 (a) E.g. make the three objectives into a numbered list ***(1 mark)***; make the manager and contact details into a table ***(1 mark)***.

(b) (i) E.g. desktop publishing software is generally used to create documents that contain text and graphics, whereas word processors are generally used to create documents that contain text / desktop publishing software is frame-based, whereas word processors aren't ***(1 mark)***.

(ii) Word processor: e.g. a letter / essay / memo / report ***(1 mark)***

You could mention any documents that are mainly text.

Desktop publishing software: e.g. a poster / catalogue / leaflet / magazine / flyer / newspaper / brochure / business card ***(1 mark)***

You could mention any documents that contain text and graphics.

7 (a) It's the process of automatically recording data using sensors and computer equipment ***(1 mark)***.

(b) (i) It's the total length of time that data will be collected for ***(1 mark)***.

(ii) the logging interval/the time between one measurement and the next / the total number of measurements to be taken ***(1 mark)***.

(c) e.g. =IF(C2>65,"Yes","No") ***(1 mark for using correct IF function, 1 mark for using appropriate true and false values)***

(d) E.g. one advantage of data logging is that it can be used to collect information in places where humans find it hard to operate, e.g. underwater ***(1 mark)***. Another advantage is that data logging equipment can measure at more accurate intervals than humans ***(1 mark)***. A third advantage is that data-logging equipment can function all of the time, whereas humans will need breaks ***(1 mark)***. One disadvantage of data logging is that the equipment can be very expensive ***(1 mark)***. Another disadvantage is that people need to be trained to use the data-logging equipment, which costs time and money ***(1 mark)***.

8 (a) (i) A LAN is a network of computers contained in one place, e.g. a building or office ***(1 mark)***. A WAN is a network of computers in different places that are quite far apart ***(1 mark)***.

(ii) Advantage: e.g. peripherals can be shared between many users / software can be shared between many users / centralised file storage reduces the danger of losing files due to an individual workstation failing / communication between users of the network is easy, cheap and fast ***(1 mark)***.

Disadvantage: e.g. cabling can be expensive to install and replace / a faulty server can disable the whole network / security measures are needed to restrict access to the network / networks can be disabled by viruses ***(1 mark)***.

(b) (i) It's where large numbers of computers/workstations are directly connected to a central computer/server/mainframe ***(1 mark)***.

(ii) Advantage: e.g. a failure anywhere but in the central computer will not affect every workstation / it's easy to add more computers to the network ***(1 mark)***.

Disadvantage: e.g. a failure in the central computer will disable the whole network / star networks use a lot of cabling so they can be expensive to install ***(1 mark)***.

(iii) line/bus network / ring network ***(1 mark)***

(c) (i) web browser ***(1 mark)***

(ii) e.g. RSS feeds / hyperlinks / animations / hotspots / forms / marquee text / navigation bars / counters ***(1 mark for each, up to a maximum of 2 marks)***

(d) E.g. your card details could be intercepted by a third party and used to make unauthorised purchases ***(1 mark)***. This risk can be minimised if the on-line shop encrypts any sensitive information using an algorithm ***(1 mark)***. This information can only be decrypted with a key ***(1 mark)***, so if the encrypted data is intercepted it will be useless ***(1 mark)***.

9 (a) It will find all customers who live in Burnhart ***(1 mark)*** and have a balance of less than zero/a negative balance ***(1 mark)***.

(b) Paul would create a standard letter in a word processor and then insert merge fields ***(1 mark)*** from the database query into the letter for details that will be different on each one, e.g. name, address and balance ***(1 mark)***. Then Paul would merge the data from the query ***(1 mark)*** with the document and each of the 38 letters would contain the details from one record of the query ***(1 mark)***.

(c) E.g. a national database would hold the information, e.g. DNA profiles, of every person in a country ***(1 mark)***. Some people do not like the idea of their personal information being stored without a good reason ***(1 mark)***, and some people are worried about the cost of the technology needed ***(1 mark)***. Other people think national databases would make crimes easier to solve ***(1 mark)*** and there would be less identity theft ***(1 mark)***.

With discussion questions you're best off starting by briefly describing the topic you're asked to discuss. The main thing to get across in your answer is a balance of viewpoints — even if you have your own opinion on the topic.

10 (a) E.g. an OMR device could be used ***(1 mark)***, e.g. the teacher could fill in a form which is then scanned and the registration data is automatically entered into a computer ***(1 mark)***.

You could suggest just about any type of automatic data capture method — the important thing is that you describe how it would be used in the new system.

(b) E.g. spreadsheet software could be used to process the data ***(1 mark)***, e.g. the SUM/COUNT function could automatically add up/count all of the children that are present ***(1 mark)***. Database software could be used to produce a daily absence report ***(1 mark)*** as it usually has report tools, with formatting options and the ability to make graphs ***(1 mark)***.

You could use spreadsheet or database software to both process the data and produce the report.

(c) presence check ***(1 mark)***

(d) Erroneous data — this is data that the system should reject / normal data — this is data that should work in the system / extreme data — this is data that is at the limit of what should work in the system ***(1 mark for each, up to a maximum of 2 marks)***.

(e) User documentation is designed to help people who are going to be using the system ***(1 mark)***. It's written in simple language with some technical terms that are used in the system ***(1 mark)***. Technical documentation is designed to help computer engineers and programmers repair or upgrade the system ***(1 mark)***. It's written in technical language with complex diagrams ***(1 mark)***.

(f) Direct implementation could be used ***(1 mark)***. It's when the old system is decommissioned and the new system started up at the same time ***(1 mark)***. An advantage of this method is that the benefits of the new system are felt as quickly as possible ***(1 mark)***. A disadvantage of this method is that any bugs that weren't picked up during testing could cripple the whole system ***(1 mark)*** and there would be no alternative system to use ***(1 mark)***.

Or

Phased implementation could be used ***(1 mark)***. It's when different parts of the system are introduced one at a time ***(1 mark)*** and the old system is kept running while this happens ***(1 mark)***. An advantage of this method is that bugs in one part of the system can be fixed before implementing the next part of the system ***(1 mark)***. A disadvantage of this method is that it might take a long time to completely implement the new system and see the benefits of it ***(1 mark)***.

Or

Parallel implementation could be used ***(1 mark)***. It's when the new system is introduced all in one go but the old system is kept running whilst the new one is tested ***(1 mark)***. An advantage of this method is the new system can be tested very quickly ***(1 mark)*** and problems can be sorted out without important operations being affected ***(1 mark)***. A disadvantage of this method is that all tasks need to be done in both systems ***(1 mark)***.

11 ***Maximum of 10 marks available:***

- *Start your answer by talking about ways of using the Internet safely. Make sure you give examples whenever you can. For example,* 'when communicating with someone over the Internet, e.g. using an instant messaging service, you should never give out your personal details, e.g. your full name, address or bank details. Someone could use this information to pretend to be you or to purchase things using your money.'
- *Other ways of behaving safely online include not opening suspicious-looking e-mails and attachments (e.g. if they're from someone you don't know), avoiding pornographic websites, not meeting people in real life that you met on the Internet (e.g. in a chat room), and only using a webcam if you completely trust the person you are chatting with.*
- *You should describe the consequences of not behaving safely, for example,* 'when you are using a webcam, the person at the other end of the conversation might not be alone or they could be recording the conversation. This means that anything you do during the conversation could come back to haunt you.'
- *Then you should move on to ways of using the Internet ethically.*
- *You should always write in full sentences for long-answer questions and it's important to use technical language when it's appropriate. For example,* 'defamation is when people make up rumours about other people that are deliberately offensive. It's easy to publish these sorts of rumours on websites and blogs, but if you are caught doing it you might have to pay compensation to the person you lied about.'
- *When you've finished your answer, read it through again and correct any spelling, punctuation and grammar mistakes. It's also important that the person marking your answer can read everything — if something isn't clear, you might not get a mark even if it's correct.*

Index

Index

Index

Index